SOCIAL WELFARE

Dedicated to
Charles I. Schottland
and to the memory of
Milton Wittman

SOCIAL WELFARE
Structure and Practice

David Macarov

SAGE Publications
International Educational and Professional Publisher
Thousand Oaks   London   New Delhi

For information address:

SAGE Publications, Inc.
2455 Teller Road
Thousand Oaks, California 91320

SAGE Publications Ltd.
6 Bonhill Street
London EC2A 4PU
United Kingdom

SAGE Publications India Pvt. Ltd.
M-32 Market
Greater Kailash I
New Delhi 110 048 India

Printed in the United States of America

Library of Congress Cataloging-in-Publication Data

Macarov, David.
  Social welfare : structure and practice / David Macarov.
      p.   cm.
  Updated ed. of : The design of social welfare. 1978.
  Includes bibliographical references and index.
  ISBN 0-8039-4939-1 (acid-free paper).   —   ISBN 0-8039-4940-5 (pbk. :
acid-free paper).
  1 Social service.   2. Public welfare.   I. Macarov, David.
Design of social welfare.   II. Title
HV40.M128   1995
361—dc20   94-46668

This book is printed on acid-free paper.

95 96 97 98 99 10 9 8 7 6 5 4 3 2 1

Sage Production Editor: Diana E. Axelsen

Contents

Preface

Social welfare changes as society changes: Although certain aspects seem to remain constant, many others change, sometimes very rapidly. This book is an acknowledgment of both the constants and the changes in social welfare. It is a redesigned, rewritten, updated version of a textbook—*The Design of Social Welfare*—published in 1978 and now out of print. Permission to use some of the contents of that book has been graciously granted by the publishers, Holt, Rinehart and Winston.

As is true of every scholarly or scientific endeavor, "We may be pygmies, but we sit on the shoulders of giants." Everyone who engages in writing owes an enormous debt to the writers, researchers, and teachers who have gone before. It is, truly, an irredeemable obligation, and one of which I am constantly mindful. Consequently, I have tried to recognize those persons or sources whom I have quoted directly; but I am unable to credit the myriads of people with whom I have spoken, whose lectures have informed me, and whose articles left deep impressions on me without my being aware of it at the time. I am also grateful to my students, who worked with me, challenged me, inspired me, and required me to put complex situations into understandable words. As the Ethics of the Fathers says: "Much have I learned from my teachers, but more have I learned from my students."

I nevertheless feel compelled to recognize the kindness of certain people in reading and commenting on what I have written, in helping me to locate sources, or in allowing me to quote from their published and unpublished works. These include Louise Skolnik, Mimi Abramovitz, Ralph Kramer,

Leonard Schneiderman, Stuart Rees, and in particular, Armand Lauffer, whose extensive comments were extremely helpful.

Because the proper role of educators is to clarify questions rather than to supply answers, I have tried to outline some of the complexities of social welfare without attempting to indicate in which directions my own preferences lie. I am aware that I have not always been successful in making this distinction, and I hope that readers will make allowances for this fallibility.

DAVID MACAROV

Introduction

Social welfare is an enormous, varied, and complex institution. Changes in welfare policies, programs, and practices affect millions of people. Even experts have difficulty predicting the effects of what may at first seem to be relatively minor shifts in goals, methods, or activities. In the United States, social welfare has become so complex that entire fields of study are devoted exclusively to federal-state-local relationships and to each area of service, type of problem, and category of client. As needs constantly change, new agencies arise to deal with them. Here's just a sampling of the new volunteer agencies that have formed since the first edition of this book in 1978:

MADD (Mothers Against Drunk Driving)
OWL (Older Women's League)
PWP (Parents Without Partners)
PA (Parents Anonymous)
SASG (Sexual Assault Support Group)
ACOA (Adult Children of Alcoholics)
GAIN (Greater Avenues to Independence)
Mothers Without Custody
Recovery
Women for Sobriety

New professional groups include ACORN (Association of Community Organizers for Reform Now), ACOSA (Association of Community Organizers and Social Administration), and AASWG (Association for Advancement of Social Work with Groups).

As a result of its size and pervasiveness, today's social welfare system is often taken for granted. People don't think of the millions of fellow citizens who have been helped through a crisis or supported for long periods of inability to work. Neither do they usually consider those who collect social welfare payments not as a reward, but as a repayment. The media pay little attention to the health, education, or cultural attainments of social welfare programs, attainments that give legitimacy to welfare efforts.

On the other hand, social welfare is constantly under fire from a number of directions. Those who design the programs and pay the bills invariably see social welfare as too costly. They may believe that it is destroying the moral fiber of recipients, including their incentive to work. Those who receive social welfare benefits criticize the low level of payments, the difficulty of working through the bureaucratic maze, and the stigma attached to accepting welfare payments. Most taxpayers, neither making the programs nor bene-fitting directly from them, see the system as clumsy, expensive, and inefficient—except when they, or a relative or friend, need to rely on welfare or Social Security payments.

For social workers to practice within the existing welfare system, to use it properly to help their clients, to understand the reasons for criticisms, and—most important—to try to change it, they need insight into the deep-seated religious, moral, and ideological factors that created social welfare, as well as the political, economic, and social realities that shape it. Any change, no matter how small, must be reconciled with these forces if it is to succeed. Consequently, traditional methods of studying social welfare must be sup-plemented by an examination of the organizing concepts that inform the whole.

This book deals with a number of those concepts. The intention is to illum-inate (a) some of the major motivations resulting in social welfare policies, programs, and practices; (b) some important attitudes, values, and beliefs that influence the resulting structure; and (c) some contemporary problems.

Structure of This Book

This book is divided into four parts. To summarize briefly, Part I includes a thumbnail sketch of social welfare, both historically and in its modern U.S. incarnation. It also describes the human needs or problems social welfare is designed to solve.

Part II consists of eight chapters examining the major motivations that gave rise to social welfare. These include the desire to engage in mutual aid, religious beliefs, political factors, economic reasons, and various ideologies that affect social welfare.

Constantly acting on this congeries of motivations is a series of attitudes and beliefs that can be traced back to, or identified with, certain seminal philosophers. Part III includes two chapters that describe some of these important influences. The morality attached to work can be traced in large part to the influence of Martin Luther. Charles Darwin's "survival of the fittest" has been transmuted to apply to social institutions and to individuals, rather than to species, in the form of Social Darwinism. As a result of Adam Smith's laissez-faire economic theory, social welfare is often viewed as unwarranted interference by the government in the economic system.

In Part IV, some of the salient contemporary challenges to social welfare are outlined: permanent poverty, ubiquitous unemployment, changes in the welfare state, and efforts at welfare reform.

The future of social welfare is discussed in the final chapter.

Definitions and Terminology

Social welfare is not an easy concept to define. Like all definitions, it is beset with the problem of infinite regression—every word in the definition is itself subject to further definition, as is every word in that definition, and so on, ad infinitum.

For example, one published definition of social welfare consists of only ten words—"Social welfare policy is collective strategy to address social problems"[1]—but this is followed by three pages defining *collective, strategy, social,* and *problems.* Indeed, the very words *social* and *welfare* are subject to many interpretations. *The Encyclopedia of Social Work* traces the term *social welfare* to the beginning of the twentieth century but notes that it was "never clearly defined." For clarity, the following definition, derived from a definition in *The Social Work Dictionary,* will be used throughout this book:

Social welfare is a nation's system of programs, benefits, and services that help meet those psychological, social, and economic needs that are fundamental to the well-being of individuals and society.

Note that this definition speaks of people in general, not just the needy and disadvantaged, and that health and education are included. Also, the well-being of society, not just individuals, is social welfare's goal.

This book deals with social welfare as an institution: an amalgam of money, manpower, and material providing a wide range of services, from public assistance for the poor, to care for the mentally retarded, to aid and support for the elderly. However, most of the chapters are involved with *policies* more than *practice*. Policies include both goals—the Aid to Families with Dependent Children (AFDC) aims to sustain children growing up in poverty —and rules governing implementation—an AFDC policy requires that the assisted child must live in the home of a relative.

Social welfare policies are implemented through social welfare *programs* carried out by *social workers*. Social workers usually hold a bachelor's or master's degree in social work, and they are certified by the state in which they practice. Most are members of the National Association of Social Workers (NASW). In 1991, NASW had more than 130,000 members. About 30,000 undergraduates were studying social work full time, and another 20,000 had proceeded to graduate work.[2]

Style Used

Finally, a word about style. Readers will find no parenthetical names and dates interspersed in the text to indicate sources of information, because these tend to distract from comfortable reading. A sprinkling of notes will provide the sources of direct quotations and statistical material, and a table, *Read More About It,* at the end of each chapter will direct readers to other works dealing more specifically with the chapter's topics. Both the notes and the tables are supplemented by a master reference list at the book's end. Newspaper articles are referenced by author or title when available.

Notes

1. The definition is from Jansson (1984).
2. The statistics are from the following sources: on NASW members, from "Data Study" (1993); numbers of students, from Council on Social Work Education (1992).

READ MORE ABOUT IT ...

For more information on:	*See these sources:*
New social welfare organizations	Perlmutter, 1988
Definitions of social welfare	Barker, 1991; Leiby, 1987; Rescher, 1972; Titmuss, 1974

PART I

The Nature of Social Welfare

Part I of this book begins with a chapter outlining the history of social welfare, some different conceptions of what it is or should be, an indication of its scope and structure, and an overview of some pertinent social welfare programs. This is followed by a chapter discussing the different kinds of needs social welfare attempts to meet.

1. The Scope of Social Welfare

This chapter provides a capsule history of social welfare, covering government involvement from ancient times to the emergence of the welfare state; the growth of voluntary social welfare; different conceptions of social welfare; the growth and structure of public social welfare; and different types of social welfare programs.

Governmental Involvement

The beginnings of social welfare lie in the prehistoric period, when mutual aid was necessary for survival, and the tribe or the clan took care of its members. Later, both religious and political entities—for many centuries they were the same—offered help to those who needed it. Vanished religio-civilizations, such as the Sumerians, planned and organized aid for helpless citizens; the Sumerian goddess, Nanshe, was particularly concerned with equity and social justice. More than four thousand years ago, Hammurabi, in his famous Code, decreed that in the event of a calamity, it was society's duty to help the victim. The ancient Athenian state distributed grain to citizens during times of famine and inflated corn prices; it provided pensions for disabled soldiers and for the orphans of those killed in battle; other orphans were supported until their eighteenth birthday.

THE ELIZABETHAN POOR LAWS

Following a long intervening history of governments attempting to relieve citizens' problems in some way, Anglo-American government social welfare is usually considered to have begun formally with the Elizabethan Poor Laws of 1601. Earlier laws dealt with the aged and the destitute, but the statutes of 1601 codified the state's responsibility for dependent people as a whole. Although these laws helped children and those with disabilities, they were also intended to repress begging, to use work as the major vehicle for overcoming need, and to punish the idle poor. Responsibility for these activities was assigned to local parishes.

Although many changes have been made in these laws—as thinking about society and social welfare evolved—they remain to this day the basis for much government social welfare policy throughout the Western world. Such features as distinguishing between the deserving and undeserving poor, restricting eligibility, specifying residency requirements, and determining relatives' responsibility (all of which will be discussed later) continue to be used in many parts of the world.

BISMARCK'S SOCIAL INSURANCE PROGRAM

The next major government involvement in social welfare took place on the European continent nearly three hundred years later. In the 1880s, Chancellor Otto von Bismarck introduced several pieces of legislation in Germany that amounted to social insurance—an innovation that soon spread to many other countries. During World War I, a movement in Great Britain to broaden government social welfare activities led to wide reforms in housing, employment, and other basic areas. The suffering of soldiers at the front inspired this reaction, which was popularly expressed in terms of building "a home fit for heroes." The postwar depression dampened these plans considerably, and it was not until the Great Depression of the 1930s that additional basic steps were taken to ensure people against more of the vicissitudes of life. This brought about massive changes in social welfare programs throughout the world, mostly in the form of increased government responsibility; individuals or private agencies were unable to deal with the massive problems. In the United States, the answer to the Great Depression came in the form known today as Social Security.

War—this time World War II—also provided the impetus for the next large step toward a deliberately conceived plan to guarantee help for citizens in most of the unforeseen exigencies of life. In England, the magnitude of the war effort, the sacrifice required of everyone, and the shared losses contributed to a feeling that the war could not be won unless millions of ordinary people were convinced that their government had something better to offer than their enemies had—not only during but also after the war. This was codified in what was generally referred to as "The Beveridge Plan," which provided a wide range of insurance-like programs to protect people against many of the exigencies of life.

In the United States, the 1960s brought the concepts of the Great Society and the War on Poverty, and a great deal more responsiveness to the needs of women and minority groups—African Americans, Chicanos, Hispanics, Native Americans—as well as concern for poverty in general. Governments took on broader responsibilities for the social welfare of their citizens, a process resulting in what has been termed the *welfare state.*

Voluntary Social Welfare

The beginning of institutionalized public, nongovernmental social welfare is usually thought of in terms of the creation of the Charity Organization Society (COS) in England in 1869. As its name implies, the basic idea of the COS was to coordinate the many charities—estimated at 640 in London alone[1]—that operated individually, sometimes in competition with each other. From such coordination grew planning, exchange of information, and research. This tradition spread and is reflected in today's United Fund drives, federations of agencies, and information and referral services.

At almost the same time, the first Young Men's Christian Association (YMCA) was established in Boston in 1851, the first Young Men's Hebrew Association (YMHA) began in Baltimore in 1854, and Toynbee Hall, the prototype of settlement houses, was established in London in 1884. Whereas the COS dealt primarily with relieving poverty, the settlement houses involved themselves in education, recreation, employment, intergroup relations, and counseling. And, to a much greater extent than the COS workers, settlement house workers engaged in social action (usually referred to as "social reform") and encouraged their members to do likewise.

As a result of the Great Depression, government activities began to overshadow the work of all voluntary and public organizations, because only the national government had the resources and the structure to attack the widespread problems. Voluntary groups then attempted to be innovative in a way government bureaucracy could not be: to serve special groups, such as religiously identified bodies or new immigrants, for which the government had no special apparatus; and to help those who fell through the cracks between government services.

Conceptions of Social Welfare

There are differing conceptions as to what social welfare is or should be. Estes has identified three distinct but overlapping models in use. The first is termed the *conventional* social welfare model, the second the *social development* model, and the third the *new world order* model. Goodin also identified three models but described them somewhat differently. One model is based on ideas concerning minimum standards, poverty thresholds, and the like.[2] The aim of this version of the welfare state is to bring everyone up to some social minimum, usually calibrated in terms of people's needs. A second model involves the concept of "social equality." The aim of the welfare state in this version is to redistribute the resources of society to achieve more equality and, ideally, to make everyone equal, in some sense or another. A third view of social welfare revolves around such notions as "fraternity" and "community." In this version the aim of the welfare state is to promote social solidarity, from a neighborhood to a national level.

FOUR MODELS OF SOCIAL WELFARE

Combining Estes's and Goodin's formulations results in four models of social welfare.

The traditional model consists of activities and programs designed to help individuals, groups, and communities to cope with their current problems or to keep such problems from arising. These activities consist primarily of financial aid, help with interpersonal relations, help with intrapsychic problems, advocacy on behalf of clients, and some social or political action that includes organizing clients into political or pressure groups. This has been termed a "problem-solving" approach because it arises from and deals with felt and perceived problems in the here-and-now.

The redistributive justice model is an attempt to solve the problems of individuals and groups by making the economic and social systems more equal, drawing from one sector to provide for another. In some cases making society more equal is seen as the goal of social welfare in its own right, without regard for problem-solving.

The social development model has come to the fore more recently and has less clarity. At one time, social development referred primarily to the developing countries, with the implication that they should be helped to develop more fully, both economically and socially. International organizations, such as the International Fellowship for Economic and Social Development, continue to focus on the developing countries. Later, the term *social development* also began to be used to refer to local community organizing in disadvantaged communities. Social institutions were encouraged to expand service and capacity by fostering the growth of mutual-aid and self-help groups, community centers, councils, neighborhood associations, and social action coalitions.

More recently, the term *social development* has come to include the empowerment of marginalized and disassociated groups: women, African Americans, the poor, gays and lesbians, the unemployed, new immigrants, the homeless, and others. Empowerment is sought through the legislative and the judicial systems and through organizing pressure groups and self-help and mutual-aid groups. Today the term is used by some to encompass individuals engaged in efforts to strengthen their coping mechanisms. This development has been expressed in a number of ways, including "enabling," "empowerment," and "capacity building."[3] It should be noted that these various conceptions of social development are not always compatible—for instance, some think mutual-aid groups are antithetical to social action efforts.

The application of social development concepts to social welfare or social work is relatively new. When the first version of this book was written, the term did not yet appear in the 1987 edition of *The Encyclopedia of Social Work,* or in its most recent supplement (1990), or in *The Social Work Dictionary.* Yet the notion of development as central to welfare is being expressed in a variety of ways. For example, China has announced that it is changing its social welfare system because the current system is no longer "meeting the needs of social development." In an announcement of a World Summit for Social Development in 1995, the Secretary-General of the United Nations described social development as a commitment "to put people at the centre of development and international cooperation" with the goal of "satisfying social needs as an integral part of efforts for greater national and international stability."[4]

However, this aspect of social welfare is far from new. It has its roots in the very origins of social welfare, when helping people to help themselves was coeval with helping those who could not help themselves; this is why it has been termed an "old/new" concept.[5]

The new world order model of social welfare aims to restructure the global social, political, economic, and ecological order. The underlying principles emphasize maximum participation of people in their own development, the pursuit of peace, the satisfaction of the basic needs of people everywhere, and the protection of the planet's fragile ecosystem.

Not everyone committed to a radical restructuring of society or of social welfare takes this global viewpoint. Some are more concerned with restructuring their own society and/or the welfare provisions within it. Islamic fundamentalists, for example, are interested in instituting or maintaining Islamic law in their own countries, drawing the ideology and structure of social welfare from the Koran. The "Shining Path" movement in Peru opposes and attempts to eliminate all present forms of social welfare as diversionary palliatives and would—if successful—institute its own way of meeting human needs.

Nor are all approaches to radical changes in society and/or social welfare violent or subversive. Sweeping changes—they amounted to dismantling social welfare—were proposed as a political platform by ultra-conservative Senator Barry Goldwater during the 1960s. More recently, there has been a call for abandonment of all government social welfare besides unemployment insurance. Others have called for drastic changes, such as breaking the link between work and welfare and supporting people for no reason other than that they are alive. Indeed, an entire school of so-called radical social workers holds that "radical practice begins with the fundamental premise that the circumstances of at-risk populations can be traced to political or economic relationships that exist in the larger social order."[6] This school often advocates changes that—although far-reaching—seem incremental in contrast to the revolutionary movements mentioned above.

These four views of social welfare's function are not always disparate and not necessarily inimical to each other. Indeed, they often overlap. However, in discussing social welfare issues, people sometimes move from one conception to another without being aware that these differences in views can result in far-reaching divergences in policies and practice.

The Growth of
Public Social Welfare

The result of government's involvement in social welfare has been almost continual growth of the populations covered and the problems tackled. For example, in 1928-1929, state and federal social welfare services cost almost $4 billion; by 1970, they cost $75 billion; and in 1983, the tally had risen to $187 billion. Public income maintenance programs alone cost $2 billion in 1940; by 1989, they cost $402 billion.[7]

In the United States, literally millions of people depend upon some facet of the social welfare system for survival. In 1991, more than 40 million Americans were receiving Old-Age, Survivors', and Disability Insurance (Social Security). In fiscal terms, the federal expenditures for income security exceed expenditures for defense. In most states, such programs constitute from one third to well over one half of all state government expenditures.

Examples of the increasing cost of social welfare abound. In 1950, expenditures for public social welfare programs in the United States were 8.8% of the gross national product (GNP): In 1989, this had risen to 18.6%. Total expenses for social welfare, both public and private, rose from 26.4% of the GNP in 1980 to 29.2% in 1989.[8]

The Structure of
Public Social Welfare

A complete diagram of the Department of Health and Human Services (which is charged with primary responsibility for social welfare at the federal level) and the relationship between its various sections and agencies would resemble a wiring diagram for a new kind of space vessel. Even then, state, county, and local services would be left out. A number of attempts have been made to clarify the structure of social welfare by categorizing the fields of service in which it engages. One such attempt is the following:

family agencies
services to children
school social work
services in health care

services in psychiatric settings
correctional services
services for the aging

Another effort to categorize social welfare describes types of services:

adjunctive social services
advocacy and legal services
vocational rehabilitation
homemaker and home-help services
community-center, settlement, and group services
family planning
job placement and training
participation

Social welfare may be grouped according to broader headings—justice, education, health, and urban families.

There are also attempts to portray the totality of social welfare by describing the methods used in its implementation: social casework, social group work, community organization, social policy and planning, social administration, and research. Finally, there are many combinations of these various approaches, usually emphasizing one over the other.

Social Welfare Programs

Programs that offer help can be categorized variously:

1. those that give financial aid—directly to clients, to third parties, or through third parties to clients
2. those that give goods rather than money (often referred to as "in-kind" programs)
3. those that offer services

Financial aid programs, in turn, can be divided between (a) the insurance-type programs that require would-be recipients to have paid a sufficient amount into the program over a specified period, as for Social Security in the United States, or require that someone else has paid premiums for them, as in the case of unemployment insurance or workers' compensation; and (b) grant programs, which require no prior contribution or participation.

INSURANCE-TYPE PROGRAMS

Although they are called insurance-type programs, they are not insurance in the classical sense: The insured holds no written policy; has no control over premiums and benefits, which are changed arbitrarily; and has no choice as to coverage. As a matter of historical record, the Social Security Act of 1935 was not passed as an insurance program. Besides fearing congressional opposition, the legislation's sponsors were afraid that any law they passed would be annulled by the Supreme Court as government engagement in private business. Hence the Social Security Act included a separate title instituting a payroll tax and a separate title establishing old-age benefits. The intention was "to get away from an insurance plan altogether, but to establish the equivalent of such a plan without resorting to a definite insurance scheme."[9]

Regardless of such intricacies, the purposes of programs that at least appear to be insurance are not only to provide a source of revenue for the program but also to create the feeling among recipients that they are entitled to the benefits because of their own previous performance or payment— eliminating any stigma that might be attached to noncontributory social welfare programs.

GRANT PROGRAMS

Grant programs, on the other hand, do not rest on prior performance or payment but are based on demonstrated need coupled with absence of sufficient resources. Need and resources are determined in what is usually called a "means test," and it is almost axiomatic in most social welfare thinking that being subjected to a means test is inherently degrading and that participation in means-tested programs is stigmatizing.

So ingrained is this feeling that one of the first proposals for a guaranteed minimum income was intended as, and entitled, "A Way to End the Means Test."[10] During the 1960s, an attempt was made to simplify the means test and to accept simple declarations of income, with little attempt to investigate except for spot checks. By the 1970s an agency verification model had come back into general use.

Means tests need not be stigmatizing. The normal citizen undergoes many means tests, for example, when he or she applies for a credit card, wants to open a charge account, or applies for a mortgage. Indeed, income tax returns are also a type of means test. Consequently, there have been proposals to link payments to means—among the upper level of Social Security recipients, for example.

A few programs give grants without requiring a means test or prior contributions; however, they are often based on some type of prior perform-ance. Such programs include veterans' bonuses after World War I and the GI Bill of Rights after World War II. Indeed, all Veterans' Administration programs can be seen the same way.

IN-KIND PROGRAMS

Programs that give material goods sometimes offer the goods directly—food, clothing, toys for Christmas, or the like. Meals on Wheels for the elderly and hot lunches for schoolchildren provide this type of in-kind benefits. Perhaps the most widespread in-kind benefit in the United States today is the Food Stamp Program, which distributes stamps that can be used to buy food. Some programs have experimented with using vouchers for educational costs, and vouchers are often used to pay rent or other bills of welfare clients. When vouchers are usable at a number of places or for a number of items, they can be viewed as a liberating device, freeing recipients to seek the best buys and providing them with bargaining power. Indeed, this is the strongest rationale among those who favor vouchers instead of goods or services. When vouchers can be used at only one place or for only one purpose, they have a controlling effect, and the rationale is to make sure that the grant is used only for the purpose for which it was given.

UNIVERSAL VIS-À-VIS CATEGORICAL PROGRAMS

Another way of labeling programs is universal vis-à-vis categorical or selective. Universal programs are designed for, or open to, everyone within the population designated, for example, for every family, every family with children, or everyone over a certain age. Selective programs are for individu-als in need and are usually means-tested. Thus universal versus categorical can often be rephrased as means-tested versus non-means-tested programs.

These divisions of programs are obviously not clear-cut. The universal programs deal with categories, albeit large ones, such as the elderly; the selective programs may deal with *everyone* in a certain category, such as all families with dependent children, and thus may be somewhat universal. The issues of universality and selectivity are dealt with in greater detail later in this volume.

A full description of all, or even the major, governmental social welfare programs in the United States is beyond the scope of this book, which is devoted to how social welfare comes into being and acquires its shape, rather than to descriptions. However, many specific programs are described as they become pertinent to the discussion.

In addition to governmental programs, there are the services of the non-governmental public sector and the private sector, on both the local level and the national level. Some of the national organizations operating under secular auspices include

American Cancer Society
American Diabetes Association
American Foundation for the Blind
American Heart Foundation
American National Red Cross
Arthritis Foundation
Big Brothers
Boy Scouts and Girl Scouts
Child Welfare League
Family Service Association of America
National Council for Homemaker-Home Health Aide Services
National Council on Aging

Sectarian organizations include

B'nai B'rith Youth Organization
Jewish Community Centers Association (formerly the Jewish Welfare Board)
National Catholic Community Service, Inc.
National Conference of Catholic Charities
National Council of Jewish Women
The Salvation Army

United Church of Christ, Board of Homeland Ministries, Health and Welfare
Division
United Presbyterian Health, Education, and Welfare Association
Volunteers for America

On the local level, there are literally thousands of organizations providing
for various needs of people, and although some of these make financial
grants, most provide services intended to solve intrapsychic, interrelational,
or societal problems. These lists do not exhaust the totality of social welfare
institutions, activities, and organizations, but they should give some indication of the enormity of the social welfare enterprise in the United States.

SUMMARY

Social welfare, both government and voluntary, has a history dating
back to ancient times, but the size and structure of the present system
are relatively recent. In general, social welfare programs presume
government involvement at the national, local, and even international
levels. However, voluntary welfare systems exist in many societies.
Four modes of social welfare were identified: traditional, redistributive justice, social development, and new world order. Government
programs can be divided between financial and in-kind types. The
former may be insurance-type or outright grants, although these categories are not always exclusive. Voluntary programs lean more toward
providing services than finances, although this, too, is not an absolute.

EXERCISES

A. When figures, especially dollar figures, reach a certain size,
they lose all practical meaning. To retain an understanding of some of
the proportions of the various government and other expenditures
mentioned here and later in the book, think of each dollar as a second
in time. Then change the seconds into minutes by dividing by 60; the
minutes into hours by dividing by 60; the hours into days by dividing

by 24; and if the result is large enough, determine the years by dividing by 365.

1. Do this for $1,000.
2. Do for $100,000.
3. Do for $1,000,000 (a million).
4. Do for $1,000,000,000 (a billion).[11]

B. Translate every dollar in each of the above amounts into inches; divide by 12 to get feet; divide by 5,280 to get miles.

Notes

1. The figure comes from Woodroofe (1962).

2. For detailed description of models, see Estes (1992) and Goodin (1985).

3. "Enabling" is from Gilbert and Gilbert (1989), "empowerment" is from Nichols-Casebolt and McClure (1989), and "capacity building" comes from Nanavatty (1992).

4. China's decision is discussed in United Nations (1992d), while the Secretary-General's statement is included in Economic and Social Council (1992).

5. Atherton (1990) is the source of "old-new" concept.

6. The quote is from Burghardt and Fabricant (1987).

7. March and Newman (1971) provide the 1928-1929 figures; Doolittle (1987) adds the more recent comparisons; and Bixby (1992) gives public income maintenance costs.

8. The U.S. Department of Health and Human Services (1991) provides statistics on the number of Americans receiving insurance and on expenditures as a share of the Gross National Product (GNP).

9. The quote is from Witte (1962).

10. Schwartz (1963) is the author of this program.

11. Note that in Britain and some other countries, a thousand million is called a "milliard," and a billion there means a million million. Throughout this book a billion will mean a thousand million.

READ MORE ABOUT IT ...

For more information on:	*See these sources:*
Nanshe	Jacobsen, 1965
Hammurabi and his code	Harper, 1955
Athens	Hasebroek, 1933
The Elizabethan Poor Laws	deSchweinitz, 1943
Bismarck's contributions	Schottland, 1974
Great Depression	Bird, 1966
The beginnings of Social Security	Altmeyer, 1966; Witte, 1962
YMHA	Kraft & Bernheimer, 1954
Toynbee Hall	Pimlott, 1935
Traditional model of social welfare	Jansson, 1984
Redistributive justice model of social welfare	Abramovitz, 1989; Atherton, 1990; Specht, 1992
Incompatibility of social development definitions	Kahn, 1991
International Fellowship for Economic and Social Development	Dixon, 1984
New world order model of social welfare	Estes, 1992
Proposals for sweeping social welfare changes	Macarov, 1980; Murray, 1984; A. D. Smith, 1955
Radical social workers	Cloward & Piven, 1975; Galper, 1980; Glennerster & Midgley, 1991; Wagner, 1989, 1990
Lists of social welfare categories	Fink, 1974; Kahn, 1973
List of voluntary organizations	*Service Directory,* 1974

2. Human Needs

Social welfare deals with human needs, and thus a distinction between needs and wants is necessary. Human needs are categorized as common needs, special needs, and societally caused needs. Methods of need detection and measurement for societal and individual problems are classified as relative, normative, or absolute. Finally, the ways in which human needs change are addressed.

Social Welfare as Meeting Human Needs

Social welfare can be defined as a direct or indirect response to human need. The goal may be to prevent new categories of need from arising or to prevent recognized categories of need from affecting still untouched individuals or groups. It may be to maintain people or groups at their present state of need fulfillment. Or it may be to help those with unsatisfied needs or unsolved problems. These categories are often spoken of, respectively, as the preventive, maintenance, and rehabilitative functions of social welfare. The preferred method of meeting needs might involve any or all of the four major conceptions of social welfare mentioned in Chapter 1—traditional social welfare, redistributive justice, social development, or societal reconstruction.

However, Goodin points out that all societies hold as dogma that social welfare deals with needs, rather than wants.[1] He explains that although there is no good, clear-cut reason to give meeting needs systematic priority over satisfying desires, almost all social welfare programs define themselves as meeting needs—and indeed attempt to defend themselves from the charge that they are answering "mere" desires.

17

On Needs and Wants

Assuming that social welfare addresses needs rather than wants, the distinction between them becomes important, even if it is difficult to pin down. For example, it is not sufficient to say that social welfare meets needs while the market addresses desires, as one formulation puts it. As a definition, this is simply a tautology, holding that social welfare meets needs, and therefore needs are what social welfare meets, which defines neither social welfare nor needs. In addition, the market supplies the answer to many needs, such as medicine, whereas social welfare makes possible the fulfillment of many desires, such as retirement from work.

The Social Work Dictionary defines needs as: "Physical, psychological, economic, cultural, and social requirements for survival, well-being, and fulfillment." However, it has been pointed out that the word *need* is used in at least five different ways in social work: impulse, lack, requirement, resource, and problem. Others add a complication by distinguishing between wants, needs, and demands, and still others differentiate between social needs and social problems. So elusive is the difference that some writers simply hold that no definitive list of needs can be given.

When asked to specify basic human needs, many people reply almost automatically: "Food, clothing, and shelter." Need is thereby equated with staying alive; that is, if one is alive, no other needs matter or are important. Under this formulation, the role of social welfare would be just to keep people alive.

It is true that in order to live, everyone needs food and water, although the amount and kinds of food that people require can differ vastly. However, increasing numbers of homeless people in large cities—estimates range from 350,000 to 3 million in the United States[2]—manage without shelter: They live and sleep on sidewalks and in parks. Nomads sleep on the desert sands, and cowboys—at least in western movies—sleep on the ground. It's the same with clothing: Australian aborigines went naked for untold centuries, and some native tribes in Africa, South America, and the Pacific islands still go naked, or wear only loincloths or grass skirts, and do not suffer as a result. Whether "everyone" needs clothing and shelter is thus thrown into question. Also, to assume that people who have food, clothing, and/or shelter have no other needs is unfeeling, if not arrogant.

More sophisticated conceptions of social welfare assume that there are other things people need, even if these things are not necessary to stay alive. These are things that people have been socialized to see or to feel are equally important as, if not more important than, some biological needs. They have been referred to as "growth needs." For example, does the hungry person "need" food more than the well-fed person "needs" social prestige? Or more pragmatically, 75 million Americans, or 25% of the total U.S. population, are defined as needing daily care and supervision because they are children or frail elderly, or they have disabilities, and therefore they are not fully self-caring, although they may have food, clothing, and shelter.[3]

COMMON HUMAN NEEDS

Although it is possible to distinguish among different types of common human needs—for example, between physiological, psychological, and sociological needs—the close links between various kinds of needs are becoming increasingly apparent with growing knowledge in psychosomatic medicine and related areas. For example, the strenuous dieting that occurs in anorexia nervosa—a physical condition—may arise from a distorted self-image—a mental condition—which, in turn, may have been derived from social isolation or rejection—a social condition. Similarly, the mother who deprives herself of food so that her child can be well dressed, the soldier who volunteers for a dangerous mission because of patriotism or loyalty to his fellows, the person who assumes guilt in order to spare someone else shame—each of these is an example of how the demands of one need may be subordinated to the satisfaction of another. Psychosocially determined needs can, and often do, assume a value as high as that of survival.

Maslow postulates a hierarchy of human needs, with each becoming potent as the previous need is relatively well satisfied. In this formulation, the most basic needs are physiological, and until they are more or less satisfied, other needs are not felt, at least not strongly. When physiological needs are satisfied, security needs become potent, followed by the need for love and then the need for self-esteem. The highest or final level of need in Maslow's view is the need for self-actualization—the need to become everything one is capable of becoming, to use all of one's powers and abilities to the utmost. Others approach the subject differently, classifying needs as those of having, loving, and being.

SPECIAL HUMAN NEEDS

In addition to common needs, there are needs that affect only certain individuals or groups, or that affect many individuals occasionally. It might be useful to view these in five categories.

The incapable are people who cannot fend for themselves, at least not completely, owing to some characteristic that puts them at a disadvantage. Included are children, the frail elderly, and those with mental or physical illnesses and disabilities.

The unprepared are capable, but not prepared: individuals or groups, including the illiterate, the uneducated, those with few or no usable skills, and those who have not learned social skills or behaviors. Included, too, are those who are not prepared for the normal tasks and vicissitudes of life. For example, for those unprepared for marriage, there are premarital counseling services; for expectant parents, there are "prospective parents" groups. There are also programs to prepare people for retirement and for old age in general. There are increasing numbers of books, articles, and discussions about death and dying, with a view toward preparing people for this certainty or preparing their support persons. Because most people do not participate in efforts to prepare themselves for what have been called these "transformations of identity,"[4] many of the needs that are served by social welfare in such cases are ex post facto; that is, they arise after the transformation, because people were unprepared.

Disaster victims are those who are capable and prepared for the normal exigencies of life but who are struck by catastrophes or undergo crises for which they need at least temporary help. Crises have been classified as those caused by:

1. natural disasters such as floods and earthquakes
2. environmental situations such as air or water pollution
3. civil disturbances such as riots

To these may be added crises caused by:

4. removal of a person—for example, a loved one or a charismatic or authoritarian leader

5. economic upheavals such as the stock market crash of 1929
6. social dislocations such as mass migrations
7. criminal and terrorist activities, such as skyjackings or bombings

Crises also may be categorized as those that are accidental, situational, or un-anticipated; those that are maturational, developmental, or normative; and those that arise during predictable periods of disorganization. Each of these can be scaled down to the individual level—a home burned out, rats running loose, a sudden arrest, runaway children, job loss, or a move to a new neighborhood.

The unconforming are those who seem capable, prepared, and spared from disaster but who nevertheless violate the norms of society. Included in this group are juvenile delinquents, criminals, prisoners, and all of those who are generally subsumed under the heading of deviants. Increased understanding of how environmental and social factors help create deviance has led some to view much deviance as something the so-called deviant cannot control—even as a functional reaction to the deviant's situation. However, the general public distinguishes between sickness and deviance, based on the assumed ability of deviants to control their behavior. Therefore, people perceived as ill get different treatment than people perceived as deviant, and the methods of meeting their needs are dissimilar. Deviance is often met with punishment; illness is met with care.

The unmotivated. Motivation cannot be observed or measured; it is inferred from action (or lack of action). When people who are able to engage in certain activities do not do so, the inference is that they are unmotivated. Although lack of motivation could affect persons in each of the other four categories, most people believe it is responsible for enough social problems to deserve separate mention. In some cases, the lack of motivation is viewed more or less benevolently, and a search is made for the best method of creating motivation—to study, to relate to other people, to be concerned about personal appearance or behavior, or to join in some endeavor. In other cases, the lack of motivation is viewed malevolently as unwillingness to work, to work hard, or to take care of one's parents or children. In these cases, negative sanctions are more apt to be used. Purported lack of motivation is one of the most salient reasons for current "welfare reform," and a strong controlling factor, under the guise of fear of work disincentives, in determining welfare rates and benefits.

In addition to common and special human needs, there are also needs that affect the whole society or flow from difficulties or gaps in the society itself. For example, all developed countries are moving from an economy based on industry to one based on services. The resulting dislocations in employment patterns do not affect everyone, nor are they confined to one of the groups specified above. They arise from societal changes. In the same manner, countries that are moving from an agricultural to an industrial economy are affected by lack of suitably trained workers, by housing shortages, and sometimes by abandoned land. In societies with officially sanctioned discrimination, needs flow from being discriminated against; in those countries with discrimination despite official bans, such as remnants of the caste system in India, the needs are no less great. Countries that "import" foreign workers create a whole array of needs. Countries that maintain, and occasionally call into active duty, large reserve armies create dislocations that require welfare services.

Sometimes societally caused needs are defined as deprivations. These include the following:

material resources deprivation
mental or emotional deprivation
cognitive deprivation
interpersonal deprivation
deprivation of opportunity
deprivation of personal rights
physical deprivation

Need Detection and Measurement

The emergence of social welfare is not dependent solely on the existence of needs. Any social intervention requires that needs be "recognized" or defined. Before action can be taken, someone or some group or institution must identify a condition as a problem or as arising from unfulfilled needs. Unless this happens, the condition is not likely to receive attention or to become the object of social intervention activity. Some occupations are more likely than others to detect and measure needs or problems.

For example, problem detection is more advanced and formalized in medicine than it is in social welfare. In the United States, physicians are required by law to report cases of certain contagious diseases and suspected child abuse. and some other items. Physicians often voluntarily report interesting, baffling, or novel cases to the local health authorities or to a professional journal. In social work, there is almost no mandatory reporting, although agencies and government departments may require certain statistics. Social workers who learn of a new problem or who learn that an existing problem is getting worse are not usually required to report it. There may be no formal channels to communicate it voluntarily. Individual instances seen by social workers are rarely reported to a central body charged with correlating such reports and assessing need. Reporting in social work tends to take place within the context of professional supervision or case management, and little machinery has been established to allow for, or to demand, data that would result in action.

Exceptions to this are cases of child abuse or neglect and elder abuse. In the United States, cases of child abuse or neglect must be reported by anyone aware of their existence—doctors, nurses, policemen, social workers, and others. In 1981, only sixteen states required the reporting of elder abuse, but this had grown to forty-three states by 1990, suggesting a growing awareness of a problem or need. Some areas are moving toward mandatory reporting of wife battering and rape, although this has proved more complicated. As a general rule, new social welfare services do not arise from the reports of social workers as much as they come from other sources.

SOCIAL INDICATORS

Because welfare agencies have no formal methods to detect problems, some have identified certain factors they believe may indicate the presence of trouble. Such "social indicators" have been the focus of considerable interest. In some places, density of population, or the crowdedness of dwelling places, is seen as an indicator of such problems as physical and mental illness and crime. In the United States, unemployment and pockets of high unemployment are often seen not only as problems in themselves but as indicators of a high incidence of related problems.

PROBLEM EXPOSURE

Some of the most dramatic and influential exposures of social problems have taken place outside the social welfare establishment. For example, a widely read and commented-on 1963 essay by Dwight MacDonald, in *The*

New Yorker, titled "Our Invisible Poor," was published in the same year as Michael Harrington's seminal book, *The Other America*. This concatenation was termed the "discovery of poverty" in the United States, because it focused public attention on what had been an obscure problem. It was a forerunner of and immediate impetus for the War on Poverty programs during the Johnson administration. Both MacDonald and Harrington were journalists, not social workers.

Problems are sometimes dramatized and publicized by well-known or charismatic figures. Franklin D. Roosevelt's own problem with polio focused attention on the organizations active in that problem area, and John F. Kennedy's interest in mental retardation gave impetus to organizations dealing with that problem. In her day, Dorothea Dix did the same thing for the incarcerated mentally ill, as did Margaret Sanger for birth control. Similarly, Dr. Martin Luther King Jr. brought racism to America's attention in a number of dramatic ways.

One of the traditional ways voluntary organizations arise is through the shared concerns of victims of a situation or their relatives. Sometimes these begin as mutual-aid groups and sometimes as social action or public information groups.

However, public demand for services is not limited to small groups of sufferers. Widespread agitation—voiced in letters to newspapers and officials, in rallies and advertisements, or in protest marches and riots—is a potent factor in calling attention to a problem and demanding action. The public apathy or fear that accompanied the onset of AIDS was changed—at least to some degree—by the publicity garnered by groups of sufferers and their sympathizers.

NEED MEASUREMENT FOR SOCIETAL PROBLEMS

Whether a detected need is considered a problem depends on its extent and intensity as compared with some norm. Hence, it is necessary to measure needs. Conventionally, such measurements have been relative, normative, or absolute.

Relative Need

A relative need is one that exists as compared to some non-need situation. Statistics are often used as the measure. Poverty may be defined as the economic condition of people within the lowest tenth percentile, or quintile, or some other percentage of the income distribution. The educationally disadvantaged or deprived may be defined as those achieving the lowest scores on national achievement tests. Relative need can also be determined longitudinally, for example, the amount of crime, drug abuse, or mental illness at one time as compared to the amount at some other time. The comparison can also be made with different countries; Per capita income in India as compared to Israel might indicate the relative affluence of Israelis, whereas comparing Israelis to Americans might indicate relative poverty in Israel. Similarly, the infant mortality rate in the United States is seen as a problem when it is compared to the lower mortality rates in other, less developed countries.

Not only statistics but lifestyles may be compared. For example, poverty can be defined as absence of indoor toilets, inability to plan ahead, lack of motivation—or as something affecting people who are "immoral, uncivilized, promiscuous, lazy, obscene, dirty, and loud."[5] Customs in some times and places—swaddling infants or binding feet, setting the elderly adrift on ice floes, or isolating sufferers from Hansen's disease (previously called leprosy)—might be seen as a social problem in societies that do not have such customs.

Finally, definitions may be relative to some norm or reference group that once existed, exists, or is hoped for or fantasized. Financial inequality, of whatever degree, may be seen as a problem by those who envision or desire a society of complete equality. Lack of mutual aid, neighborliness, or viable and meaningful neighborhoods may be defined as a problem by those who view these as desirable attributes of the past or future. Even lack of happiness may be relative to the presumed happiness among primitives of the past or among citizens of future utopias. In these cases, the existence of a problem is seen as relative to some other group, situation, time, or place.

Normative Need

Some needs are considered normative, in that they are expected to exist. For example, some people see poverty not only as inevitable but as necessary for a number of economic and social reasons. The aged are expected to be ill, to the point that their problem is viewed as a result of age, not illness. It is generally assumed that people in institutions (homes for the aged, hospitals for the mentally ill, homes for disturbed children, and the like) are living in poverty, although both reflection and logic indicate little basis for this belief.

The normative view also operates to obscure problems: If all homeless people are seen as mentally ill or chemically dependent, then providing affordable housing is not a solution for their problem. Homelessness is thus seen as a "mere symptom," and not the "real problem." Again, if the members of religious cults are seen as immoral, antisocial, or disturbed, by virtue of their joining such groups, there is no reason to deal with their problems, which can more easily be solved by dissolving the cults in some manner.

Absolute Need

Besides relative measures and normative views, there are also absolute measures of problems. Thus the poverty level in the United States is now around $14,000 for an urban family of four.[6] This is an absolute measure of poverty, rather than a relative or normative measure. Illness is also usually determined by absolute measures—the number of hospital admissions, office visits to doctors, house calls, and so forth. Infant mortality rates, longevity and life expectancy, deaths due to starvation or various diseases, and many other measures of the extent and intensity of social problems are determined with reference to absolute scales.

Similarly, there are legal definitions of blindness, deafness, and of disability. Both workers' compensation and Veterans' Administration staffs spend time and effort determining not only the existence of disability but also its degree. The difference between a 10% hearing loss and a 20% hearing loss incurred in military service is not only statistical; compensation varies with the amount of loss. There is even a 0% disability classification, which entitles the veteran to some benefits but not to compensation.

NEED MEASUREMENT
FOR INDIVIDUAL PROBLEMS

Measures are also needed for determining the extent to which individuals' needs are defined as problems. Again, the method may involve relative, normative, or absolute measures. Poverty usually involves measurement of income and sometimes of assets. The degree of mental retardation is often determined by a series of verbal, written, and motor tests. Individual health measures almost invariably begin with thermometer, stethoscope, and sphygmomanometer, and the ascertained fever, heart rate, and blood pressure determine whether more tests are necessary. Like adult crimes, juvenile delinquency is determined with reference to a guilty or not guilty verdict. These, and others like them, are absolute measures.

Some examples of normative measures applied to individual cases include when a Down's syndrome child is assumed to be mentally retarded, when a widow or widower is assumed to be sad and lonely, or when a drug addict is assumed to be desperate for the next fix.

Relative measures—comparisons with some other group, all the rest of society, or some norm or standard determined as a nonproblem—are usually used to resolve the questions of how much marital discord constitutes a problem, whether mental illness is present, or whether social isolation is healthy independence or neurotic withdrawal. Indeed, the difference between normal, neurotic, and psychotic behavior is based on relative measures.

Changing Needs

As society changes and societal norms and behaviors evolve and become transmuted, situations once considered problems are no longer viewed that way. Situations once considered normal become identified as problems, and entirely new problems arise.

Homosexuality was once seen as both a societal and an individual problem, and until 1973 it was officially labeled as a mental illness by the American Psychiatric Association. Today, in the United States, it is increasingly being viewed as a condition, a situation, or one of a variety of acceptable behaviors. Pornography grows and recedes as a problem in accordance with varying court rulings. Sex, age, and racial discrimination have moved from being defined as problems to being defined as crimes. On the other hand, cohabiting unwed heterosexual individuals, unwed parents, and gay and lesbian couples—once equated with rank immorality, if not crime—now have certain legal protections. Homeless people, unknown to the general public a decade or so ago, now constitute a severe challenge to social welfare programs. So do adolescent pregnancies: The United States has the highest rate of such pregnancies among developed nations. AIDS sufferers and users of new kinds of dangerous substances, such as crack cocaine, present relatively new social problems. Among the newest problems being investigated is "fiscoholism"—uncontrollable spending.[7] Changing human needs define the problems with which social welfare deals, creating a dynamism that changes policies, programs, and practice.

SUMMARY

If social welfare is based on answering human needs, it becomes necessary to distinguish between needs, wants, and desires when devising programs. Needs can be classified as common, special, and societally caused. On both a societal and an individual basis, needs can be measured using relative, normative, or absolute standards. Differences in types of needs, and the way they are measured and defined as needs, also determine social welfare provisions. As needs change over time, programs are sometimes—but not always or immediately—also changed.

EXERCISE

A mother on general assistance asks for more money for clothes. She seems to spend most of her income on clothes of the latest fashion. Without knowing any other circumstances, given the reasons that she states below, to what extent do you see this as a want and to what extent a need? How do you distinguish, and on what basis? If it is a need, is it a normal, special, or societally created need? Would you measure it on a relative, normative, or absolute scale?

1. I feel depressed when I am not well dressed.
2. Shopping is my hobby.
3. I want my husband and children to be proud of me.
4. I'm getting back at my husband for spending so much on liquor.
5. My husband won't give me money for clothes.
6. I'm looking for work as a model and must be well dressed.

Notes

1. See Goodin (1988) for this material.
2. The number of homeless is from Connell (1987).
3. Miles (1985) describes growth needs; Macarov (1970b) asks if food is more important than prestige; the figures on needy Americans are from Schneiderman (1992).

4. "Transformations of identity" is Strauss's (1962) phrase.
5. The quote is from Rodman (1950).
6. The poverty level is from Teegardin (1992) and Fisher (1992).
7. Case Western Reserve University (1992) discovered fiscoholism.

READ MORE ABOUT IT . . .

For more information on:	*See these sources:*
Discussion of needs and wants in social work	Doyal & Gough, 1991
Definition of social welfare	Goodin, 1985
Uses of *need* in social welfare	Hoffman, 1958
Defining and classifying needs	Allardt, 1973; Dixon, 1987b; Johnson & Schwartz, 1991; Maslow, 1954; McKillip, 1987
Death and dying	Bertman, 1991; Kamerman, 1988; Lieberman & Black, 1987; Paul & Miller, 1986
Categories of crises	Eddy, Lawson, & Stilson, 1983; Stallings, 1973
Deviants	Jones et al., 1984; Page, 1984; Palmer & Humphrey, 1990
Different treatment of deviant and ill	Macarov, 1970b
Lack of motivation as reason for welfare reform	Macarov, 1980
Social conditions creating needs	Jansson, 1984; Macarov, 1988a, 1989; Macarov & Yanay, 1974
Need to identify problems	Loewenberg & Dolgoff, 1972
Novel medical cases	Roueche, 1965
Required reporting of child abuse	Saltzman & Proch, 1990; Suffolk County, 1974

For more information on:	*See these sources:*
Required reporting of elder abuse	*Reports on Elder Abuse,* 1991; *Summaries of Elder Abuse,* 1990
Social indicators	*Compendium,* 1988; Miles, 1985; Strumpel, 1976
Margaret Sanger	Chesler, 1992; Kennedy, 1970
Measures of need	Macarov, 1970b
Measures of poverty	Sherraden, 1988, 1991a
Necessity of poverty	Macarov, 1970b
Views of the aged	Macarov, 1991a
Views of homosexuality	Babuscio, 1988; Kus, 1990; Richan, 1987; Savin-Williams, 1990
Homelessness	Stoner, 1989
Teen pregnancy	Bell, 1987; Miller, Card, Paikoff, & Peterson, 1992
Crack cocaine	Sharp, Register, & Leftwich, 1992

PART II

Motivations for Social Welfare

The determination to help meet human needs is a theme running through all definitions of social welfare. This determination may arise from a number of motivations. Part II discusses five of the major motivators for engaging in social welfare: mutual aid, religious commandments, the desire for political advantage, economic considerations, and ideological factors.

These motivations coexist and intermingle; one may strengthen another, weaken it, oppose it, or have little relationship to it. Social welfare policies arise from combinations of motivations. It is only in order to clarify each motivation and the relationships of one to another that they are presented here as separate entities.

3. Mutual Aid

Among the historical roots of social welfare is the need and desire to engage in mutual aid, with the family as the primary locus. However, the structure of the family is changing from the "traditional" family to a myriad of different forms, some of which have been recognized in law and in social welfare regulations, and others which have not.

One of the oldest and most ubiquitous motivations for meeting human needs is the desire or the necessity to engage in mutual aid. In the past, and in some places even today, social welfare has consisted almost entirely of mutual-aid activities. Voluntary social welfare organizations often originate as a sharing of resources between people with common problems or needs. These resources are not limited to finances but may include psychological support, social relations, information, and activities. Mutual aid is one of the mainsprings of such movements.

For some social welfare programs, the goal is to enlarge mutual-aid activities in families, neighborhoods, and other settings. Mutual aid, in short, is one of the basic motivations for social welfare policies and programs, and one can comprehend these in their entirety, or in depth, only by understanding the influence of mutual aid in their development and existence.

The Roots of Mutual Aid

The roots of mutual aid lie in human prehistory. Aggression, territoriality, and the need to hunt are traits that humans share with animals, traits that may have originated in prehuman times. Similarly, mutual aid recalls a period when individuals could not stand alone against the vicissitudes of nature and banded together in herds or tribes to survive. In that phase of society, individual survival was not important; the continuation of the tribe was paramount, and all else was subordinated to it. Mutual aid was thus neither purposefully willed nor consciously undertaken; it was a normative condition, the only way that life could be lived. Kropotkin's seminal study of mutual aid in animals and humans leads to the conclusion that the species that have survived have not been those most able to dominate or destroy others but those most able to cooperate with one another.[1]

When people were undifferentiated parts of a tribe, they may have shared the same thoughts and emotions, giving birth to the concept of a collective unconscious—a "timeless and universal psyche"[2]—and the archetypes that are central to Jung's psychoanalytic theories. This assumption also underlies the concept of empathy, but some modern understandings and usages of that concept have been questioned.

Those who subscribe to recapitulation theory, which holds that the stages of the species' evolution are repeated in individual development, often argue that the need to become a member of a group is programmed into the human phylogeny. Others may not accept recapitulation but nevertheless emphasize that the individual "self" cannot emerge as a distinct entity without constant reference to other selves in the human community. These others, by their reactions, mold the individual: "He is what he is insofar as he is a member of this community, and the raw materials out of which this particular individual is born would not be a self but for his relationship to others in the community."[3]

The dependence of individuals upon mutual aid is nowhere more dramatically illustrated than in the universal experience of birth. Here is "the special, unique case in which the loved one really was once a spatial, corporeal 'part' of the one who loves" and is completely dependent upon the latter for life maintenance.[4] Nor is this a one-way relationship, for, as the folk saying has it, "More than the calf wants to suck, the cow wants to suckle." Mutual aid, then, is the very essence of human relationships, as well as the basis for individual and societal existence. Consequently, one way of viewing social welfare is as "that patterning of relationships which develops in society to carry out mutual-support functions."[5]

Although new ways of living have evolved since mutual aid began in the distant past, the same kind of mutual aid that once made life possible in herds and tribes may still exist today. Among Bedouin in the Near East, Gypsies in Europe, and people in many parts of Africa, in the South Pacific, and elsewhere, the basic structure of society is still based on mutual aid. In China, fostering a collective spirit is said to be of prime importance.

Families as the Primary Locus of Mutual Aid

Over time, the tribal structure evolved into clans; locality, ethnic, and language groups; and other kinds of associations. However, none of these is as universal or influential as the family, which has been described as "two or more people in a committed relationship from which they derive a sense of identity as a family."[6] Not only did the family take over mutual-aid activities as it emerged, but the very definition of family often includes the extent to which mutual aid is practiced.

As families developed, differences in family structure also came into being. The "traditional" family is usually an extended family including cousins, in-laws, and several generations, customarily living under one roof or in close proximity to one another, sometimes on communally owned land. In the Middle East this is called, in Arabic, the *hamula*. The patriarch of the family usually receives all income, dispenses all funds, and makes all decisions regarding both the family as a whole and each individual member. Mutual aid is so built into the structure of the extended family that it has been termed a source of security more time-honored than any social security system.

Mutual aid is an important aspect of the extended family, and every member is expected to pitch in on many essential activities—house building, sowing, reaping, and so forth. So important is the mutual-aid aspect of the extended family that where the extended family system is strong, the role of the state in social welfare has been found to be weak. The extended family takes care of its own, reducing the need for outside help. This is not always seen as a social good. In China, for example, policies aim to curtail the extended family's influence to create more dependence on government and/or collective institutions. Furthermore, one should be careful not to confuse correlation with causation. To say that strong families require less welfare does not mean that less welfare will create strong families. Even when family support grows after social welfare declines or stops, the result may well be weakened, rather than strengthened, families. Mutual aid extended under outside pressure does not necessarily result in good relations.

THE EMERGENCE OF THE NUCLEAR FAMILY

Historically—and particularly in the industrialized West—the extended family was long ago overtaken by the nuclear family, which consists of parents and unmarried children living at home. In Norway, for example, all welfare is provided to the individual, and the importance of the extended family is minimized in favor of the nuclear family. Although the nuclear family is more prevalent than the extended family in most developed countries, even there substantial segments of the population cling to the older tradition.

Social problems, such as anomie, alienation, intrafamily discord, and intergenerational problems, often arise from the interface of the traditional extended family and modern types of family structures. The conflict of values between parents and children is one part of this problem, leading to familial tension. Also, the claims of the extended family on the income of its members may conflict with the individual-success ethic of "getting ahead."

Countries that receive immigrants from societies with a differing family structure also face this problem. Immigrants from a traditional society are often bewildered and resentful of the values (or, to them, loss of values) in the nuclear family structure. The same problem is found in countries that experience migration from rural areas or small towns, with their extended family tradition, to the large cities, which are often characterized by an atomistic and anonymous existence.

CHANGES IN FAMILY STRUCTURE

In the United States, social policies affecting families have long defined the normative family as a working father, a nonworking mother, and two or more children under age 18 at home. Many social and social welfare policies are based on this pattern, giving rise to what Abramovitz calls a "family ethic." Today, this supposedly normative pattern represents less than 6% of American families.[7] Most families have no children under age 18 living at home. Because these changes have occurred in the last ten years or so, it is not surprising that social welfare policy has not yet been amended to reflect the new situation.

Adult children living at home, although not part of the supposedly normative pattern, are another matter. Over the last twenty years, adult children in the parental home have become more common. In 1988, nearly three fourths of adults between ages 19 and 25 had lived with parents for at least some period after age 19; in one survey of parents ages 45 to 54, almost half had an "unlaunched" child at home; more than 30% of all 25- to 30-year-olds are estimated to be living in the homes of their parents.[8] Indeed, the "empty nest" is being replaced by the "crowded nest." Again, this is a relatively new situation.

Most families in the United States today are neither extended nor nuclear, as defined above. A number of other variations have been identified: single-parent, divorced, widowed, separated, reconstituted, gay or lesbian, foster and adoptive, two-career families, and cohabiting never-married couples who may also have children. To this list can be added childless couples, dyadic-nuclear families, dual-work families, two-earner families (not necessarily the same as dual-work or dual-career families), multigenerational families, families with remarried spouses, middle-aged or old-aged couples, second-career families, institutional families, grandparent/grandchildren families, mixed-religion families, mixed-race families, and families containing children, half-kin children, adoptive children, and combinations of these.

Statistics concerning some of these patterns are revealing. More than 50% of all couples marrying in the United States have spent extended periods living together before marriage, and 40% of cohabiting unmarried families include children, which makes it increasingly true that children born of unwed mothers are not necessarily children of single parents.[9] Despite increasing public acceptance of nonmarried cohabiting partners, many governmental programs still require proof of marriage before extending certain benefits. This is, in fact, a relatively modern convention; before 1753 a ceremony was not a condition for the validity of marriages. Furthermore, despite growing public acceptance of same-sex couples, no state in the United States recognizes marriage between two people of the same sex. However, the connection between marriage and family and between family and parenthood is becoming looser, and this inevitably brings with it a less clear image of the family. Indeed, there are those who speak of "marriage-related" families and "non-marriage-related" families.

ONE-PARENT FAMILIES

From 1970 to 1984 the number of one-parent families doubled from 3.2 million to 6.7 million. Eighty-eight percent of these were mother-child families, but there are also about one million single fathers whose children reside with them all or most of the time. In 1984, 15% of white families and

50% of African American families were headed by one parent, and more than 50% of American children will spend some time in a single-parent family.[10]

MORE WORKING
WIVES AND MOTHERS

Although it is not itself a change in family structure, the entry into the labor force of increasing numbers of women—wives and mothers among them—brings changes in family functions. In 1930, women constituted 22% of the American labor force; in 1960, 33%; and in 1988, 45%. It has been estimated that by 1995 at least 60%, or three in five, of all women will be working. Between now and 2000, 64% of all new entrants to the labor force will be women. Some 70% of females now working are in their childbearing years, and 80% of these are expected to become mothers during their working years. By 1998, the labor force participation of married women will equal that of married men. Half of women with children under 18 work, 50% of mothers of children under 6 work, and 55% of mothers of children under 3 work. Although many women work for career fulfillment, self-esteem, or other reasons, the great majority give income as their main reason.[11]

The growth in the number of working mothers has given rise to the burgeoning child care business, private, volunteer, and governmental. The programs known as workfare acknowledge that welfare parents cannot be required to work unless arrangements are made to care for their small children. The Family Support Act of 1988 recognizes this problem and attempts to solve it.

Under the Family Support Act, states must provide twelve months of child care to recipients who leave the welfare rolls and who need such help if they are to work. In 1988, day care providers tended more than one fifth of all children under age 5 whose mothers were employed. The availability of day care is often the determining factor in whether mothers work—57% of nonworking, low-income single mothers said they would seek employment if acceptable child care was available.[12]

DIVORCE AND REMARRIAGE

The U.S. divorce rate has grown steadily for the past several decades; it doubled between 1960 and 1980 and increased 111% between 1970 and 1988 alone. In 1990, there were almost 2.5 million marriages and 1.17 million divorces. Seventy-nine percent of divorced men and 75% of divorced women remarry, but 60% of second marriages also end in divorce. One of the resulting problems is that a quarter of divorced women fall into poverty for some time during the first five years of leaving a marriage.[13]

The divorce-remarriage cycle has resulted in what has been variously termed *merged families, blended families, reconstituted families, second-chance families*, and others. The result is family patterns very far from the model family on which policy is based, including families with children, stepchildren, half-siblings, stepgrandparents, and many more complexities.

In addition, there are "informal marriages" to consider. The number of unmarried cohabiting couples tripled during the 1970s and tripled again by 1983, although this total does not distinguish between what were once called "common law" marriages and couples living together without considering themselves married, couples living together before marriage, and couples living together for relatively short periods.

There has also been a rising trend toward interfaith marriages, although homogamous marriages have been found to be more satisfying. Reuben points out that "Catholics are marrying Protestants, Methodists are marrying Lutherans, Baptists are marrying Episcopalians. There are currently 300,000 to 400,000 Jewish/non-Jewish interfaith marriages alone in America, and the numbers increase annually."[14]

THE CONTINUING ROLE OF THE FAMILY

With all of these changes in family structure and function, a common thread of familial mutual aid remains. When people are in trouble or in need, they naturally turn to the family first. The family is seen as the first line of defense, both by society and by family members, and all needs that can be satisfied within the family are generally expected to be handled that way. That "blood is thicker than water" is a widely accepted axiom, and throughout society the family is considered to be one of the major sources of need satisfaction.

Although policy problems are caused by such varying and changing family forms, some social welfare policies and practices also may cause or contribute to family difficulties. Some social workers, for example, have been accused of aggravating family problems by viewing the extended family as encouraging immature dependency patterns in its members and by defining appropriate or "healthy" behavior as the breaking of traditional kinship ties and establishment of closed nuclear families. It has also been charged that social work intervention, education, and policy have shared with other counseling disciplines the tendency to sanctify and encourage the nuclear family, when other less traditional structures might be more appropriate for some people. Other critics point to the fact that some social welfare policies or social work practices may weaken or eliminate mutual dependence of parents and children, or encourage removing one of them from the home, or inculcate values in children that are at variance with parents' values.

The impact of social welfare on families, and the place of families in social welfare programs, will be examined in the next chapter. Nonfamily aspects of mutual aid will be discussed in Chapter 5.

SUMMARY

One of the major motivations to engage in social welfare is the need or the desire to participate in mutual aid. Although the family has almost always been the central focus of mutual aid, the structure of families is changing to include many new types of relationships. Some of these may be adversely affected or not even recognized by social welfare policies and programs. Nevertheless, social welfare in general aims to provide support to individuals when traditional forms of family and other supports are not adequate.

EXERCISES

1. To whom do you refer when you speak of your family?
2. To what extent do you consider your family an extended family? a nuclear family? a different category of family?
3. With which of the types of families mentioned in this chapter are you personally familiar?
4. Can you add other types of families to the ones listed in this chapter?

Notes

1. Kropotkin (1925) discusses the primacy of cooperation.
2. The quotation is from Campbell (1971), who discusses Jung's collective unconscious.
3. The quotation is from Strauss (1956).
4. The quotation is from Scheler (1954).
5. The quotation is from Gilbert and Specht (1974).
6. The quotation is from Chilman, Nunnally, and Cox (1988).
7. The term is from Abramovitz (1992), and the number of "normative" families is from the *Wellness Newsletter,* 5(1).
8. The number of families with children at home is from *The Futurist, 23*(6); "unlaunched" children survey is from Aquilino (1990); children in parents' homes is from Schneiderman (1992).
9. These statistics are from Schneiderman (1992).
10. Statistics are from the following sources: on one-parent families, Norton & Glick (1986); on children residing with fathers, Greif (1990); on European American and African American families, Norton & Glick (1986) and Berrick (1991); on children in single-parent families, Schneiderman (1992).
11. Statistics are from the following sources: on percentages of women in the labor force, Lingg (1990); 1995 estimate, Conference Board (1985); on new workers and childbearing years, Barton (1991); on married women equalling married men, Davis (1984); on mothers of children 6 to 18, Conference Board (1985); on mothers of children under 3, U.S. Department of Commerce (1987). Reasons for mothers working are from Moss & Fonda (1980).
12. The proportion of children in day care is from Aquirre & Marshall (1988); the data on mothers who want to work are from Berrick (1991).
13. Statistics are from the following sources: the 1988 divorce rate and data on remarriages, from Visher & Visher (1988); the 1990 figure, *Demographic Yearbook* (1990); marriages ending in divorce, Furstenberg & Spanier (1984); the poverty of divorcées, Morgan (1984).
14. The quotation is from Reuben (1987).

READ MORE ABOUT IT . . .

For more information on:	*See these sources:*
The concept of mutual aid	Lee & Swenson, 1986
Territoriality, hunting need	Ardrey, 1966, 1976
Aggression	Lorenz, 1971
Empathy	Macarov, 1970a, 1978b; MacKay, Hughes, & Carver, 1990; Stotland, Mathews, Sherman, Hansson, & Richardson, 1978

For more information on:	*See these sources:*
Recapitulation theory	Lorenz, 1971
Mutual aid in the South Pacific	Gilbert & Specht, 1974
Collective spirit in China	Dixon, 1992
The family	Aptekar, 1967; Kates & Millman, 1990
in China	Dixon, 1992
in Norway	Tutvedt & Young, 1991
Types of families	Chilman et al., 1988; Macarov, 1991a
Early conventions of marriage	Eekelaar, 1978
New forms of U.S. families	Saltzman & Proch, 1990; Schneiderman, 1992; Wingen, 1992
Family Support Act	Tatara, 1990
Informal marriages	Glick, 1984; *Jerusalem Post* (August 2, 1987; p. 2)
Interfaith marriages	Heaton, 1984
Contributions of social work to family problems	Constantino, 1981; Leichter & Mitchell, 1967; Tutvedt & Young, 1991

4. Social Welfare and the Family

Social welfare programs that affect families can be divided into two some-times overlapping types. The first is the attempt to affect families as such, either strengthening them—the original intent of the Aid to Families with Dependent Children (AFDC) program—or limiting them, as in some recent state-level AFDC regulations. The second thrust is the desire to use families for social welfare purposes, as, for example, making family members legally responsible for one another.

Besides mutual aid, families are expected to carry out many other functions, such as socialization, control, and continuity. The family is not the only element charged with these responsibilities. The desirable "mix" of government, voluntary services, the market, and the family varies from time to time and location to location, with respect to responsibility for religious beliefs and practices, education, health, deportment, inculcation of values, and career choices, among other things. Some societies hold that education is the family's responsibility, religion the church's, and defense the government's. Others have entrusted religion to the family, education to the state, and health to voluntary organizations. Transnational studies indicate a number of additional permutations.

The same is true of social welfare. However, because mutual aid is one of the most distinguishing characteristics of families, and because the family is the basic unit in most societies, social welfare policy is inevitably affected by the extent to which families engage in mutual aid. The amount of mutual aid in families is also conditioned by the extent and type of social welfare available.

Family Policy

Family policy may be understood to mean attempts to influence the structure and functions of families by means of conscious and deliberate planning. Governmental policies regarding families, in this sense, did not become generally established until after World War II, and these—including social welfare policies—have a number of motivations:

- The desire to maintain strong family structures so that the family can carry out the normative activities mentioned above—education, training in deportment, and so forth
- The desire to provide a healthy environment for growing and living, which will avoid or minimize psychic and interrelationship problems
- The instrumental goal of avoiding social welfare costs and activities by increasing the amount of mutual aid that families extend to their members

These motivations are expressed in the two main thrusts of social welfare policies regarding families. The first is to affect families by strengthening, enlarging, or limiting them. The second is to use, exploit, or rely on families in carrying out social welfare activities. Those who would like to see families carry more of society's need-fulfilling activities can be expected to take steps to maintain or strengthen families. Those who see strong families as a social good might see the need for families to undertake more mutual-aid activities as an instrumental device for strengthening the family, or they might see a reverse effect in the legal requirement that family members be financially responsible for each other. In either case, family size is often considered an important target of family (welfare) policy.

POLICIES DESIGNED
TO AFFECT FAMILIES

Some countries have deliberate policies intended to influence the size of families. In 1990, 56% of all countries reported that their level of fertility was either too low or too high—twenty wanted higher fertility rates, and seventy-four did not. Sixty-four countries have policies devised to lower the fertility rate; twenty countries have policies to raise the rate, and sixty-six countries do not intervene directly. Both the United States and Canada reportedly view their present situation as satisfactory, and neither intervenes directly to affect the fertility rate.[1]

LIMITING FAMILIES

In India, the major preoccupation of social welfare policy is limiting the size of families. Very few agencies exist to help families cope with problems, and these tend to be located only in certain urban areas. Similarly, China has engaged in a "one child per family" campaign for many years, with various penalties imposed on families having more than one child. Only recently have the possible negative consequences of this policy been examined. Limiting family size is not necessarily the only response to a high birthrate. In Thailand, the family is considered so important that at one time the challenge was to find foster homes for children: So many families had taken the children of relatives or servants into their own homes that they had no room to receive other children.

Although increasing life expectancy is as important a factor in population growth in many countries as a high birthrate, the birthrate seems easier to manipulate. Population control seems easier and cheaper than increasing resources or attempting to solve the problems caused by overpopulation. This has been phrased: "Money spent to reduce births will be as much as 100 times more effective than money invested to raise output."[2] Another indirect method of encouraging smaller families is through legislation that favors small families through tax structures, housing policies, employment policies, and social welfare programs. In some Indian states, for example, workers are threatened with dismissal if they have more than two children. In other countries, income-tax exemptions grow progressively smaller with additional dependents, or children's allowances are reduced. Singapore makes it difficult for employed women with more than three children to get maternity benefits and for large families to find housing. Some countries pay bonuses to men who undergo vasectomies.

These measures have been called "inducements," in contradistinction to voluntarism and compulsion. More direct measures are used to encourage voluntarism in the area of population control. These include education, the availability of legal and inexpensive abortions, voluntary sterilization, and widespread distribution of contraceptives. In Pakistan, contraceptives are sold at more than 35,000 pharmacies, tea stalls, general provision stores, and elsewhere. No prescription is required, and as a sales incentive, the shopkeepers are permitted to keep 40% of the sales price.

Even more direct measures are involved in compulsion, which, taken to its logical extreme, means enforced sterilization. Although no country admits

to this practice, there are charges that so-called voluntary sterilization plans
are enforced under various kinds of pressure. Reports of such cases in the
United States led to an investigation and, in 1974, to strict measures against
the practice. However, evidence suggests that these measures are not being
enforced and that coercion, linkage to other health measures, and misleading
information may be employed. Shapiro holds that involuntary sterilization
continues to be performed.[3]

RELIGIOUS ATTITUDES
TOWARD BIRTH CONTROL

The extent and efficacy of the direct measures rest, in large part, on the
religion, culture, and laws of the country concerned. Religious attitudes vary.
The Roman Catholic Church, as expressed by the Vatican, officially opposes
all methods of birth control except the rhythm method. Protestants generally
favor contraception as a method of preventive birth control. The Orthodox
Jewish faith condones use of contraceptive methods by women but forbids
them for men, including coitus interruptus. Conservative and Reform Jews
tend to condone contraceptive devices employed by either sex. Hindu belief
systems provide little barrier to the use of family planning, although Gandhi
saw artificial birth control as reprehensible. Buddhism has neither the injunc-
tion to multiply nor strict prohibitions on birth control: The well-being of
the living is considered paramount. In Islam, abortion is absolutely forbidden,
but contraception is allowed for pressing reasons, providing both marriage
partners agree, the agreement is voluntary, and the time period is limited.
Because of their differing circumstances, Saudi Arabia forbids the sale of
contraceptives, Pakistan encourages and subsidizes such sales, and Bangla-
desh is reported to be moving toward legalized abortion. Nevertheless,
culture continues to play an important role in setting family policy.

Cultures may view large families as a manifestation of lower-class values.
Some individuals and groups consider more than two children per couple a
form of environmental pollution and aim for zero population growth. In other
cultures, having many children (particularly boys) is considered proof of the
masculinity (*machismo*) of the father and the good fortune of the mother. In
Hinduism, a son is looked on as one of the greatest blessings because the
father's fortune in the next world depends on the exact execution of the
funeral rites by his son. Similarly, in some branches of Judaism, a son must say
the memorial prayers (Kaddish) for the departed.

Some societies value children as laborers. In U.S. history, children were employed in factories or home sweatshops, and the employment of children continues among some immigrant groups. Children may also participate in income-generating activities on farms. In other countries, children may be given specific income-generating tasks, and these may replace school in terms of importance. Examples include picking flowers, making rugs, and working in other specific occupations. In some cultures, such as African countries in which the life expectancy is short, parents may have large families out of the desire to have enough grown children to provide for their old age.

Finally, the laws of a country may mandate birth control measures; may legalize some, but not other, contraceptive activities; or may outlaw any such measures. In some countries, government involvement is illegal or otherwise impossible, but voluntary organizations may be permitted, or even encouraged, to engage in such programs. The law may permit dissemination of information but not devices. Information and devices may be permitted but abortions outlawed. Finally, abortions may be permitted but not those paid for by public funds. In addition, states or local authorities may be permitted to do what the national government cannot, or vice versa.

THE HISTORY OF BIRTH CONTROL

Although individuals and couples have probably practiced some sort of birth control since the earliest times, the nineteenth century saw more widespread use of such methods. In 1807, the *Code Napoléon* in France gave daughters the same inheritance rights as sons. French workers and peasants immediately embraced the advantages of family limitation, using folk methods handed down for generations. The first birth control clinics in the world were established in Holland in 1878, and subsequent acceptance of contraceptive techniques in England is said to have caused the sudden drop in the English birthrate. The term *birth control* came into use in 1914, winning out over phrases such as family limitation, conscious generation, neo-Malthusianism, voluntary parenthood, voluntary motherhood, race control, and birthrate control. *Family planning* has become the preferred expression recently, conveying a somewhat different approach.

The growth of birth control or family planning throughout the world is forever linked with the name of Margaret Sanger, who virtually single-handedly brought the importance of population questions to the attention of governments and people. Jailed eight times, she persisted in contending that birth control information is not obscene, that it is an integral part of public health and education, and that both societies as a whole and individuals have a right to decide population questions on the basis of knowledge, rather than ignorance.

The development of the birth control movement can be traced through a series of important events. The first issue of Margaret Sanger's magazine, *Woman Rebel,* appeared in March, 1914, and the first birth control clinic in the United States opened in Brooklyn in 1916, only to be closed by police. In 1921, the National Birth Control Association was founded, and in 1925, the International Birth Control Association was formed. In 1931, as a result of such activities and growing interest, the Federal Council of Churches of Christ in America called for the repeal of federal and state laws that prohibited communication about birth control by physicians and other qualified people, and the Vatican sanctioned the rhythm method of birth control in the early 1930s. In 1936, court rulings made it legal to mail contraceptive materials and information to and from doctors and other qualified people. In 1942, the Birth Control Association changed its name to the Planned Parenthood Federation of America. After continuing interest and agitation, the American Public Health Association, in 1959, passed a "stunning" resolution stressing the importance of birth control.[4] In 1960, the birth control pill was released to the general public, and family planning became a generally accepted activity. In 1965, the U.S. Supreme Court found in *Griswold v. Connecticut* that the constitutional right to privacy guarantees the right to decide "whether and when to bear or beget a child." As a result, distribution of contraceptives and contraceptive information became legal in all states.

Two caveats regarding this history of birth control and family planning are in order. The first is that it has been concerned solely with the activities of voluntary organizations, rather than with those of governments. The second is that the history concerns information and materials about birth control but not abortions, which have their own record.

THE ABORTION ISSUE

In 1942, the U.S. Surgeon General ruled that states could use federal funds for family planning services, but few states did so. Government, rather than private medicine, became interested in communicating knowledge about family as evidence suggested that poverty and large families were correlated. After the Supreme Court ruled in 1965 that married couples had a constitutional right to practice contraception, the Office of Economic Opportunity began to make grants to finance family planning projects. In 1967 this became an object of "special emphasis."[5] In the same year, the Social Security Act was amended to offer educational and practical services to families with dependent children.

Family planning activities can be divided into giving information, giving or implanting devices, and performing abortions. Although the controversy over the first two activities was heated, deterring their usage, the passions, controversies, and campaigns about abortion have been far more prominent. The abortion issue arouses deep moral fervor on both sides, and it has medical, legal, sociological, philosophic, demographic, and psychological aspects. Nevertheless, abortion is now a widespread method of limiting birth. The number of pregnancies terminated each year by induced abortion throughout the world is not known. Some form of abortion has probably been in use since the earliest days of mankind, and it had evidently become widespread enough in relatively modern times for Pope Pius XI to feel constrained in 1679 to condemn the notion that the unborn fetus may be killed to escape personal or social complications. Nevertheless, until 1869 the Catholic Church held that abortion was not a punishable act if it occurred in early pregnancy.

Indeed, the widespread use of illegal abortions, which often resulted in injury or death to the mother, motivated many people to support contraceptive measures. Margaret Sanger, for one, was originally opposed to abortion and urged contraception as a measure that would make abortion unnecessary.

In the United States, a number of forces combined to change attitudes and the law regarding abortions. The rediscovery of poverty in the 1960s led to recognition that the poor, dependent on societal resources and agencies, were denied the goods and services available to others through the private market, including birth control information, devices, and abortions. Simultaneously, the student revolt and the civil rights movement led to more concern about individual freedom and rights, and the women's movement built on these beginnings. The evident correlation between large families and societal problems affected attitudes toward abortion, as well as other methods of birth control. The question of legal abortions came up dramatically in the early 1960s when the use of a tranquilizing drug, thalidomide, widely prescribed for pregnant women, was found to result in badly deformed babies, and requests for abortions were refused.

The mid-1960s appear to have been a watershed in the liberalization of abortion laws throughout the world. Until then, U.S. laws had generally been strict—in some states, even stricter than those of the Catholic Church.

However, in Japan and certain parts of Europe, abortions—safely performed—
were associated with spectacular drops in birthrates. In the 1960s, there were
about a million abortions a year in the United States. Most of these were illegal:
Legal abortion was permitted only to save the life of the mother. Beginning
in 1967, about a dozen states enacted somewhat more liberal laws, and the
Roe v. Wade U.S. Supreme Court decision in 1973 invalidated the antiabor-
tion laws of most states. By late 1975 this decision had not yet been fully
implemented in every state. In 1973, between 600,000 and 750,000 legal
abortions were reported in the United States, and this has since risen to about
1.6 million legal abortions per year. In 1975 there were 33.1 abortions for
100 live births in the United States; by 1987 this had increased to 42.2. The
number of illegal abortions is obviously not known, although anecdotal
evidence suggests it is even higher than the legal rate.[6]

The move toward more liberal attitudes about abortion in the United
States has not been without opposition. Those who oppose abortion on moral
grounds hope to override the Supreme Court decision with a constitutional
amendment. The attitudes of presidential candidates toward such an amendment have become an issue during election campaigns. Aside from morality,
one of the most controversial issues is whether abortions should be made
available through welfare programs, thus using tax payments for what some
people consider illegal and immoral acts. The battle for legalized abortion
involves deeply held ideological and moral positions, the poles of which
have evolved into the right-to-life and the right-to-choose positions. Owing
to the passionate intensity of views on both sides, laws and activities will
probably continue to fluctuate from side to side with political, judicial, and
administrative changes.

ENCOURAGING LARGE FAMILIES

At the opposite end of the spectrum from population control are what are
termed *pronatalist* policies. Early legal codes dating back to Hammurabi and
the Emperor Augustus contained pronatalist provisions. The Declaration of
Independence said of King George III of Britain: "He has endeavored to
prevent the population of these states."

A widespread motive for pro-natalist policies is quasi-xenophobic fear
that other groups, countries, philosophies, or races are threatening by virtue
of their very size. Unable to affect their growth, policy makers turn their efforts
inward, toward increasing population. Other countries are simply short of

labor, and some see a minimum population figure as necessary for viability and independence: Denmark's population of 4 million people is sometimes cited as a model. Argentina and Brazil have been called "frankly pro-natalist," with their large tracts of empty land given as the reason. In India, despite a change in the inheritance law in 1956, custom still limits succession to males, exerting a pronatalist effect because "a family which already has several daughters will want more children in the hope of producing a son, in order to keep property within the family."[7]

Another influence is the tradition, which the women's liberation movement seeks to alter, that the proper role of women is to have babies and raise families—or, more precisely, that a woman is or should be happy only when she has a baby on the way or in the family. Finally, some practices are implicitly pronatalist: In Egypt, Indonesia, Iran, and Sri Lanka, a woman can be unilaterally divorced on one of many grounds and find herself without alimony, job opportunity, or custody of her children; this policy forces her to bear as many children as her husband demands.

Whatever their motivations, certain activities are generally directed to enlarging populations. Tax exemptions that consider the cost of raising children are perhaps the most universal of such devices. Generally speaking, these are of limited utility, because tax exemptions can be exploited only by those with a sufficiently large income; poor people pay lower income taxes in any case. Such exemptions act to subsidize the more affluent, who generally do not refrain from having children for financial reasons, rather than the poor, who might.

MATERNITY BENEFITS

Another method of encouraging higher birthrates, as well as healthy parents and children, is maternity benefits. In many countries, these are limited to working mothers and take the form of financial help during time off from work, guarantees of a job on return, and reduction in work hours for a specified period. Some countries, such as Israel, give a direct grant for initial childrearing expenses and repay the cost of transportation to the hospital. Some maternity benefits may be available to all mothers, not just those who work—Israel includes adoptive parents, and Sweden pays for paternity leave. Israel also has a network of maternal- and child-health clinics that give prenatal and postnatal care to all mothers and are patronized by all strata of society.

Children's and Family Allowances

Of all measures avowedly designed to increase the birthrate, children's or family allowances are the most ubiquitous. In some cases, the original motivation was mixed: a combination of low birthrates and difficult economic conditions for large families. In other cases, it was straightforward: "With its present rate of reproduction, the British race cannot continue and children's allowances can at least help to restore the birth rate." In Europe, the early stages of family policy were explicitly pronatalist, because the policy was formulated against the background of the declining birth rate between the two world wars.[8]

The terms *children's allowances, family allowances,* and *demogrants* are often used synonymously, although they are technically different. Family allowances are paid to all family units, children's allowances are linked to the number of children, and demogrants are paid to each individual. There is no known instance of demogrants, and the term is often used in a generic manner, encompassing both of the other two. As noted previously, such allowances began in Europe, when employers paid differential wages based on family size—a method that was later taken over by governments. Such programs have grown from seven in 1940 to sixty-three in 1991. Of the countries with children's allowances or family allowances, 67% are work-related—that is, they either are for workers only or require prior work and/or payment records.[9] Almost all of these are universal—that is, not means-tested—programs. The United States has no childrens' or family allowances as such but makes payments through its means-tested Aid to Families with Dependent Children program.

There is no consistency in arrangements for family or children's allowances. Although most countries pay more as the number of children increases, some have limits; others pay less with each additional child. In some countries, one-parent families get paid as for an additional child. In others, the allowance rises with the age of the child, in recognition of increasing needs. Although twins do not result in disproportionate payments, some countries pay more for triplets and/or quadruplets. Great Britain has specified that family allowances belong to the mother, rather than to the father or to the children. Finally, some countries tax family allowances as part of income, whereas others declare them nontaxable. Children's and family allowances were originally instituted to increase birthrates and thus enlarge populations. France was one of the first countries to institute such a program, and aid to families is largest in that nation. France's policy of encouraging a higher birthrate is also seen in the increase of family allowances provided for the third and fourth children.

EFFECTS OF CHILDREN'S AND FAMILY ALLOWANCES

The success of children's allowances can be evaluated from a number of different assumptions, as emphasized by a 1975 World Health Organization report. Some of the side effects that can occur have been mentioned in a Swedish report that finds children's allowances tend to reduce other types of child- and family-oriented programs, such as summer camps for children and vacations for housewives. But France's program was the prototype of the use of children's allowances to raise birthrates, and the French experience is instructive.

In 1939, France extended coverage of its previous children's allowance program to the entire population. Immediately after World War II, the average number of births per year rose from 630,000 to 856,000. However, during the same period, the United States experienced a comparable increase, without a children's allowance, and the birthrate in Sweden declined, despite that country's family-allowance system. In 1945, Canada instituted a family allowance program, but its birthrate continues to parallel that of the United States, which has no such program. It seems, therefore, that children's or family allowances do not create higher birthrates. Even if taken together, family allowances, tax measures, and maternity benefits for working mothers have not increased birthrates. On the other hand, compulsory education, child labor laws, and social security do seem to nudge fertility downward.

An argument can still be made for family allowances, not as an incentive for population increase but as a method—or even the preferred method—of fighting poverty and its related ills. Such a program, as opposed to existing antipoverty programs, embodies the dilemma of universal versus categorical programs that was mentioned briefly in Chapter 1.

CHILDREN'S AND FAMILY ALLOWANCES AS A UNIVERSAL PROGRAM

Proponents of a children's allowance in the United States point out that universal programs, by making benefits available to every stratum of the population, ensure that there will be an influential, sophisticated body of users who will demand and receive good service. They point out that services only for poor people almost invariably become poor services. Furthermore, they argue that because payments are based on the number of children, large families will receive the bulk of the payments, and—because they constitute the portion of the population most at risk—their problems will thereby be solved or alleviated in disproportionate numbers. They also argue that payments going to everyone and being paid automatically will eliminate the need for a means test and all other stigmatizing features. Finally, it is argued that because everyone in the country, regardless of class or position, will benefit from such cash payments, there will be little political opposition to such a program, as there is to programs that aid only the poor. Indeed, some say that the dismantling of some current programs that a universal allowance would make possible is enough reason to support such an allowance.

Proponents of categorical, or selective, programs contend that the limited money available to fight social problems should be concentrated on those with problems. They view children's allowances as a bonus to middle- and upper-class families at the expense of the poor. They hold that the amounts to be paid would be insignificant to the affluent, although they might be the difference between hunger and satisfaction, or dignity and humility, for the poor. They point out that services for the poor need not become poor services, provided they are adequately funded and clients are allowed to participate in policy determination and organized into self-interest groups. They contend that means tests need not be degrading, as people are asked their financial status in a number of nonstigmatizing situations. Finally, they hold that making "something for everybody" the price for political support is polite bribery. Proponents of these programs argue that there is little evidence that the affluent would object to more efforts to eradicate or alleviate poverty, or even that they would be unwilling to sacrifice to do so, if they were convinced that the effort would bear fruit.

On the question of the affluent's willingness to aid the poor, it should be pointed out that many taxpayers subsidize services for others: Childless couples pay school taxes, and people who own no car pay highway taxes. In a survey in Israel, 54% of those asked indicated a willingness to pay more taxes to fight poverty, but 10% demurred on the grounds that the money collected would not, in fact, be used for that purpose.[10] Public opinion polls do not, of course, determine policies, and the major argument for a universal children's allowance, family allowance, or demogrant remains its supposed political feasibility.

U.S. POLICY TOWARD
POPULATION GROWTH

The United States has no policy dealing with population growth as such. One report points out that in 1982, 1.3 million pregnancies in the United States resulted in unwanted or mistimed births; 1.6 million pregnancies were terminated by induced abortion; and 400,000 unintended pregnancies were miscarried. The report ends by asking, "Can there be any doubt that family planning in the United States is inadequate?"[11] In other parts of the world, social welfare agencies and workers have taken the lead in population-control activities, carrying almost the entire burden in some countries.

Strengthening Families

The importance a society ascribes to families as such, attempts to affect them, and the means by which such attempts are made vary from place to place. In most Western countries the family is seen as a social good, and policies are adopted to aid them. Some policies are governmental, whereas others emerge from the voluntary or private sectors.

For example, a number of European businesses began adjusting salaries to family size at the end of the nineteenth century, and this practice spread widely after World War I. After World War II, this policy tended to become a government activity, and by now a majority of the world's nations—and all of the industrialized West, except the United States—have either a children's allowance or a family allowance. In Israel, salaries of employees were originally geared to the sizes of their families, and although this has been reduced to an almost symbolic amount, many fringe benefits are based on family size. Israel's family policy is also reflected in its universal children's allowance, maternity leave, maternity pay, and a maternity grant.

The closest thing to a family allowance in the United States is the Earned Income Tax Credit: Working couples with dependent children whose salaries—as attested by their tax returns—are below a certain level are "forgiven" part of their taxes. However, not only are the amounts involved very small, but this policy provides no help to those whose incomes are so small they are not taxed.

THE FAMILY AS THE FOCUS
OF SOCIAL WELFARE ACTIVITIES

The history of social welfare in both England and the United States is replete with references to the importance of the family. For example, one of the pioneer social reformers at the beginning of the nineteenth century saw the "kindness of relatives" as one of the essential founts from which flowed beneficial work. The Charity Organization Society in England firmly adopted the position that the family was to be considered as a whole. Thus, voluntary activities in charity, reform, and welfare work can be viewed as being family- and child-oriented since their inception. The very names of the Family Service Association and the Jewish Family Service bespeak the concern of voluntary agencies for families.

However, critics point out that despite the Charity Organization Society's stated concern with families, it was 1919 before its name was altered to include the word *family*. There was limited concern with the family as a unit or with the interaction between family life and social institutions.

GOVERNMENTAL FAMILY POLICY

In the United States, government policies were not much more supportive. When the U.S. Secretary of Health, Education, and Welfare appointed an ad hoc committee on public welfare in 1961, its recommendations were "designed to reinforce and support family life through rehabilitation, prevention, and protection."[12] However, eight years later, in 1969, Congress debated a Family Assistance Plan but did not muster enough votes to adopt it. Nevertheless, the 1974 Code of Federal Regulations dealing with social welfare clearly includes the goal of strengthening family life. In 1980, during President Carter's term, a White House Conference on Families took place. It helped set in motion developments that led to the 1988 passage of the Family Support Act. In 1993, state programs for "family preservation" received $295 million, and the Clinton administration was seeking funds to substantially widen this program. These are state programs that provide services and finances that will help abused and neglected children remain with their families rather than being moved to foster homes or institutions.

LACK OF GOVERNMENTAL FAMILY POLICY

However, some question the validity of the belief that families have always been at the center of governmental family concern: "The United States does not have an overall, official, explicitly stated family policy" and "There is no family policy in this country. The United States has no family ministry, no high-level family commission, and no programmatic legislation or administrative orders which are called 'family policy.'"[13] Some critics are more emphatic:

> To its disgrace, the United States does not have a family support policy. There is no federal law mandating that wages be sufficient to support a family: there is no requirement that jobs provide fringe benefits such as health care and pensions. Nor does the public benefits systems address these deficiencies.[14]

These critics hold that although there are programs that contain the word *family* or that purport to serve families as such, they do not do so and even have other aims:

> There are 63 federal programs and a greater number of state programs, with the word "family" in their title or with an explicitly stated objective of aiding families.... The word "family" in the title or preamble of a piece of legislation is not, however, a particularly good indicator of the importance of the program to families.[15]

Thus, the so-called Family Assistance Plan was actually a proposal for a guaranteed minimum income, and it was supported by some legislators, such as former Senator Goldwater, primarily as a method of doing away with *all* welfare programs. Similarly, although the welfare reform act of 1988 was called the Family Support Act, one of its major provisions was designed to require mothers on welfare to put their children into child care facilities and go to work. The extent to which this strengthens families can be questioned. The White House Conference on Families in 1980 did succeed in highlighting the needs for a family policy, but family values did not prevail in most of the actions that followed the conference. The opinion that the United States has no family policy was succinctly expressed by a former commissioner in the Department of Health, Education, and Welfare: "The United States has no explicit national policy with respect to family life" and a former Commissioner of Social Security details this charge:

It is surprising how little attention has been given to a "family policy" by the United States government. This is in contradistinction to the family policy goals of other countries. Some nations have formally enunciated policies encouraging large families through rewards of various kinds. For example, the Soviet Union, Japan, India, and others have established goals to reduce family size; some nations have clearly established policies of financial assistance to large families to help in lessening the economic burden of children through a system of family allowances; and others have set forth family goals in their constitutions or in a variety of programs.[16]

AMERICA'S "REAL" CONCERN FOR FAMILIES

The difficulty in determining America's "real" concern for families lies in the fact that almost every area of social services involves families in some way. Explicit family policy is illustrated by programs such as adoption services, foster care, family planning, and so forth. Family policy is implicit in programs such as special education for mentally handicapped children and institutionalization/deinstitutionalization of family members. As a matter of record, American social welfare programs usually begin with individuals and only later take into account the fact that individuals are parts of families. To some, this lack of policy regarding families has been so disturbing that a proposal was once made to establish a Department of Marriage and the Family on a par with other cabinet posts—a proposal that did not get very far. Moynihan, for one, holds that this neglect of legislative concern for the family as an institution is not accidental but, rather, a conscious and deliberate form of "benign neglect."[17] It is said to have arisen from a fear of "great" families, on the one hand, and, on the other, a laissez-faire attitude that defined families as inviolate and private. This avoidance was reinforced by immigration that contained diverse family patterns. Recently, growing concern for American families has been created by the rising U.S. divorce rate, now the highest in the world.

In summary, it seems clear that despite a belief in and a desire for whole, healthy, functioning families, few U.S. government policies have the enhancement of healthy family functioning as their goal or result.

Despite what might be seen as a lack of overall family policies, some organizations and programs are specifically designed to help families. Among voluntary agencies, the names previously mentioned—Jewish Family Service, Family Service Association, and others—speak for themselves. In addition, specific programs, including government programs, are at least nominally aimed at strengthening families, for example, Aid to Families with Dependent Children (AFDC).

THE CASE OF AFDC

The major exception to the government's neglect of families in social welfare is the program originally called Aid to Dependent Children (ADC). Mounted in a deliberate effort to keep families together and to ease their lot, ADC had some interesting precursors. In 1898, the New York State legislature passed a bill allowing children in an institution to be released to their parents and directing city comptrollers to pay the parents the same amount it had been paying the institution for the children's upkeep. The bill was vetoed as being immoral—that is, paying parents to take care of their own children. But New York City (which dealt with the bulk of such cases) agreed to refer applications for commitment of dependent children to voluntary agencies, which would "assist in keeping homes together by granting relief to as many families as possible."[18]

From such experiences grew the "Mothers' Aid," or "Endowment of Motherhood," laws, which were first adopted by Illinois in 1911 and spread rapidly to other states. When the states proved unable to cope with welfare needs during the Great Depression, the federal government took over such programs through the Social Security Act of 1935. The ADC program, as enunciated by the U.S. Committee on Economic Security in 1935, was

> designed to release from the wage-earning role the person whose natural function is to give her children the physical and affectionate guardianship necessary not alone to keep them from falling into social misfortune, but more affirmatively to make them citizens capable of contributing to society.[19]

A premise of the original ADC program was that the well-being of children raised in fatherless homes was closely linked to their mothers' not having to work outside the home. An official congressional document states: "When AFDC was created a half-century ago, recipients were neither required nor expected to seek work outside the home."[20]

In its history, the program underwent a number of changes, some reflected in name changes: Aid to Dependent Children (ADC); Aid to Families with Dependent Children (AFDC); Aid and Services to Needy Families with

Children; and Aid to Families with Dependent Children—Unemployed Parent (AFDC-UP). This program was initially aimed at one-parent families, and in fact, no program for "whole" families was ever attempted. However, it was at least directed toward families rather than individuals, and later in its metamorphosis it embraced two-parent families, if the breadwinner was unemployed.

Thus, despite rhetoric concerning the importance of the family in American society, the only program directed exclusively at families was AFDC and this, as will be discussed in Chapter 15, became increasingly punitive, until it was almost antifamily. In fact, nearly one third of all children living in poverty in the United States are without medical assistance because their families have lost eligibility for Medicaid.[21]

Selective Policies

Social welfare policies regarding population control or family planning do not always apply to the entire population. Some programs aim to control growth of only segments of the population or to offer family planning help to selected groups. Back points out that "It is rare . . . to find direct statements that too many people of one's own kind constitute a calamity. Population restrictions . . . are usually directed toward others."[22]

Selectivity in population growth (or control) seems to have arisen when the danger of overpopulation was seen as receding because food production kept pace with or outdistanced populations. Then the population problem became not a question of numbers in general, but of the kind or quality of people. Selective population policies have become a serious bone of contention, with disadvantaged groups sometimes convinced that such measures are designed solely to decimate or weaken them. For this reason some developing countries are known to view family planning as a type of colonialism, designed to keep them small and weak.

THE EUGENICS MOVEMENT

The eugenics movement was spurred by a book published in 1877. Richard Dugdale, a prison inspector, became interested in the large number of prisoners who bore the family name Juke, and on tracing 1,200 people of Juke blood, he found 280 on relief, 200 criminals, 50 prostitutes, and numerous others with similar records. Blaming heredity, *The Jukes* created a sensation. Two books published in 1912, one in London and one in New York, purported to demonstrate how much certain families of "hereditary criminals" and mental defectives had cost society. These works contributed to the foundation of a eugenics movement that called for the repression of "defective stock." Eugenics theory powerfully influenced late nineteenth- and early twentieth-century U.S. policies toward groups then known as "the dependent, defective, and delinquent classes."[23] It was implicit that those who should be allowed— perhaps encouraged—to reproduce were mature, well-to-do, college-educated citizens. As a result, by 1915 twelve U.S. states had adopted sterilization laws.

President Theodore Roosevelt had remarked, around the turn of the century, that the "worst evil" in population-growth rates in the United States was the relative infertility of the "old native American stock, especially in the North East, as compared with the immigrant population."[24] Furthermore, during lectures on population problems at the University of Chicago in 1929, one participant called for action that would prevent the overwhelming of the white race by colored people. The fact that this person was one of Mussolini's chief spokesmen is obviously not without significance.

Such suspicion of the true intent of population control measures, and even of family planning programs, continues to apply to current activities: Whispers of "planned starvation"[25] emerged from the economic crisis of 1967, after huge cotton production cutbacks and highly automated farm machinery left the Deep South with thousands of no-longer-needed, unemployed African Americans, and concentration of family planning programs in ghetto areas gave rise to the suspicion that this was simply a ploy to try to reduce the African American population.

Even today, eugenics arguments occasionally make their way into debates about such matters as population growth and crime control. The question of whether drug-abusing mothers, whose children may be born as addicts, should be allowed to continue bearing children, or even whether AIDS sufferers should be allowed to procreate, sometimes enters into current discussions of family planning and population control. Lately, the eugenics question has been raised from the opposite direction, so to speak. With gene splicing, frozen sperm, and the latent possibility of cloning, the question of whether some types of people will be brought into being "in preference to" other types has become a matter of debate.

Suspicions of selective policies are deep. The 1967 amendments to the Social Security Act ruled that public welfare programs for families with dependent children should include educational and practical services in family planning. Rather than being seen as an attempt to give poor families equal access, these amendments were interpreted in some circles as singling out the poor as promiscuous. Many social workers balked or inwardly resisted them on the grounds that by designing the program for the poor alone, the government might arouse feelings of undue pressure in the minds of some families.

These charges indicate the strength of emotions around the entire question of population control or family planning. When the government withholds family planning information, it is accused of depriving the poor of what is available to others. When it offers such information to the poor, it is accused of discrimination. When it offers information on a universal basis, it is still accused of discrimination, because only the poor participate in government social welfare programs.

SUMMARY

Many family policies are, by intent or consequence, aimed at encouraging or limiting family growth. Although culture may play a major role in this, public policy decisions are often more pragmatic— a response to the social system's need to expand the population base or to limit population growth. Population policies may include such devices as children's allowances and special family services (intended to increase growth and strengthen families) or laws limiting family size (intended to decrease the family's influence and the need to create costly supportive programs).

EXERCISES

A. If the United States were to adopt a children's or family allowance, do you think that it should be universal—that is, paid to every child or family—or selective—that is, paid to only those who are below some selected income level? Why?

B. Do you think a children's allowance would:

1. generally encourage a higher birthrate in the United States?
2. encourage a higher birthrate among certain population groups only? If so, which ones?
3. have no effect on birthrates?

Notes

1. Figures on efforts to control fertility are from the U.S. Department of Health and Human Services (1992); Davis & Abramovitz (1992) record attitudes of the United States and Canada.

2. The quotation is from Enkes (1967).

3. Shapiro (1985) is cited here.

4. The term *stunning* is Guttmacher's (1968).

5. The phrase *special emphasis* is from Oettinger & Stansbury (1972).

6. Statistics are from the following sources: 1973 legal abortion figures, Tietze & Murstein (1975); the 1.6 million figure, Callahan (1991) and Francome (1986); abortion rates, United Nations (1992e).

7. The quotation is from *Law and Population*, n.d.

8. The impact of low birthrates and economic considerations is from Holgersson & Lundstrom (1975); the quotation is from Beveridge (1942); early stages are discussed by Wingen (1992).

9. The statistics on children's and family allowances are from U.S. Department of Health & Human Services (1992).

10. The Israel survey is from Macarov (1977a).

11. The statistics and quotation are from "Security for America's Children" (1992).

12. The quotation is from Axinn & Levin (1975).

13. The first quotation is from Zimmerman (1988), and the second quotation is from Bane (1980).

14. The emphatic criticism is from Roberts & Schulzinger (1988).

15. The quotation is from Bane (1980).

16. The preceding quotation is from Zimmerman (1988), and the one that follows is from Schottland (1963).

17. Implicit policies are mentioned by Zimmerman (1988) and Kamerman & Kahn (1978); Rue (1973) proposed the cabinet position; Moynihan (1967) coined the phrase *benign neglect*.

18. The quotation is from Coll (1969), which describes the 1898 legislation.

19. The quotation is from Berrick (1991).

20. The quotation is from Congressional Budget Office, 1987.

21. The one third figure is from Mishra (1990).

22. The quotation is from Back (1989).

23. *Defective stock* is from Lubove (1973), and the subsequent quotation is found in Rafter (1992).

24. President Roosevelt's remark is in Kennedy (1970), and the lectures in Chicago are documented by Lader (1955).

25. Kotz (1971) writes of *planned starvation*.

READ MORE ABOUT IT . . .

For more information on:	See these sources:
Transnational studies of family responsibilities	Dixon, 1987a, 1987b; Dixon & Kim, 1985; Dixon & Macarov, 1992(b); Dixon & Scheurell, 1990, 1991
Goals of welfare policies	Wingen, 1992
Thailand's foster care problems	Department of Public Welfare, 1962
Contraceptives in Pakistan	United Nations, 1976
Sterilizations in the United States	Rothman, 1977
Islamic attitudes on contraception	Maududi, 1974
History of birth control	Lader, 1955
Margaret Sanger	Chesler, 1992; Douglas, 1970; Sanger, 1938
Catholic Church on abortion	United Nations, 1992a
Pronatalist policies	*Law and Population,* n.d.
Traditional "woman's role"	Peck & Senderowitz, 1974
Maternity benefits in Israel	Macarov, 1987b
Family allowances and their impact	Ambassade de France, n.d.; British Information Services, 1975; Gilbert & Specht, 1974; Holgersson & Lundstrom, 1975; Schorr, 1965b
Ways to reduce fertility	Oettinger & Stansbury, 1972
Charity organizations	Woodroofe, 1962
The Charity Organization Society	Axinn & Levin, 1975
Family Assistance Plan	Moynihan, 1973
1974 Code	General Services Administration, 1974

For more information on:	See these sources:
Family preservation program	Murphy, 1993
White House Conference on Families	Zimmerman, 1988
Mothers' Aid laws	Axinn & Levin, 1975; Clarke, Cochrane, & Smart, 1987
The Great Depression	Bird, 1966
Previous names for AFDC	Macarov, 1970b
Eugenics	Dugdale, 1970; Goddard, 1912/1973; Pearson, 1912; Rafter, 1992; *Time* (November 8, 1993, p. 56)

5. The Use of Families and
Other Institutions of Mutual Aid

This chapter indicates how families are used within social welfare policy and practice. One way is to place responsibility for family members' support on relatives—both as a method of strengthening families and as a way to ration services and save money. Mutual aid is also a feature of unions, mutual-aid societies, collectives, cooperatives, and communes, as well as communities and neighborhoods. Proximity and relationships are necessary aspects of mutual aid, so it is usually confined to people in the immediate area. This has given rise to residency requirements.

The second thrust of social welfare regarding families includes all those policies and programs that attempt to use, exploit, or build on family relationships and mutual aid. The most prominent and widespread example seem always to have centered on relatives' responsibility.

Relatives' Responsibility Laws

Most societies that view the family itself as important seem to take for granted that families should be responsible for their own members. Indeed, this is one of the functions that makes the family important. Where mutual aid in families is strong, outside social welfare measures tend to be weak. These outside measures —whether under church, voluntary agency, or government auspices—are often intended to reduce costs, on one hand, and not to weaken the structure of the family or the "moral fiber" of the individual, on the other.

Together, they transform family mutual aid from a desideratum into a responsibility. In many places, the law then foists upon families responsibility for their members or, conversely, denies help to persons with families that could help them. The notion of mutual aid in families is so deeply ingrained in individuals and in society that moral outrage usually greets the idea of a child of wealthy parents living on social welfare or, conversely, of wealthy children allowing their parents to live only on Social Security benefits.

THE HISTORY OF RELATIVES' RESPONSIBILITY POLICIES

Before Elizabethan Poor Laws were enacted in 1597 and 1601, children were never expected to be responsible for their parents. However, rising costs of social welfare caused changes in the law. Because the law reinforced public attitudes, at least insofar as parents' supporting children was concerned, the responsibility of family members for each other was insisted on, even if it meant—as it sometimes did—breaking up the family. The Charity Organization Society, for example, ruled that, if possible, a husband should be forced to support his family, and if he disappeared, the family should be broken up and its members placed in public institutions where they could receive needed care.

At times, moral judgments combined with administrative and fiscal considerations to create policies intended to dissolve families, in some cases, and to neglect individuals in the family in the name of family solidarity, in others. Thus, the wife of a drunkard was required to leave him to obtain help for herself and her family, and she was thenceforth treated for social welfare purposes as a widow. But if a husband deserted his wife, she could not get a widow's benefits; for if she did, other men might presumably be induced to desert their families. The records do not reveal how many men arranged to have themselves called "drunkards" rather than "deserters," so that their families could receive benefits.

The history of social welfare is full of such policy-induced choices. For example, a 1965 Wisconsin law stipulated that a woman deserted by her husband must file criminal charges of abandonment against him to be eligible for Aid to Families with Dependent Children (AFDC)—a requirement hardly conducive to domestic harmony.

REDEFINING RELATIVES' RESPONSIBILITY

In recent years family responsibility has been redefined. As the extended family has been replaced by the nuclear family and new family forms have arisen, the Poor Law legacy of relatives' responsibility has been successively limited. This may be owing to new views about and definitions of individual liberty and rights. For example, U.S. courts have ruled that selecting certain relatives as liable for others deprives them of equal protection under the law, because family membership is an unreasonable classification for separating the liable from the nonliable.

As long ago as 1965, Medicaid law limited responsibility to a spouse for a spouse and to a parent for minor children or those with disabilities. The 1974 Code of Federal Regulations regarding public welfare said, "In family groups living together, income of the spouse is considered available for his spouse and income of a parent is considered available for children under 21."[1]

Although the responsibility required of various relatives has been consistently weakened, children are generally entitled to financial support from their parents, and the states generally require spouses to support one another. Furthermore, the 1988 Family Support Act strengthened the requirement that fathers, especially absent fathers, pay child support, authorizing legal action and withholding of wages for this purpose.

USING FAMILIES TO "RATION" SERVICES

Despite the narrowing of relatives' legal responsibility, the practical effect is often unchanged. Program administrators, with limited resources, sometimes seek out other relatives (and even friends) as potential financial resources. Any relative, whatever the degree of relationship, may be considered a potential resource for public assistance clients, even though this responsibility is not legally enforceable.

In social work jargon, this is referred to as the concept of "past management." Clients who apply for assistance may be asked how they managed previously—although it is illegal to do so in some states. Unless they can prove some drastic change in their situation, they are told to go on the same way, even if this involves depending on a nonresponsible relative. The invocation of relatives' responsibility or past management is not necessarily due to malevolence on the part of program administrators or practitioners. They are simply trying to stretch available resources to cover the largest number of needy clients—a process that is part of "rationing services," to be discussed later.

Even if the requirement that families (and other relatives) support the needy is not written into laws, budget cuts in social welfare services may have the same result indirectly. More and more people find their grants and pensions insufficient and are therefore thrown on the benevolence of others. Between 1982 and 1988, for example, government funds for social welfare services in the United States were cut by 42%. Partly as a result, much of the help that families receive comes from local, informal support systems for families and family members.[2]

EXPLOITATION OF RELATIVES' RESPONSIBILITY LAWS

Narrowing the concept of relatives' responsibility leads to methods of exploiting the social welfare system in ways probably neither foreseen nor intended by legislators. For example, limiting responsibility to "family groups living together," as the Code of Federal Regulations does, means that those who move away from their families become eligible for welfare help, regardless of the family's income or resources. Thus, students who live away from home at college, even youngsters sent to expensive private schools, and young people setting up their own households—all are technically the financial responsibility of the government, rather than of their families. Although they are living together, couples who postpone or waive marriage formalities are also technically not living in a family group.

Emancipated minor is the term in use for a young person living away from home and legally declared no longer the responsibility of his or her parents,[3] with all of the positive valence that emancipation contains. Indeed, for some young people, no longer being financially dependent on their parents may have sound psychological results. However, from another point of view, dependence has simply been shifted from parents to taxpayers. Despite the greater ease and sense of freedom this may give the recipients, both the justice of such arrangements and the extent to which the public will continue to condone them may be questioned. In 1976, for example, there were eleven thousand cases of emancipated minors on the relief rolls in New York State.[4] In order to limit the growing expense in this area, it was ruled that eligibility would henceforth depend on a family court order that declares the emancipation necessary or desirable or on the minor's petition asking parents for support—evidence of attempts to invoke relatives' responsibility.

In summary, the institutionalization of mutual aid into relatives' responsibility laws proceeded from two bases. One was the belief that supporting one's family was moral, good for family members, and created family cohesion, and that failure to require such support would lead to "catastrophic consequences" for family cohesion and morality.[5] Therefore, relatives' responsibility laws were believed to enhance families and their functioning by placing responsibility upon them. The second basis is that such laws remove from the government, the taxpayers, or the contributors to voluntary organizations burdens that are felt to belong rightfully on families.

RELATIVES' RESPONSIBILITY
LAWS AS STRENGTHENING FAMILIES

As far as the first contention is concerned, most empirical evidence shows that responsibility imposed from without tends to destroy rather than enhance families. Finch says:

> The historical evidence suggests that . . . when government was attempting to impose a version of family responsibilities that people regarded as unreasonable, many responded by developing avoidance strategies: moving to another household, losing touch with their relatives, cheating the system. It seems that it is not in the power of government straight-forwardly to manipulate what we do for our relations, let alone what we believe to be proper.[6]

REDUCING WELFARE COSTS
THROUGH RELATIVES' RESPONSIBILITY

As for the second contention, caseloads tend to rise when relatives' responsibility laws are repealed, and vigorous collection methods with responsible relatives result in increased income to the state. However, less is known about the effects on the financial situation of relatives. When all relief was terminated in an Ohio county early in the 1960s, "Clients did not magically become self-sufficient nor did responsible relatives come out of the woodwork. . . . Instead, the burden of support was shifted . . . to landlords, grocers, physicians, churches, schools, and other civic groups."[7] Similarly, in Michigan, when General Assistance was ended, most clients obtained other forms of public assistance. Because the relatives of poor people tend to be poor themselves, the net result of widespread relatives' responsibility laws may have been to save taxpayer money at the cost of family cohesion and inter-relationships. In turn, this may have created other costly problems.

The family is the major provider of mutual aid, and in technologically underdeveloped countries it is often the sole source of mutual support activities. However, as societies become more complex, other groups, organizations, and agencies are developed to carry out mutual support activities.

Guilds, Unions, and Mutual-Aid Societies

GUILDS

Although mutual aid is often dispensed in families, unions, mutual-aid societies, and small groups, including mutual-aid and self-help groups, also depend on mutual aid. In addition, some communities and neighborhoods are characterized by mutual aid, as are cooperatives, collectives, and communes. Because one necessary aspect of mutual aid is proximity, the activity is often confined to persons in the immediate vicinity, giving rise to—in social welfare terms—residency requirements. Many of these have been declared illegal, but they still abound under various guises. Mutual aid is also characteristic of various voluntary organizations. In some cases, mutual aid becomes institutionalized as a form of social welfare; in other cases, it decays and thus necessitates other forms of help.

One example of extrafamily mutual aid was the medieval guild. Guilds were either social-, craft-, or merchant-based; they all tended to be small closed groups that emphasized brotherhood among members and cooperative help. Guild members were required to help each other in time of need, but such help was confined to members of the same guild.

LABOR UNIONS

From the guild flowed the concept of labor unions, and in the original small unions mutual aid was a primary concept. Members spoke of the organization as a brotherhood, and belonging to the same union created a bond that resulted in mutual aid. As unions began to grow in size, their social welfare activities became institutionalized, with results that will be discussed later. In some cases, the social welfare benefits of unions outstripped those of both government and voluntary agencies. The railroad union in the United States was known for its excellent social welfare benefits. When the Social Security Act was passed, railroad workers asked not to be covered, because their union benefits were greater than those promised by the new law. The social welfare demands of unions have become a major factor in bargaining negotiations, outweighing salary demands in many cases. A growing number of unions, including most of the large ones, employ social workers, and the element of mutuality—that this is "our" service, and benefits are a right rather than a privilege—is an important aspect of such services.

MUTUAL-AID SOCIETIES

As their name implies, mutual-aid societies are another vehicle for the expression of people's concern for one another. Most of these societies are based on some commonality between members—place of origin, religion, neighborhood, political affiliation, or belief. As government and voluntary social welfare agencies grew, the need for such mutual-aid societies diminished, but a surprising number still exist. Fraternal orders are usually larger than mutual aid societies, and some of these—Benevolent Protective Order of Elks, International Order of Oddfellows, and so on—are national or even international. They offer interest-free loans, sickness funds, funeral benefits, and other help, in addition to their social events. Mutual-aid societies and the local chapters of fraternal orders usually start as small groups, because one of the requirements of mutual aid is a continuing interaction among the members.

SMALL GROUPS

Even smaller mutual-aid elements in society are the groups people become part of throughout life. Social welfare activities—usually in the form of improving interrelationships, mental health, citizenship education, leisure, and rehabilitation—include work with or through groups. This is the method in social work practice known as social group work. Unlike other types of group leadership, in which task completion is paramount, the social worker's role in this practice is to strengthen the group as a whole so that the members are enabled to help one another. That the help in the group flows from peers, rather than only from the social worker, is fundamental to social group work. All group work recognizes the importance of "we feeling"—the recognition by members that they are bound together by virtue of their membership.

The belief that people need one another and, given the proper circumstances, can help one another finds expression in self-help groups. During the Victorian era, the new industrial society was rising with no governmental action to ease the friction this caused. Self-help groups sprang into being among the working class, and during the nineteenth century organized mutual aid in the form of "friendly societies" made a major contribution to social welfare. After World War II there was a fresh proliferation of self-help groups, dealing with a wide range of conditions and problems, including groups of AIDS sufferers, battered women, alcoholics, the chemically dependent, and others.

Incidentally, although mutual-aid groups and self-help groups are often spoken of as synonymous, there is a difference. Mutual aid is usually given without a condition of reciprocity, whereas in self-help groups the pursuit of self-interest remains. In fact, self-help groups are usually an alternative or a distinct complement to professionally sponsored assistance programs. Furthermore, not everyone sees mutual-aid groups as a public good: They may hinder rather than help the development of welfare services.

Self-help groups with goals such as improving the neighborhood or empowering people can be distinguished from those dealing with the problems of individuals. As for the latter, whether the problem is as obvious and acute as chemical dependency or as nagging and chronic as obesity, the basis of such groups as Synanon, Alcoholics Anonymous, and Weight Watchers is that only people who suffer from the same problem can help others and, in doing so, be helped themselves. The other members of the group are seen as the source of help, although in many groups the social group worker is used as an initiator, facilitator, resource person, and so forth.

Social Group Work

Social group work has gone through a number of phases. Although some of the earliest activities of social workers involved working with groups, as in Toynbee Hall and the YMCAs, YWCAs and YM-WHAs mentioned in Chapter 1, the "psychiatric deluge" that followed widespread dissemination of Freudian psychology in the 1920s engulfed social work as a whole and also caused group work to take a therapeutic bent. In the following decades, this was eclipsed by the proliferation of community centers, settlement houses, and neighborhood houses, in which much work was done with and through groups, with an emphasis on the use of leisure time activities.

In the 1960s, groups were used for "consciousness raising" in many areas, including feminist movements, ethnic groups, and others. This fostered the "sensitivity training" period that pervaded many areas, including business management and education. Although some of these activities undoubtedly remain part of social group work, the present emphasis seems to be on rehabilitation through self-help. Since the 1970s, the self-help movement has mushroomed in North America. There are groups for people with disabilities, for battered wives, battering husbands, homeless women, families of homicide victims, child sexual abuse victims, rape survivors, and many others. During the 1970s, Alcoholics Anonymous increased by an annual 7% worldwide, and self-help groups in general grew at an annual rate of over 8%. In the 1990s U.S. self-help groups are expected to become the major method of mental health care, involving over 10 million members by the year 2000. Thus it seems that the small group will remain one of the basic units springing from and expressing mutual help in social welfare.[8]

COMMUNITIES AND NEIGHBORHOODS

The mutual-aid approach also characterizes community organizations. Although some see the proper role of the social worker as coordinating services and agencies for the benefit of clients, identifying gaps in services, and initiating new services, others are more deeply committed to increasing cooperation among people in solving their own problems. This approach can be used by those who see the end result in terms of roads built, garbage collected, or problems solved and by those who see the desired result as self-images improved, attitudes changed, and relationships strengthened. The latter group may view mutual aid as a goal or an instrument, but even when community organization efforts are directed toward agencies and organizations, rather than toward individuals, collaboration—that is, working together for mutual benefit—is usually preferred to either cooperation or coordination.

Focus on communities is subject to various definitions, and in some cases the community is almost synonymous with a neighborhood. Organized concern with neighborhoods or communities can be traced back to the work of Canon Barnett and others like him, culminating (or beginning) with the establishment of the previously mentioned Toynbee Hall in London and the YMHA in Baltimore. From these separate beginnings grew the settlement house (or neighborhood/community center) movement. By 1970 there were more than three thousand neighborhood multiservice centers in the United States alone.[9] To these must be added the Jewish community centers, YMCAs and YWCAs, and settlement houses—in all, a vast network of social welfare agencies, all flowing from the concept of neighborhood or community.

Since medieval times, at least, neighbors have been considered an important source of help. In the eighteenth century this was institutionalized to the point that when a poor person was without family and was sick or feeble, a neighbor was reimbursed for assuming the responsibility for his or her care. Societal changes have taken away from local neighborhoods many of their former functions. The amount of "neighboring" that goes on in modern life has been reduced by mobility, expressed in the number of cars, ease of car ownership, and proliferation of highways; changing residential patterns, mainly through suburbanization; centralized services, as represented by huge shopping malls; and the anonymity of metropolitan living. To overcome some of the problems flowing from urbanization, and recognizing that mutual-aid activities flourish better in small or contiguous settings, there have been calls to return services to local units. This movement received considerable impetus during the 1960s and the War on Poverty, followed by concurrent African American and student revolts. As a consequence, services were required to offer local residents "maximum feasible participation." This resulted in a plethora of local groups designed to take control of certain aspects of social welfare activities and policy. Neighborhood cooperative nursery schools and credit unions are examples of this type of locally based mutual aid.

COOPERATIVES, COLLECTIVES, AND COMMUNES

There have also been attempts to go beyond mere communities to cooperatives and collectives. The early charities in the United States were cooperatives—not gifts of the rich to the poor, but a sharing. Much of the cooperative aspect faded away in the nineteenth century when charity organizations came into being, but a surprising number of cooperatives and collectives remain. The United States has a strong communitarian tradition; it was and is home to an enormous number of attempts to create "utopian" communities. Many of these were and are small and comparatively obscure, representing tiny religious groups: Hutterians, Amish, and others. Others sprang from purely secular philosophies: Owenites, Waldenites, and so forth.

The emergence of the counterculture in the 1960s brought a resurgence of collective groups, many of them small, individual, and unaffiliated—the product of the youth revolt. Since then, some have continued to search for a communitarian lifestyle. There are now approximately 3,000 communes in the United States—the preferred term today being *intentional communities.* In each of these, mutual aid is an important element of living, and in many cases the groups were formed in order to facilitate mutual aid, which is seen as a value in itself. Therefore, there are calls to try to build all large decision-making structures of society on the strongest possible collective units at the local level—units in which people come together around a range of common concerns and build their lives with each other.[10]

A common theme running through group work, self-help groups, community organization, and communes is belief in the efficacy of smallness. Once the group becomes too large, the involvement of all members in helping every other member begins to break down, and mutual aid becomes structured and institutionalized.

Residency Requirements

Another theme in the neighborhood, community, village, or small-town approach is proximity. At one time, social welfare policy and law were based on the idea that only people who live close to one another are responsible for one another on more than a one-time or indirect basis. This was referred to as residency requirements and has been termed *face-to-face relationships* as opposed to *stranger relationships.*[11]

In ancient and medieval times hospitality to travelers was enjoined. However, this was not mutual aid, because the traveler rarely had help to give the resident, other than news from afar and a break in routine. Aid that was extended over time from one person to another was confined to small groups. Thus, the codification of mutual aid into law brought with it limits as to who should be aided: usually only those within the group or the locality.

EARLY RESIDENCY REQUIREMENTS

Athenians were jealous about restricting citizenship to a narrowly limited body. In 451 B.C. both parents had to be Athenians if their offspring was to be a citizen. The first English law of settlement was promulgated in 1388: Able-bodied beggars were subject to punishment; those unable to work were permitted to beg, but only at their current place of residence or their birthplace. The Poor Laws of 1601 not only relieved a locality of the burden of supporting people from other places, but it also protected residents from strangers, guaranteed a supply of labor by not allowing people to leave freely, and reduced the number of vagrants, who often became criminals. The Law of Settlement and Removal of 1662 went further and made it possible to eject persons and families from the parish who, in the opinion of the local authorities, "might in the future become dependent."[12] This long-standing and emotional basis for residency requirements is expressed in the subtitle of Morris's 1986 book: *Rethinking Social Welfare: Why Care for the Stranger?*

The purpose of residency laws is to dissuade poor people from leaving areas offering parsimonious benefits to go to places where benefits are higher, thus becoming a "strain drain" from some communities at the expense of others. The belief that this is a widespread phenomenon seems to be false. From 1988 to 1991, California offered social welfare benefits more than twice as high as those in some other states, but growth in the number of welfare recipients in states with limited benefits more than doubled the increase in California. Nevertheless, efforts continue to limit payment from other countries and states.

EROSION OF RESIDENCY REQUIREMENTS

As it became clearer that people left poor areas because of the total situation or for personal reasons, rather than mendaciously, application of residency laws relaxed in some areas. The erosion of residency requirements in the United States reached its legal culmination in 1969, when the Supreme Court declared them unconstitutional in *Shapiro v. Thompson*. However, the consequent specter of hordes of indigents migrating to Arizona, for example, gave politicians there an excuse to reduce benefit payments to AFDC recipients. So strongly were residency requirements embedded in tradition and emotions that New York State attempted to evade the court decision by withholding welfare from newcomers who had not managed to find standard housing and by threatening them with the offer of only emergency relief and a ticket back to where they had come from. A one-year residency requirement was also imposed—and again declared unconstitutional.

Remnants of residency requirements persist. In 1979, for example, sixteen states had no residence requirements for general assistance—they assisted all eligible persons in the state, including transients and migrants. Sixteen states had durational residence requirements, that is, the applicant must have lived for a specified period of time within the state, within the local jurisdiction, or both. Typical periods of time were one year for the state and six months for a local jurisdiction. Nineteen states require that the applicant be residing in the state.

Social welfare for migrant workers is a continuing problem, even where there are no residency laws, because local populations feel little responsibility for temporary residents. Approximately 1 million Americans move with their families from place to place to meet seasonal labor demands. Mexican labor is used in parts of the the western United States and Canadian Indians are brought to Maine to pick potatoes every year. In countries dependent on foreign labor, the difference between social welfare benefits for residents and those for nonresidents may be striking. By contrast, England and the Netherlands, among other countries, extend their social welfare services to visitors as well as to residents.

Volunteers and Voluntary Organizations

A final aspect of mutual aid has to do with volunteers and volunteering. People volunteer to help one another for a variety of reasons: the desire for status, the need to feel useful, the public approbation derived, the inability to refuse a request, religious beliefs, and many others. However, certainly a major motivation for many people is pure altruism—the desire to help others.

It is useful to distinguish between voluntary organizations—that is, nonprofit structures that may use professional staff, mixed professional-volunteer staff, or all-volunteer staff—and volunteers as such. The former are bodies, agencies, services, and so forth; the latter are individuals. Furthermore, not all voluntary agencies are mutual-aid bodies—they may be one-way services consisting of people or services that only give aid.

The amount of volunteering that takes place in America is staggering. In 1983 there were an estimated 92 million volunteers, of whom 20% to 30% were helping out in government-operated agencies. In 1984, volunteers donated hours of work equivalent to almost 5 million full-time workers, with a cash equivalent of $66.5 billion.[13]

The Institutionalization of Mutual Aid

Despite the widespread existence of mutual-aid functions in families, groups, neighborhoods, and collectives, the activity is subject to various forms of decay, many of which lead to the institutionalization of mutual aid, a departure from its basic nature. One form of decay arises from an inequality of necessary or desired resources within the group. Some members then become constant givers, while others become permanent receivers. These roles usually lead to a series of rules and regulations that govern the kind and amount of help and the procedures to be followed to obtain it. The givers do not necessarily insist on such structures, although they often do. Sometimes the recipients of help, in their desire for equality, resent and resist their role and demand different methods of being helped.

The type of help needed, or its quality, can also contribute to the decay of mutual aid. When members of a group are incapable of providing the skills or resources needed and outside professionals are called in, the mutual-aid function begins to change form. Mutual aid is sometimes spoiled by success. When a small group is successful in helping its members, other people understandably want to join, and large size makes mutual aid difficult, if not impossible. This is precisely the path followed by some mutual-aid societies that began as small groups of neighbors, compatriots, or workers but are today huge, institutionalized mutual building and loan associations or international fraternal bodies, such as those mentioned previously.

Finally, members of a group may change their attitudes toward mutual aid for a number of reasons. When aid comes to be based on a "put in, take out" psychology and judgments are made about whether one has contributed enough to deserve others' help, a difference has been established between helping another by inclination and helping as a result of reasoning; the latter is no longer mutual aid. In Whyte's seminal study of factory workers, for example, those who contributed too little to the group's objectives—the goldbricks—and those who went beyond the work quota set by the group— the rate-busters—were not seen as helpful by the others.[14]

Mutual aid is not an "all or nothing" phenomenon. Some elements of mutual aid exist in many other types of undertakings, and mutual aid itself may benefit one party more than another. For example, when schoolchildren help younger children with their homework, or when the needy or people with disabilities help those even more needy or with more serious disabilities, the "helper therapy" principle may apply: The helper benefits at least as much as the person helped. However, this is stretching the meaning of mutual aid very thin.

The Future of Mutual Aid

Some discussions of social welfare assume that mutual aid no longer is a significant factor in social welfare or that it has decreased in scope and importance. Much of this thinking seems based on a nostalgic view of an idealized past. Whether there is less mutual aid today than at some given point in history is subject to empirical investigation, but the continuance of considerable mutual aid in families, groups, and neighborhoods—among other places—seems irrefutable. Given the gaps in social welfare alone, and the levels at which help is given, many people would not be able to survive if they could not call upon relatives, friends, or neighbors. No reliable studies record the amount of neighboring that goes on in American communities, but some indications are that it is greater among inhabitants of slums and ghettos than among more affluent people.

Although the amount of mutual aid usually increases in crisis situations, the type of event will dictate whether it unites the community, defeats it, or causes controversy and conflict. Crisis-induced mutual aid does not tend to become either permanent or institutionalized. Even in Homer's time it was pointed out that one's neighbor "can be expected to contribute once or twice, but not forever." Mutual aid remains part of the mix of motivations and methods that constitute good social welfare systems.

Some mutual-aid activities arise from religious motivations, and some religiously sponsored social welfare activities derive from mutual aid. Chapter 6 looks at this aspect.

SUMMARY

The impulse to impose responsibility for one another on family members often has the opposite result. Nevertheless, a major aspect of family life remains mutual aid, and, conversely, the great bulk of mutual aid resides in the family. Mutual aid exists outside the family in various settings, and it is sometimes incorporated into the social welfare system by laws and regulations. It is also subject to decay, requiring other forms of social welfare to take over. Despite the growth of the formal social welfare system, the amount of mutual aid that people extend and receive remains considerable.

EXERCISES

A. To whom does Charles "belong"? Alice, at age 20, married Bert, age 22. Within a year they had a son, Charles, but in another year Bert met and fell in love with Doris, a widow three years older than himself, who had three small children—Eileen, Ferris, and George. He divorced Alice and married Doris. Within five years Bert and Doris had two children, Herbert and Ingrid. Convicted of "insider trading" on the stock market, Bert was sentenced to twenty years in prison. Doris divorced him and was reduced to living on AFDC for her five children until she unexpectedly won the state lottery and become wealthy.

In the meantime, after two years of being alone with Charles, Alice married Jerry, an older man whose wife had been killed in an accident. Jerry had a grown daughter, Kathy. Alice and Jerry had two children, Lewis and Maurice, but three years later Alice was mugged on the street and killed when she resisted. Jerry went into a deep depression and was institutionalized. Kathy, who was unmarried, took Charles, Lewis, and Maurice to live with her in her small apartment. When Kathy met fabulously wealthy Norman and they decided to get married, he told her he had divorced his former wife because she insisted on having children—they had four—and he found that he couldn't live with children around. Jerry's mother therefore offered to take care of Lewis and Maurice, and Norman undertook to pay all their expenses, but both Jerry's mother and Norman said they felt no responsibility for Charles.

1. Who, if anyone, is legally responsible for Charles?
2. Who, if anyone, do you see as morally responsible for Charles?
3. To which relative would you appeal for help for Charles?
4. Where else would you seek help for Charles?
5. Because AFDC makes payments only to responsible relatives living with the child, to whom, if anyone, can payment for Charles be made?

B. To whom would you turn for help if you needed:

1. a few dollars for a short time?
2. a thousand dollars for an indefinite time?

3. counseling and advice?

4. sympathy?

5. housing during a temporary emergency?

6. help in finding a job?

   C.   A group of new immigrants to the United States has formed an association with the stated aims of:

1. discussing problems of mutual concern and seeking solutions to them;

2. engaging in social action to acquire more rights and resources for new immigrants;

3. establishing a free loan fund for members;

4. raising funds by raffles, dances, dinners, and so forth, with part of the ticket sales retained by the member selling them;

5. requiring members to employ other members of the association if their skills are appropriate for the job to be done; and

6. employing outside experts to give professional help to various subgroups of the association.

   Which of these activities would you consider to be mutual aid, and which not?

   D.   Over the course of time, as often happens, members leave the group as they become adjusted to the larger society or as their problems no longer require such a group. The remaining members are the most problem-ridden, and with very few resources to share with others. To whom do you think they should turn?

Notes

1. The quotation is from General Services Administration (1974).

2. The 42% cut is from Johnson (1989); on informal systems, see Kagan, Powell, Weissbourd, & Zigler (1987).

3. *Emancipated minor* is from Saltzman & Proch (1990).

4. The number of emancipated minors is from *The New York Times* (May 11, 1976; p. 11).

5. *Catastrophic consequences* is Bell's (1960) phrase.
6. The quotation is from Finch (1989).
7. The quotation is from Steiner (1966).
8. The growth of AA and the 10 million figure are from Kurtz (1990).
9. The 3,000 figure is from O'Donnell & Reid (1971).
10. The 3,000 figure is from Gauthier (1992); the description of people coming together is from Galper (1975).
11. *Face-to-face relationships* is from Watson (1980).
12. The quotation is from Coll (1969).
13. The number of volunteers is from Manser (1987); the volunteer hours are from Wolch (1990).
14. Lorenz (1971) distinguishes between inclination and reasoning motives; Whyte's study is from 1955.

READ MORE ABOUT IT . . .

For more information on:	*See these sources:*
Early instances of relatives' responsibility laws	Coll, 1969; Schorr, 1960
U.S. examples of relatives' responsibility laws	Eagle, 1960; Handler & Hollingsworth, 1971; Norris & Thompson, 1995; Saltzman & Proch, 1990; Spindler, 1979
Guilds	deSchweinitz, 1943
Labor unions	Kropotkin, 1925
Social group work	Glassman & Kates, 1990
Mutual-aid and self-help groups	Hatch, 1980; Katz & Bender, 1990; Manser, 1987; Powell, 1987; Schindler, 1980
"Friendly societies"	Hatch & Hinton, 1986
Division of community work activities	Macarov & Fradkin, 1973
Cooperation among agencies	Feine, 1974
Canon Barnett	Barnett, 1921

For more information on:	See these sources:
Toynbee Hall	Pimlott, 1935
The YMHA	Kraft & Bernheimer, 1954
Origins of neighbor mutual aid	Rothman, 1971
Utopian communities	Levitas, 1990
Hospitality to travelers	Coll, 1969
Early residency requirements	Axinn & Levin, 1975; Coll, 1969; deSchweinitz, 1943; Gouldner, 1969
Benefits in California	Norris & Thompson, 1995; Schneiderman, 1992
Court ruling on residency requirements	DiNitto & Dye, 1987; Patterson, 1986; Rosenheim, 1969
Arizona AFDC payments	Graham, 1970
New York residency requirements	Axinn & Levin, 1975
Remnants of residency requirements	Spindler, 1979
Distinction between volunteers and voluntary organizations	Kramer, 1993
Mutual aid in the ghetto	Stack, 1974
Impact of crisis on mutual aid	Coleman, 1959; Constantelos, 1968; Macarov, 1975

6. Religion as a Motivator of Social Welfare

Among the prime motivators for social welfare are the religious commandments concerning charity. Almost all religions enjoin their followers to practice charity. This may take place in individual behavior or through the institutionalization of charitable acts. Some religious institutions engage in charity; others establish groups of members who do so. At issue for many religiously inspired social welfare programs is the definition of its recipients. In some countries, the question of the relationship between religions and government requires ongoing clarification, particularly where there is a clear distinction between the two.

The History of Religious Welfare Activities

Almost all religions have obliged their followers to engage in acts of charity, either to co-religionists or to everyone in need. The Egyptian Book of the Dead, which predates the Bible, records acts of charity. The Jewish Torah, often referred to as the Old Testament, describes the responsibilities of Jews toward others and mandates them. About 500 B.C., Siddhartha Gautama, known as Buddha, established the foundations of Buddhism, with its interpretation of and relief from poverty. Prince Asoka of India, a Hindu, endowed hospitals and shelters for both people and animals 300 years before the beginnings of Christianity.

In antiquity, only the Greek world had no underlying and widespread spirit of philanthropy. Although Athenians could be said to live off the state, they were not living on charity, because the nature of society was such that the citizens were the state and the state provided their needs.

Both the Eastern and the Roman branches of Christianity engaged in charity at many levels. Indeed, it has been observed that the "Byzantines [were] a nation . . . characterized by its many works of practical philanthropy . . . a virtue not only of the rich and prominent, but of all organizations and classes of people." The differences between these groups have been summarized as the Christian model of charity, the Greek model of magnanimity, and the Jewish model of *tzaddakah* (righteousness).[1]

Among the first organized social welfare institutions of the Roman Catholics was a hospital in Rome for sick slaves. This type of activity expanded rapidly. Between the years 500 and 1500, Christian hospitals sheltered the homeless and orphans, as well as the sick. In Arab countries, hospitals were magnificently built and equipped as early as the twelfth century, while in Europe the needs of Crusaders on their way to the Holy Land resulted in many kinds of help. Catholic social work was first conceptualized along modern lines by Vives (1492-1540). Saint Vincent de Paul (1581-1660) established voluntary local groups for those in need, which became institutionalized as the Ladies of Charity in 1617 and as the Society of Saint Vincent de Paul in 1833.

At first, the emergence of Protestantism had little impact on social welfare activities. Indeed, in some respects, the "Protestant ethic" was inimical to charity because hope of salvation depended more on faith than on good works. Eventually a variety of social services sponsored by Protestant groups arose, including the YMCAs, YWCAs, and Lutheran Children's Homes, either to serve group members or to evangelize among recipients.

In 1676, the Society of Friends, more popularly known as the Quakers, established its first philanthropic endeavor, known as the Meeting for Sufferings, in London. The Mormon church appears to be more concerned with missionary activity than social welfare projects, although the latter are sometimes used for the former. Most evangelical churches are more concerned with the spiritual condition of individuals than with forces of oppression or poverty. Evangelical Christianity has "spawned a social work with an emphasis on rescuing the immoral or preventing immorality,"[2] rather than addressing other kinds of problems. This is in contrast to the "pastoral power" called for by Jacobson, which is oriented toward salvation in the present—that is, a good dwelling, sufficient welfare, as well as security and health—or by those who are concerned with the spiritual element in social work.[3]

There are said to be 1,200 distinct denominations, sects, and cults in the United States, although the majority of people give as their primary religious allegiance about two dozen mainstream religious organizations.[4] None of the new religious or pseudo-religious groups have showed strong trends toward charity or social welfare for others, although they often help provide basic sustenance to their members.

THE AMOUNT OF RELIGIOUSLY
SPONSORED SOCIAL WELFARE

The amount of religious or religiously sponsored social welfare activity in the United States is considerable. About 87% of congregations in one national survey had one or more programs in human services and welfare, including 80% in family counseling. Members of congregations donated $13.1 billion worth of volunteer time, 60% of it to nonreligious programs. About half of the time donated to religious projects and 12% of the time donated to nonreligious programs involved human service activities. In addition 60% of the congregations reported that they provided in-kind support, such as food, clothing, and housing, to human service programs managed by outside groups. The Roman Catholic church alone operates more than 7,000 elementary schools, 239 colleges and universities, and 731 hospitals.[5]

Maton and Pargament advance four reasons why religion should be given more emphasis in social welfare, especially in prevention of problems:

First, in its effort to promote a view of the world and a way of life, religious systems of thought and practice can converge with the values and practice of prevention. Second, religious systems are a natural site for prevention activities—from birth to death, most people are nested in a system of religious beliefs, practices, and institutions. Third, religious communities have greater access to many populations than the mental health community, including some of the most disenfranchised and neglected groups of society. Moreover, this access includes some right to reach out to people before problems develop. Finally, religious perspectives and practices have special contributions to make to secular approaches to prevention and promotion, such as visions and models of community life, approaches to the problems of mortality and limited resources, and notions of calling and servanthood.[6]

RELIGIOSITY IN EDUCATION FOR SOCIAL WORK

Despite the importance of religious beliefs as a motivation for social welfare and the need for social welfare policies to take into account religion, religious institutions, and the religiosity of some clients, social work education rarely includes religion or religiosity. In one study, 79% of U.S. social workers queried said that religious or spiritual issues were rarely or never addressed during their education and training for social work.[7]

As government aid has declined recently, the role of religious organizations has become more important and more urgent. On a community level, congregations are helping people directly and supplementing the operation of human service agencies with volunteers, money, goods, and other resources. Simultaneously, some of religion's role in philanthropy is being taken over by other organizations in the voluntary sector and by business.

Religious Manifestations of Social Welfare

The religious motivation in social welfare may manifest itself in the behavior of the individual and via delegation to some institution or agency.

PERSONAL BEHAVIOR

When religious beliefs are demonstrated in individual behavior, the charitable act is usually a response to a commandment or a requirement of the religion and has no ulterior motive. In other words, acts that arise from a desire to gain friendship, companionship, prestige, material advantage, or any recompense other than carrying out the will or instruction of God or the gods are not, strictly speaking, purely results of religious motivation.

In this sense Sir Thomas Browne said, "I give no alms to satisfy the hunger of my brother, but to fulfill and accomplish the will and command of my God; I draw not my purse for his sake that demands it, but His that enjoined it."[8] The altruistic act may also be a penance, as it were, for previous or other sins.

The Structuring of Individual Charity

Desires to engage personally in charity may result in individual behavior patterns, such as never passing a beggar without giving alms, never refusing a request to contribute for philanthropic purposes, or volunteering to help in a social welfare agency or institution. The motive may also manifest itself in structured ways.

Buddhists undertook to become—rather than help—beggars, because begging was considered a breeding ground for many virtues and made possible a life of contemplation, which was considered the only justification of human existence. In Europe, followers of some monastic orders took vows of poverty and maintained themselves by begging. Because obeying the command to help the needy required the existence of poor people, the desire to obey the command undermined measures to alleviate or abolish poverty and furnished a rationale (or a rationalization) for allowing demonstrated need to continue.

The absence of philanthropy in the ancient Greek world may have originated in a lack of religious commandments regarding charity. A religion worshiping gods who competed with people, manipulated people, and behaved like people did not lend itself to divine commandments about peoples' actions. Thus, Socrates, Plato, and Aristotle did not include charity in their lists of the "natural virtues": prudence, temperance, fortitude, and justice. Indeed, according to Plato's *Republic,* the aged and the handicapped were to be done away with.

However, Judaism, which existed before and during ancient Greek civilization, included a concept of a transcendental monotheistic God who issued commandments about how people should behave. Despite aberrations and transgressions, repentance, prayer, and charity would avert the evil decree that was imminent once a year, on the Day of Atonement. The decree itself, incidentally, concerned earthly torments—flood, fire, plague, and death. There is no concept of salvation or damnation in Jewish thought, and life after death is rather hazily drawn. Hence, to achieve a year of the good life, charity was as necessary as prayer and repentance, and the requirement was renewed annually.

As a matter of fact, the word *charity* is a mistranslation. The Hebrew word *tzaddakah* actually means righteousness. It is derived from the etymological root meaning "justice." Giving charity, then, meant simply being just or righteous, as one was required to be. No special effort or conscious behavior was defined as being charitable. The medieval Jewish philosopher Maimonides outlined eight degrees of charity.

The first, and lowest, level is to give, but with reluctance and regret. This is the gift of the hand, but not of the heart.

The second is to give cheerfully, but not proportionately to the distress of the sufferer.

The third is to give cheerfully and proportionately, but not until we are solicited.

The fourth is to give cheerfully, proportionately, and even unsolicited; but to put it in the poor man's hand, thereby exciting in him the painful emotion of shame.

The fifth is to give charity in such a way that the distressed may receive the bounty and know their benefactor, without being known to him.

The sixth, which rises still higher, is to know the objects of our bounty, but remain unknown to them.

The seventh is still more meritorious, namely, to bestow charity in such a way that the benefactor may not know the relieved persons, nor they the name of their benefactor.

Lastly, the eighth and most meritorious of all, is to anticipate charity by preventing poverty; i.e., to assist a reduced person so that he may earn an honest livelihood and not be forced to the dreadful alternative of holding up his hand for charity.[9]

Christianity emphasized the heavenly, or afterlife, rewards for enjoined behavior on earth. Whereas *philanthropia* in the ancient Greek world was mostly anthropocentric, in Christianity it became eminently theocratic. "The principle of philanthropy was the love of God rather than the love of man." The "theological virtues" were set forth as faith, hope, and charity, the greatest being charity. A person's behavior was to be rewarded in heaven, and good works on earth were a prerequisite. In the Eastern Church, too, "forgiveness of sins after death as a philosophic motive for philanthropic action was maintained."[10]

The Institutionalization of Charity

Inevitably, in almost every religion, personal giving or participation in charity came to be supplanted or paralleled by religiously sponsored institutions and agencies. The individual no longer gave help directly to the needy person. Instead, help was channeled to the church or a church-sponsored or church-related group that, in turn, dispensed it. Even individual behavior became, in large part, institutionalized, including that of beggars and monks:

In the course of time . . . the practice of begging was discontinued [by Buddhist monks]. The reasons for the abrogation of the ancient poverty are very noble and altruistic; they are, at present, heard frequently among well-to-do Christians. . . . Monks may possess wealth and property, even gold, silver, and silken clothes, because their possessions allow them to be more useful to others and to help them.[11]

The monasteries in Europe, too, accumulated wealth in order to help the indigent. In England, for example, "their hospitality was beyond compare . . . they kept most bountiful houses."[12]

An important aspect of the institutionalization of charity was the custom of tithing—contributing part of one's income to the church. At one time, the tithes were used mainly or entirely for the upkeep of the church and its functionaries. Gradually, however, such monies came to be used for the needy. In 1014, King Ethelred II of England decreed that the tithe should be divided three ways: for the reparation of the church, for religious functionaries, and for the poor. Some churches went further and basically divested themselves of social welfare functions, initiating and encouraging religious orders to undertake those activities.

EARLY CODIFICATION OF
SOCIAL WELFARE METHODS

As charity became institutionalized, the methods were codified. The Jewish community was enjoined that a man who was needy and asked for aid should be helped to continue his customary lifestyle. Specifically, if a man accustomed to riding a horse with an attendant preceding him could no longer afford to do so, the community was obliged to provide him with a horse and an attendant. Inherent in this interpretation is the idea that stigmatization may be worse than poverty itself, that cosmetic and psychological measures may be as necessary as economic ones. Flowing from this, and obviously arising from the agricultural economy and simple society of those days, is the idea that poverty is a transient, recurring phenomenon due to chance elements—wind, rain, natural disasters—that affect everyone periodically. Thus the horse and attendant would be needed only for a short time, as luck would change and the temporarily poor would again be self-sustaining.

Two additional aspects of poverty were enjoined in Judaism: Even the poor had to give to the poorer, but the community was not obliged to bankrupt itself or its members to take care of the poor.

The institutionalization of social welfare not only dealt with methodology and amounts but also began to establish the concept of eligibility. Individuals might have helped anyone needing help, but agencies established criteria that often carried moral overtones, such as: "The orphan, the widow, and the stranger deserve every assistance, but not the hypocritical and the lazy. To give to those who do not deserve it is to deprive those who merit it."[13]

The sanctions that religion gave to philanthropy can be summarized as follows:

1. establishing the principle that relief of distress is good for the giver, good for the recipient, and good for the community;
2. giving dignity to poverty and creating social acceptance of the poor, as being necessary for others' salvation; and
3. giving poverty the status of a way of grace because it made possible the meritorious deed of alms giving.

The institutionalization of religiously motivated social welfare has not been easily or completely achieved. Every group includes some who prefer to be personally involved, perhaps because they do not see, or trust, that contributions to institutions or services are used exclusively for social welfare or for the programs that they favor. Some question the amount of necessary overhead, and consequent reduction of help, that institutionalization inevitably involves. Others feel, perhaps irrationally, that the merit in giving comes from personal involvement.

POVERTY AS ENJOINED, DESIRABLE, OR INEVITABLE

The institutionalization of the religious value of charity has also created an underlying feeling that poverty and need are not only inevitable but in a certain sense, desirable. In part, this belief reflects the need of charity-dispensing institutions for a reason to continue existing. But it also arises from the feeling that—to reverse Lincoln's comment—if God didn't want poverty to exist, He wouldn't let people become poor. Countenancing the continued existence of poverty and other problems is thus given a pseudo-religious basis.

DEFINING RECIPIENTS

Adherents of all religions have been asked to decide whether charity should be extended only to members of the same faith, to nonbelievers as well, and/or to those who profess other faiths.

On the occasions when ancient Greeks practiced philanthropy, the recipients were usually civilized Hellenes: "The 'love of man for man' found its actual outlet in application to relatives, friends, fellow citizens, and allies."[14] On the other hand, Jewish law, as codified in Deuteronomy (14:29; 24:19-21), specifically included the stranger with the fatherless and the widow as deserving help if they had no land or sustenance of their own. Not until the fourth century was Christian philanthropy extended to believers and nonbelievers alike.

Although they can extend services to nonbelievers, most sectarian agencies have continued to render most services to co-religionists. Until recently, many Jewish agencies limited their services to Jews, and Catholic services tended to provide few services to non-Catholics. Protestant denominations have been more willing to extend services outside their own groups, primarily to other Protestants, possibly because the criteria for membership in the various groups are less clear-cut than among Catholics and Jews.

The inclination to render service only to members of the same religious group has a second, parallel root: the desire of members to receive help only from their co-religionists. They may feel that contributions of members should be used only for members (an important aspect of the previously discussed mutual aid), that only fellow members can understand the need, that it is shameful to expose one's needs to members of other groups, and—sometimes— that other groups have refused to aid nonmembers.

Since the earliest immigration to North America, members of various religious groups have expressed concern for the welfare of people. This was true of Protestants, of Catholics, of Jews, and of members of the Society of Friends from the first day they set foot on American soil. However, the bulk of such help has always gone to co-religionists. It was natural for the Catholic Church to be concerned about the needs of Catholic immigrants, just as Jewish institutions have catered to Jewish immigrants. For Jews to turn to a Catholic institution, or vice versa, would, in the public view, have tarred their own institutions as being uncaring or unable to help and the recipient as a renegade.

THE STUYVESANT PLEDGE

Perhaps the most clear-cut case of religious xenophobia due to outside pressures dates back to the arrival of the first Jews in New Amsterdam in 1654. Refused admission by Peter Stuyvesant, who was subsequently ordered by the Dutch East India Company to admit them, they were admitted on the condition that they would always be responsible for one another and never become public charges. Although there were other reasons, including a long history of Jewish separateness, the so-called Stuyvesant Pledge has been held to account for a great part of the autonomy—or separateness—that has characterized Jewish communal and social welfare institutions in the United States.

Church and State

With the advent of the nation-state, the relative roles of the church and the state in social welfare came into focus. When religious and secular authority were one, the intermingling of authority and activity was relatively unimportant. In Byzantium, for example, a sharp line of differentiation between the church and the state, the monastery, or the individual could not be clearly made.

As functions began to separate in some areas, social welfare was seen as the proper responsibility of religion, rather than of government. Thus, church wardens played a major role in providing care for the poor in England, and in Victorian times need was traditionally relieved by families, the churches, the religious orders, and neighbors. Public authorities intervened only in a supplementary way, to coordinate or to provide special types of service. Even when governments moved more massively into social welfare activities, they often did so through the church structure and personnel. In the sixteenth century, the government in England asked the established church organization to administer relief. Little conflict was seen between church and state functions, because the church not only was the established church but had become, in effect, a government institution supported by taxes.

The manner in which church-state relations have evolved will have an influence on the relative roles of both institutions in social welfare. Where the church has been the traditional dispenser of charity, areas may still be reserved, by law or by popular consent, to religious authorities, despite secular control. However, when the position of the church has been diminished or eradicated by revolution or civil reform, any social welfare activities it undertakes may be seen as competing with the state or attempting to strengthen religion. Perception of a church or a particular religion as an incipient or past oppressor, or its identification with a colonial power, will limit the extent of its charitable works. The social welfare activities of certain Christian missionaries in the province of Assam, India, immediately after Indian independence, gave rise to accusations that they were trying to establish a separatist Christian state.

CONSEQUENCES OF
CHURCH-STATE SEPARATION

In countries in which church and state are completely separated, social welfare may be the exclusive responsibility of religious bodies or of the government, or it may be administered by parallel systems that, in turn, may or may not divide up the areas of action between them or may handle them cooperatively. For example, in the United States:

> Separation of church and state has made the church's efforts distinctly private. Churches developed institutions for orphans and for the aged in their congregations. They also collected alms for the poor and provided food, clothing, and shelter to the needy. Adoption and foster care were added later. Counseling was seen basically as pastoral advice, but the clergy often found that problems required expert help.[15]

The proper relative roles of government and religious bodies in social welfare have been one of the most difficult philosophic and practical problems in countries in which separation of functions is seen as desirable. The problem is intensified because various religions have differing views.

THE PROTESTANT VIEW

In the United States, the Protestant church has traditionally held that religion's function is to be concerned with people's souls. Because salvation rests primarily on faith, concern with good works is a diversion of energy. Noted Protestant thinkers have reiterated the position that the church has no role in social welfare. Some Protestant theologians argue that the church has a pioneering role, which should be relinquished as the government recognizes its responsibility. This was enunciated by Niebuhr:

> It is the business of the church . . . to pioneer in the field of social work and to discover obligations which society, as such, has not yet recognized, but to yield these to society as soon as there is a general recognition of society's responsibility thereof.[16]

There is also the third view, more evident in practice than in theory, that although churches or religious bodies should not engage in welfare activities, secular Protestant organizations should be concerned with the state of the world and of humanity. This helps to explain the establishment and growth of such organizations as the Salvation Army, Volunteers of America, Baptist hospitals, Lutheran homes for the aged, and Methodist Fresh-Air Funds. For example, although Lutheran agencies are likely to be church-owned, the majority are not owned or controlled by churches themselves but by organizations of church members.

Coughlin presents a convincing argument as to why Protestant groups in the United States have not engaged in social welfare under their own auspices to the extent that Catholics and Jews have.

> A majority group, however, does not need . . . a bulwark to assure the preservation of its way of life, since its values are reflected in the patterns and policies of the larger society. At one time American society was practically identical with Protestant society. Social institutions reflected Protestant values, and in the field of welfare agencies, staffs and boards of directors were frequently also lay trustees of Protestant churches. Non-sectarian social work was therefore bound to reflect Protestant values, and it was easy for Protestants to adjust to secularization in social welfare.[17]

THE CATHOLIC VIEW

The Catholic view of church-state relationships in social welfare differs greatly from the Protestant views. Because good works are a requisite of salvation, the opportunity to engage in social welfare must not be taken out of the hands of church groups and individuals. For this reason Catholics have enunciated the principle of "subsidiarity," which means that smaller units and those closer to individuals should perform, and be allowed to perform, as much as they can, relinquishing to larger and higher units of society only what they cannot accomplish alone.

THE JEWISH VIEW

The Jewish view of church-state relations in social welfare has been complicated, if not ambiguous. Usually classified with the "liberal" political camp, Jews have favored government measures against poverty, discrimination, and other welfare problems. Fearful of encroachment by other religions or discrimination by a government dominated by another religion, Jews have opted for clear divisions between church and state. At the same time, they have built up a Jewish welfare establishment paralleling the government's in many important aspects. It includes hospitals, employment services, family counseling agencies, schools, loan funds, neighborhood and community centers, and immigrant-absorption services. The separation of church and state in the United States fostered a large number of welfare structures under Jewish religious auspices, including all three major groupings: Orthodox, Conservative, and Reform.

CHURCH-STATE RELATIONSHIPS

The question of church-state relationships in social welfare took on new dimensions in the United States during the Great Depression, when it was acknowledged that existing welfare organizations—sectarian and secular—could not cope with the massive need. For religious organizations, government entry into the social welfare field brought with it a sharpening of previous questions: Would it be better to encourage government action at the expense of weakening voluntary organizations, to seek government funds for sectarian groups at the risk of violating church-state separation, or to establish religious organizations for their own members, allowing the government to take care of nonmembers? Although much discussion and debate accompanied the decision making from the 1930s through the 1950s, by the time the War on Poverty programs began in the 1960s, the role of government as the prime mover in social welfare programs was well established.

The continuance of sectarian programs was usually justified to deal with peculiarly religious aspects (such as Sabbath observance among Jews or anti-Semitism in some businesses, as the rationale for Jewish employment services). In some cases, the reason is clients' comfort in being dealt with by "one's own" or in being among co-religionists: "There are people to whom religion is so critical a component of daily life that, precisely under circumstances during which they require social services, they wish sectarian services."[18] In other cases, the importance of religious identification was recognized in law, as when only parents of the child's religion were allowed to adopt (a stipulation now overridden by specifications based upon the best interest of the child).

The Professionalization of Social Work

However, the professionalization of social work—including work in community centers, with youth, in hospitals, and in homes for the aged—led to the postulation of a "value-free" agency. Even the sectarian services began to question how they helped maintain the religious group or the religious tradition—one of their own justifications for existence. This question was sometimes phrased in terms of whether there is a "Jewish," a "Catholic," or a "Protestant" casework, group work, or community organization method. In terms of center work, for example, it was sometimes half seriously asked whether there is Catholic, as opposed to Jewish or Protestant, basketball. Further questions about maintaining parallel secular institutions came with the realization that some Jewish hospitals might serve nonkosher food, and that some Catholic hospitals might allow abortions to be performed. In this connection, a study of religious beliefs and social work practice found that despite identifiable differences in beliefs, practices tended to remain the same.

Ethnic Groups and Social Welfare

Another facet of the religious motivation for social welfare is exhibited in the number of welfare services being offered by ethnic groups and organizations. Sometimes, religious and ethnic factors are intertwined. Agencies are run by and/or for Irish Catholics, rather than Hispanic Catholics or Italian Catholics. In services offered by Black Muslims, the African American element is coequal with the Muslim ethic. In other cases the religious element is not present—help is given to Koreans, or Indians, or Arabs, regardless of their religious affiliations or lack of them.

Sectarian Versus Secular Services

ACCEPTING GOVERNMENT FUNDING

Another reason for the trend away from sectarian agencies is the different quality of service provided by government compared to such organizations. The desire for good service might overcome otherwise strong sectarian identification. Again the need for funding beyond what is available from sectarian sources might lead to acceptance of funds from other, that is, government, sources. This was, for a long time, the sticking point for many sectarian agencies. Although tax exemption for church property was almost universally seen as proper, exemption for church-run enterprises was less clear, and exemption for fund-raising devices such as bazaars, bingo games, and raffles—even for social welfare purposes—raises legal and moral questions in some circles.

Accepting money from the government was seen as violating the separation between church and state, or as opening the way for secular control of sectarian activity. For a while, some agencies struggled with inadequate budgets while ignoring the availability of federal funds, eventually overcoming their scruples only on the grounds that they were doing a disservice to clients by limiting their resources. Sooner or later, most voluntary services, including church-sponsored services, not only accepted governmental funding but competed for it. They opened their services—at least technically—to nonmembers and conformed to governmental guidelines concerning mandated services, accountability, and so forth.

OFFERING GOVERNMENT FUNDING

The opposite side of the coin—whether the government has the right to fund, help, or buy services from sectarian agencies in societies in which church and state are separate—has raised an equal number of difficult questions. Beginning with court opinions that allowed funds for children in sectarian schools to be spent on lunches, schoolbooks, and supplies rather than on the schools themselves, viewing the individual rather than the institution or agency as the ultimate recipient has eased the problem in the United States for those who favor government support of sectarian agencies.

GOVERNMENT CONTROL
OF SECTARIAN ORGANIZATIONS

Besides funding questions, there are also questions concerning government inspection and licensing of religiously sponsored social welfare institutions. As the power to tax is the power to destroy, so the power to license is the power to control. That physical facilities must meet certain standards is generally agreed. Less clear is the extent to which the government can or should control the content of programs. For example, the curriculum in Amish schools in the United States or Hutterian schools in Canada has been a bone of contention, as has the right of Christian Scientist parents or those who believe in faith healing to withhold medical care from their children.

Interestingly, some religious authorities distinguish between educational programs, which are seen as legitimate opportunities for evangelism, and welfare programs, which are not. Some Africans, for example, decry missionaries "who find it hard to conceive of a school as anything except an instrument for the propagation of the beliefs of the sect."[19] Other religious authorities would accept help for needy people in the form of purchases of service and capital grants, providing that such payments do not imperil church control, compromise basic principles, or interfere with their proclamation of the gospel.

This desire or obligation of religious institutions to proclaim their gospel, or to evangelize among their clients, impresses upon some people the need for government—that is, nonevangelical—social welfare agencies, on the one hand, and the need for agencies that support, offer continuity for, or proselytize to different branches, sects, or beliefs, on the other.

In the first instance, a minority group may need to maintain its own institutions with their value orientation as a bulwark against encroachment of the value system of the majority group. In other cases, groups may compete for members. Distinctions between social service activities dictated by religious commandments and proselytizing by offering services, and perhaps material goods, are not always easily drawn. What one group views as humanitarian programs, another may see as missionary activities, and sometimes with reason. For instance, during the Great Depression, the *New York Tribune* Coal and Food Fund was used by Hebrew Christian missionaries to make converts through the distribution of tickets.

Because of this ambivalence, many want such programs to be offered by a secular body, such as the government. Conversely, the group's need to go beyond social welfare and to deal in spiritual welfare is justification for the existence of sectarian groups. For example, a Cardinal wrote, "Catholic social science will do all things for the individual that secular social science can do, but it will and must go further and help to save the soul of the one with whom it comes in contact."[20] This explains why Scout troops and youth movements are sponsored by churches and synagogues in the United States.

In summarizing this discussion of church-state relations in social welfare, it can be said that religious groups maintain their own agencies and services

1. for fear that other sectarian agencies will attempt to proselytize, missionize, or subvert their members;

2. for fear that secular agencies will lessen need or respect for religion;

3. to garner strength and continuity for the groups by serving members' needs;
4. to perpetuate their values, beliefs, and customs;
5. because appealing for help outside the group may stigmatize the group as needy, as unable to help its members, or as neglecting them; and
6. in order not to violate the separation of church and state, as a matter of principle.

Religion and Social Work Education

Insofar as religious ideals and values are seen as important components of social work practice, there is a need to imbue practitioners with such values, to professionalize work stemming primarily from religious motivations, and to bring into harmony sectarian and secular values. In the United States, few seem to feel the need for purely Protestant schools of social work. However, there are schools devoted to preparing senior staff for YMCAs, such as Springfield College, and schools sponsored by more fundamentalist groups that include social work in the curriculum. Catholic schools include Catholic University in Washington, D.C.; Boston College School of Social Work; Loyola University; Fordham University, and others. In addition, numerous books and articles discuss social work in the light of Catholic beliefs.

A Jewish school of social work, which was not organically connected with any of the three major branches of Jewish practice (Orthodox, Conservative, and Reform), was relatively short-lived, lasting only from 1925 to 1940. However, about ten social service programs exist to prepare Jewish communal workers, although they do not grant social work degrees. Several schools have joint programs with various religious bodies: Social work training is given in the secular school, and the values and practices of a given religion are added in a theological seminary or similar setting. Finally, there are Catholic organizations parallel to the International Association of Schools of Social Work and the International Federation of Social Workers.

RELIGION AS THE CAUSE OF SOCIAL PROBLEMS

Although religion and religiously oriented bodies are customarily viewed as ameliorating or solving problems, in some cases the religious aspect is irrelevant: "Consider the problem of religion in a culture of overwhelming physical and psychic scarcity. How can one express undying love for a neighbor when there is only one job for the two of you, and you intend to have it?"[21]

In other cases religion is the cause of the problem. Anti-Semitism and anti-Catholicism have engraved their marks on many individuals, with deleterious effects on self-images, motivations, and behaviors. Hope and joy have been occasioned by religious beliefs and experiences, but so have feelings of guilt and anxiety. Consider the effects of excessive religious zeal, not only on groups and mobs but also on individuals:

> Medical superintendents [of asylums] were hardly cheered by the state of religion. Psychiatrists distrusted the more successful manifestations of religious enthusiasm in the revival. The subject was not altogether a comfortable one—for belief in God was not supposed to resemble financial or political ambitions, where too much was a dangerous thing. Still, medical superintendents regularly included religious excesses among the causes of insanity. And occasionally, a movement as extreme as the Millerites afforded them the opportunity to denounce "a popular religious error" for having produced "so much excitement in the community and rendered so many insane."[22]

A modern parallel is found in a syndrome recently detected and named in Israel—the Jerusalem Syndrome. Visitors, overcome by what they have seen, identify themselves as God, Jesus Christ, the Messiah, and other religious figures, to the extent that they often require therapy. In earlier times, the excesses of the Crusaders as they pillaged their way across Europe, the tragic Children's Crusade, pogroms, and religious wars all created problems, as did the enormous wealth of some monasteries and other religious establishments.

In a slightly different vein, the attitude of religious groups has an impact on the way social problems are handled, and even on what is defined as a problem. Where the dominant church opposes disseminating birth control information, condones begging, or crusades against prostitution, the implications are clear. When the church is a minor influence, its attitudes have less impact on policy and practice. For example, the fact that nothing in the Hindu religion bars family planning makes it possible for the government of India to institute and pursue various methods of birth control.

The Future of Religiously Inspired Social Welfare

A number of factors point to a lessening in the role religious motivations play in social welfare. One is the increasing complexity of society, which is correlated with the increasing complexity of societal problems. Social welfare agencies will probably continue to grow in size, scope, and comprehensiveness, placing more distance between the giver and the ultimate recipient. Such institutionalization of the religiously motivated act may lessen enthusiasm, even while increasing donations. Second, the missionizing aspect of certain religious social welfare activities will probably become clearer as literacy and sophistication grow—not to mention political awareness— resulting in a rejection of suspect religious services in favor of secular ones. Finally, laws that prohibit discrimination on the basis of race, sex, national origin, or religion will probably continue to be expanded and enforced. As a result sectarian agencies will have to deal with increasing numbers of nonmembers, weakening their reason for being.

On the other hand, religious adherents will continue to see the commandments that lead to social welfare as immutable, and one of the major reasons why people and society engage in social welfare will continue to be—in greater or lesser degree—the desire to do God's will.

Neither mutual aid nor religious activities operate in a vacuum. Political considerations, among other factors, impinge upon them, sometimes supporting, sometimes constraining, and sometimes distorting their structure and activities. Chapter 7 turns to the political picture.

SUMMARY

Fulfilling religious injunctions is an important motivation for the emergence and continuation of social welfare. However, the institutionalization of such impulses raises questions about the proper role of religious institutions vis-à-vis other bodies in providing welfare services. Among the issues are relationships between government and religions in states with separation of powers, identification of recipients for sectarian services, and the role of religion as a help to clients, on the one hand, and as causing social problems, on the other. Meanwhile, religion does not seem to have influenced social work education to a great degree.

EXERCISE

If all social welfare activities were to be the exclusive domain of religion, what different kinds of policies and programs would you envision in a society governed by:

1. the "natural virtues"—prudence, temperance, fortitude, and justice?
2. the "Judaic virtues"—repentance, prayer, and charity?
3. the "Christian virtues"—faith, hope, and charity?

Notes

1. The quotation about Byzantines is from Constantelos (1968), and the comparison between Christian, Greek, and Jewish models is by Eisenberg, Gwatkin, & Tracy (1991).

2. The quotation is from Eisenberg et al. (1991); Jacobson (1992) follows.

3. Jacobson (1992) talks about pastoral power, and Kilpatrick & Holland (1990) discuss the spiritual element.

4. The number of religious organizations is from Thompson (1986).

5. The amount of religious social welfare is from Wineberg (1992); the numbers of Roman Catholic institutions are from Wuthnow & Hodgkinson (1990).

6. The quotation is from Maton & Pargament (1991).

7. The study of social workers was done by Sheridan, Bullis, Adcock, Berlin, & Miller (1992).

8. The Browne quotation is from deSchweinitz (1943).

9. Maimonides is quoted in the *Encyclopedia Judaica* (1971).

10. The quotations are from Constantelos (1968).

11. The quotation is from Conze (1959).

12. The quotation is from deSchweinitz (1943).

13. The quotation is from Constantelos (1968).

14. The quotation is from Constantelos (1968), as is the subsequent material on fourth-century Christianity.

15. The quotation is from Brieland (1975).

16. The quotation is from Niebuhr (1932).

17. The quotation is from Coughlin (1965).

18. The quotation is from Kahn (1973).

19. The quotation is from United Nations (1965).

20. The Cardinal is quoted by Kohs (1966).

21. The quotation is from Hampden-Turner (1975).

22. The quotation is from Rothman (1971).

READ MORE ABOUT IT . . .

For more information on:	See these sources:
Buddha	Conze, 1959
Philanthropy in ancient Greece	Constantelos, 1968; Gouldner, 1969
Vives and St. Vincent de Paul	Kohs, 1966
The Protestant ethic and good works	Faris, 1930
Quakers	Jorns, 1969
Mormons, evangelical churches	Wuthnow & Hodgkinson, 1990
Contribution of local congregations	Wineberg, 1991
Taking over religious role	Wuthnow & Hodgkinson, 1990
Buddhist beggars	Conze, 1959
Jewish charitable beliefs	Kohler, 1903
Tithe	deSchweinitz, 1943
Religious sanctions for philanthropy	deSchweinitz, 1943
Attitudes about who should receive help	Brieland, 1975; Fink, 1974
The Stuyvesant Pledge	Coughlin, 1965; Rubinow, 1966
Philanthropy in Byzantium	Constantelos, 1968
Philanthropy in Victorian England	Brieland, 1975
Government role in social welfare	Marshall, 1965
Church-state cooperation	deSchweinitz, 1943
Protestant thought on social welfare	Miller, 1961
Secular Protestant charities	Brieland, 1975
Minority group needs	Coughlin, 1965

For more information on:	*See these sources:*
Religious beliefs and social work practice	Eckardt, 1974
Humanitarian vs. missionary activities	Macarov, Akbar, Kulkarni, & Wertheimer, 1967
New York Tribune Coal and Food Fund	Feder, 1936
Jewish school of social work	Berger, 1976
Role of religious motivations in social welfare	Wuthnow & Hodgkinson, 1990

7. Politics as a Motivator of Social Welfare

Social welfare can be used to gain or maintain political power and to reduce social unrest. It can also be a side effect of the political process itself, and when that is the case, social welfare is likely to be "universal," rather than "selective" or "categorical."

With the advent of the modern era in Europe and elsewhere, church and state became separate entities. This enhanced both the opportunity and the need for governments to undertake social welfare activities. However, the extent of government responsibility for social welfare has varied from country to country. There are a number of ways in which this responsibility is divided among government, religious bodies, the family, the marketplace, and voluntary groups. For example, in the United States, the government traditionally was responsible for education and material need, the family (with some exceptions) for health care, the church for religion, and voluntary groups for recreation and preventive health care.

History

During the days of absolute rulers, especially when kings were felt to rule by divine right, charity was usually dispensed at the whim of the ruler or flowed from his desire to attain salvation (often as he lay dying). Whatever help was given usually went to the ruler's relatives, immediate retainers, military leaders, or the church. Rulers did not need the support, or even the sanction, of the ruled, and social unrest was perceived as an attempt to upset the divine order of things: It was heresy rather than revolution. Therefore, there was little political motivation to engage in social welfare.

A radical change came in 1215, when the nobles wrested the Magna Carta from King John of England, thereby establishing the ruler's dependence on at least some of his subjects. Another turning point in the process of separating church from state was Henry VIII's expropriation of the monasteries in 1536 and 1539 and establishment of the Church of England. Although the newly established religion and the state were still one, the state had established the religion, the reverse of past practice. In 1531, also during the reign of Henry VIII, the government of England first took responsibility for the relief of economic distress. It is true that Edward III had issued the Statutes of Laborers in 1349, but because this essentially prohibited giving to beggars, it is hard to view it as a social welfare measure.

In 1531, the state revised Edward's ruling by taking responsibility for licensing the right to beg. The major significance lay in the fact that a type of social welfare right was conferred by an act of Parliament. Five years later, the government took responsibility for stimulating and securing contributions from private citizens for the relief of the needy. The continuing evolution of the separation of church and state is evident in the fact that although payments to the indigent were required by government, they were secured mainly through church collections and paid out through officials of local parishes.

CONTENT OF THE
ELIZABETHAN POOR LAWS

These laws continued to be expanded and revised during the reign of Elizabeth I, who succeeded to the throne in 1558 and died in 1603. The entire complex is usually referred to as the Elizabethan Poor Laws. These laws dealt with employment of the able-bodied poor, almshouses for the unemployable, and measures for dependent children. Their significance was that achieving a better society was no longer regarded as God's task; people were to undertake this work.

The Elizabethan Poor Laws, one of the first clear enunciations of government responsibility for social welfare, contained a number of features that continue to influence social welfare to this day. The Poor Laws were based on three principles:

1. the responsibility of the state
2. limitation of this responsibility to those unable to take care of themselves, in contradistinction to "sturdy beggars"
3. administration of social welfare through local units

From these principles and later amendments flowed several important concepts. One of the most enduring is the distinction between those who cannot take care of themselves, the "deserving poor," and those who were presumed to be in need because of their own behavior, the "undeserving poor." Because the undeserving were less eligible for help—or eligible for less help—so this doctrine is often referred to as the concept of "less eligibility."

FARMING OUT AND INDOOR/OUTDOOR RELIEF

At one time, this distinction was based solely on physical ability. The healthy poor person, who would not "put himself to labor as a true man ought to do," was assigned to a workhouse or even required to work for another person. Since the employer was almost invariably a farmer, this practice was called "farming out." One side effect of this system was a distinction between "outdoor relief," given to people living outside the workhouse, and "indoor relief," including assignments to workhouses, almshouses, and other institutions. In farming out, payments were made to farmers who would house and feed the needy in exchange for their labor. One way the farmer could make more money under this system was to give the workers the cheapest housing and least food possible, leading to so many abuses that the system was eventually eliminated. In colonial America, the poor were housed with families (usually at their own request), but here, too, the allowances for their upkeep were so small that they must have resulted in semistarvation.

Indoor relief within institutions was preferred to outdoor relief for the undeserving poor, adding a certain punitive element. Indeed, people entering workhouses were often routinely given several lashes as a further deterrent to "choosing" this way of life. Contemporary legislation continues to echo these activities.

Critics find parallels to farming out in the current "workfare" requirements of Work Incentive Program (WIN) and Family Support Act regulations for assistance and AFDC: Recipients must take any available job, with only minor guarantees concerning payment or conditions. The same notion is found in the Clinton administration's approach to welfare reform.

Governments have become involved in social welfare in three ways: as a means to acquire and maintain political power, in an effort to avoid social unrest, and as a side effect of the political process itself.

Acquiring and Maintaining Political Power

As the philosophy of divine right of kings faltered, governments became dependent on the sanction, if not the support, of the populace. Rulers found many devices to gain such sanction and support. These included feasts, holidays, the release of debtors from prison, territorial acquisition, military adventures, and devices of a quite different nature—repression of opposition. Social welfare benefits have also been used to gain support for rulers or political parties.

Bismarck's introduction of social security measures (see Chapter 1) did not stem from humanitarian motives. Indeed, Bismarck opposed limited working hours for women and children in factories and state interference in agriculture and industry. However, because an opposition political party (the Social Democrats) advocated social insurance, it was adopted solely "to make German Social Democracy less attractive to the working man."[1]

POLITICAL MOTIVATIONS
FOR AMERICAN SOCIAL SECURITY

A prime motivation for the adoption of Social Security in the United States was quite analogous. As a result of the Great Depression, politicians and would-be politicians began to attract followings with proposals to overcome the effects of the economic situation. The most powerful of these was Francis E. Townsend, a retired California physician who devised a plan he said would relieve the poverty of the aged while contributing to the economic recovery of the country.

The Townsend Plan called for monthly payments of $200 to every person over age 60, provided that the money was spent within thirty days. The plan was to be financed by a sales tax. Thus the aged, many of whom were penurious, would have enough disposable income, the demand for consumer goods would rise enough to provide jobs for all, and the sales tax would be a small price to pay for the proposed prosperity. The Townsend Plan gained widespread support among the aged, with an estimated 10 million adherents at one time. Townsend clubs—1,200 of them by the end of 1934—were established in almost every city. Many of them were interracial and composed of ordinary citizens with many different ethnic backgrounds. The *Townsend National Weekly* had a circulation exceeding two hundred thousand, and many clubs had begun endorsing and nominating political candidates.

A desire to defuse the Townsend movement before it became too powerful politically was no doubt one of the taproots of the Social Security Act. As Altmeyer notes, "The political motivation was particularly strong in [the promotion of government support for] old age assistance because of the strength of the Townsend movement: The President was concerned about the Townsend plan."[2]

Even on the state level, the plight of the aged became a political issue because of the Townsend movement. Governors would write letters to recipients taking credit for any increase in old-age assistance, rather than have it credited to the Townsend movement. Conversely, candidates appealed for the votes of the elderly by using old-age assistance lists to contact them. Even after Social Security was adopted, the Townsend forces had to be reckoned with when changes and amendments were discussed. A proposal requiring the states to make uniform payments was scrapped for fear of fanning the flames of the Townsend movement, which reached a peak of intensity during the 1938 congressional elections. As late as 1939, the strength of the Townsend movement was demonstrated when more than fifty congressmen and two senators testified in support of a Townsend-endorsed amendment to the Social Security Act.

Nor were the votes of the aged the only prize at issue. Governor Huey Long of Louisiana gained national prominence with his "Share the Wealth" plan, which was intended to make "Every Man a King" and had great appeal to the poor. The details of Long's program were vague, but his personality created a following that might have taken enough votes away from the Democratic party to give Republicans a victory in 1936. The Long threat caused President Roosevelt more worry than the Townsend movement did. In California, Upton Sinclair promoted a political platform called EPIC (End Poverty in California), and he also became a considerable power. Against this background, there is little question that one of the motivations for Social Security was a desire to weaken the appeal of competing programs.

In other instances in American history, the potential political power of a bloc or group resulted in "preventive" or "anesthetizing" social welfare programs. For example, the potential political power of veterans resulted in a bonus payment to World War I veterans in 1937 and in the GI Bill of Rights after World War II. No other group was as well rewarded as veterans after the war. Although veterans' benefits were not explicitly a social welfare program, the results were the same.

The steady increase in the number of older people organized into interest groups has continued to influence the political process. This is so even when their agendas are 100% issue- rather than candidate-focused. Examples of such organizations include the 32 million-member American Association of Retired Persons and the National Retired Teachers Association. The Medicare Catastrophic Coverage Act of 1988 was passed primarily because of political pressure from the elderly, and was repealed in 1989 when 2 million letters of protest, mainly from the elderly, objected to some of its provisions. Other potential U.S. interest groups have not been as successful.

For example, poor people have rarely organized themselves into political pressure groups under that label, certainly not on a national level or for a sustained period. Referred to as "the silent poor,"[3] they nevertheless became a potent force in U.S. politics during the 1960s under other labels. Although the Black Power movement was never labeled a movement of poor people, it obviously drew strength from the shared sense of outrage stemming from the powerlessness and poverty of many African Americans. Similarly, the student, women's, and gay liberation movements were never labeled as poverty movements, but they represented people who were disadvantaged and discriminated against, a characteristic they shared with the poor. As a result, these groups often fought for the rights of poor people.

The political potential of those affected by unemployment has also played a part in the political process. Kerbo and Shaffer report that:

> While elements of the Democratic party were going after the working-class vote with concerned statements about the unemployed, Republicans could not be silent. . . . When Democrats tried to court working-class voters, Republicans mounted a counteroffensive.[4]

The amount of unemployment present has played important, if not decisive, roles in some presidential elections—including the 1992 campaign.

However, it would be a mistake to believe that majority support for social welfare legislation is enough to ensure its adoption. The role of the minority elite should not be underestimated. New and expanded welfare programs often come about only if the elite favor them and have a hand in shaping policy. This is one argument advanced for universal rather than selective programs —that if the elite benefit, they will insist on arrangements that, in the long run, benefit everyone. Thus, many social welfare measures are "spawned in the first place to maintain a political leadership, and then continuously adapted to a changing political environment" to keep or expand it.[5]

Avoiding Social Unrest

The second political motivation for social welfare, the desire to avoid social unrest, operates somewhat differently. It can be a potent force, even if those creating the unrest neither pose a political threat nor aspire to political power. For example:

The whole congregation of the children of Israel murmured against Moses and Aaron in the wilderness. . . . "Ye have brought us forth into this wilderness, to kill this whole assembly with hunger." . . . And Moses said . . . "The Lord shall give you in the evening flesh to eat, and in the morning bread to the full." (Exodus 16:2-4)

One of the major motivations for the Poor Laws was to reduce the threat from roving bands of beggars, who often turned to robbery or pillage. Far from being designed to provide a modicum of social security, poor relief was conceived of as a police measure. By preventing the despair of starvation, it was expected to diminish the potential danger of desperate action and the ensuing disturbance to society. Victorian society also was shot through with the fear that one day the masses would overthrow the existing order. Thus, in the nineteenth century:

That a good deal of the charity of this period was inspired more by fear than love can hardly be denied, the fear of revolution inherited from those who saw the French Revolution was present to their minds, and in every agitation for better conditions they saw the red terror raising its head in their own country. The provision of soup was a method of keeping the poor quiet.[6]

Governments are not alone in this concern. For example, it has been observed that Japanese management styles are intended in part to promote both industrial and social stability. In Brazil, a consortium of industries, the SESI, have designed measures to provide social services to workers in order, among other things, "to provide progress and public tranquility."[7]

Responses to social action efforts vary with the times. In 1932, during the Hoover era, veterans demanding a bonus marched to Washington and were gassed, dispersed by force, and hustled away through state after state. In 1933, during the Roosevelt presidency, bonus marchers were housed in an army camp and provided with three meals a day. The Navy band played for the veterans, and Army doctors ministered to their ills.

The distinction between measures designed to gain political power and those designed to minimize social unrest becomes clearer when U.S. history of the 1960s is examined. The rebellions in ghettos, student riots, civil disobedience, antiwar demonstrations, and draft evasion were not seen as attempts by a political body or party to gain power—perhaps because the participants were seen as essentially powerless from a political point of view. They belonged to and formed no parties of any consequence; they backed no candidates; they were divided into many small, sometimes squabbling, groups; they often rejected the entire political process and hence did not vote. To a large extent they were viewed as outside the political spectrum. However, their activities were seen as threats to internal peace and security, and perhaps to the position of groups that were not necessarily political in nature.

METHODS OF AVOIDING SOCIAL UNREST

Not all threats to internal security are met by adopting welfare measures. The responses range from attempting to reason with and convert the disaffected, through compromises, bribes, chicanery, promises, threats, bargains, and confrontation, to conflict. At various times and in differing situations, any of these might become the response of choice. One method of dealing with social threat is to co-opt the leaders of the threatening group by bringing them into the influential bodies of the threatened controlling group. Seen benevolently, this is an attempt to empower such leaders, to show them the wider picture, and to take their views into account. Viewed cynically, this is intended to buy off the leaders with jobs or prestige, create distance between them and their constituencies, and bury their views in those of a larger group.

Another method has been termed *nondecision making*: Latent or manifest challenges are suppressed or thwarted before they become threats. In "pseudo-democracy," people are given the feeling that they have participated in reaching a decision, when in reality they have not.[8] For example, Congress may respond to the pressure of interest groups by passing the legislation they request, but it may not appropriate the resources to implement it. Vast pressure on Congress, through letters, telegrams, visits to representatives, marches on Washington, and so forth, may bring passage of a bill. But appropriation of funds is a separate action that often comes later, and it is virtually impossible to remount the whole campaign a second time.

The Family Assistance Plan was proposed to Congress by President Nixon as a result of welfare scandals, public backlash, and increasing resentment toward the welfare system among recipients and nonrecipients alike. The proposal attracted adherents with various motives, but the basic reason was not humanitarian. Moynihan holds that "the proposal was made . . . as part of an overriding *short-term* strategy to bring down the level of internal violence."[9] The proposal did not pass; it was a victim of conflicting views about the basis of the unrest and its solution, as well as the political process, with its tradeoffs and logrolling. Nevertheless, modern social welfare has developed, in part, out of fears about the threat to social stability posed by an impoverished underclass.

Social Welfare as a Political Side Effect

Social welfare programs often arise as a side effect of other or previous policies. One type of side effect is referred to as a "decisionless decision." Certain actions, once undertaken, set up a sequence of steps that acquires a life of its own. This is a variation of what is referred to as "incremental" decision making. The ultimate result may be welfare programs that were not intended. For example, a desire to keep the prices of some farm commodities high led to payments for *not* planting those crops. In turn, farmers received annual payments, a motive for some of them, at least, to vote for the party or candidates keeping these payments intact. The income protection of farmers was thus a result of political, rather than social welfare, policy, but the net result is social welfare, and sometimes social welfare for the rich.

Another result of "incrementalism" is the organic growth of welfare programs. Once established, a program tends to encompass more and more participants and to offer larger and larger benefits. Because of the vested interests involved, the government is unlikely to step out of welfare programs completely, or even to reduce its participation, despite rhetoric to the contrary and some amount of divestiture taking place through privatization.

Another type of decisionless decision is the social welfare program that becomes necessary because of other government activities—social welfare as a by-product, as it were. The United States' entry into World War II led to the construction of munitions plants. This in turn required housing for workers, which necessitated schools, clinics, and welfare services. Similarly, the adoption of WIN in the 1970s and provisions of the Family Support Act of 1988 required welfare applicants to undergo vocational training or take available jobs. This necessitated the establishment of day care programs for children, so their mothers could go to work or attend classes. Not surprisingly, many such programs have no educational or developmental goals: They are basically artifacts created by other programs. Policy-mandated vocational training and other educational programs may require scholarships, subsidies, or other types of assistance payments while participants are in training. Social welfare programs and activities can thus be unintended consequences of other actions.

In addition, governments sometimes enter the social welfare field because the size and complexity of the problem are too much for the capabilities of other institutions. Income tax deductions for children are an indirect type of family subsidy, and only the government collects income tax. Controlling agriculture, stimulating the economy, or ensuring a reasonable margin of profit so that industries will not collapse and cause unemployment—each requires government intervention. Such interventions create the need to engage in other activities, which may have social welfare implications.

Once government enters an area of social welfare, the goals and methods of its programs are likely to become targets in the political process. Political parties may become identified with certain approaches, and the programs may be used to gain support for parties. The political structure, as well as the process, can affect the shape of social welfare. In 1854, President Franklin Pierce vetoed a proposal made by Dorothea Dix and passed by Congress to allocate 10 million acres of land to care for the blind, the deaf, and the insane. He based his action on "states' rights," claiming that the federal government could not properly engage in social welfare activities, although he urged individual states to do so. Since then, a complex social welfare structure has evolved, involving federal, state, local, and sometimes county jurisdictions, replete with mandated items, permitted items, and forbidden items, as well as underappropriated mandated and permitted programs. Hence the existence or absence of a program may be the result of jurisdictional infighting, rather than conscious decision making.

The Future of Politically Motivated Social Welfare

The political motives for engaging in social welfare described here are not the only reasons why governments become so involved. Other possibilities are humanitarian purposes, economic reasons, religious beliefs and commitments, or the need to deal with population problems. However, to the degree that motivations are political, the growing size of, complexity of, and demands on the social welfare establishment will probably require more political attention. Benefits, costs, recipients, and policies will become much more significant as political issues.

SUMMARY

Two major motivations for social welfare arising from the political structure are the desire to gain and maintain political power, on the one hand, and the desire to reduce social unrest, on the other. In other cases social welfare policies and programs arise as a consequence of other political moves.

EXERCISE

Since mid-century the government has taken responsibility in several areas that were once the exclusive province of other institutions. For example:

1. guaranteed loans to students
2. loans to industries (e.g., Chrysler Corporation)

3. the Family Assistance Program
4. the Family Preservation Plan (in some states)
5. motivational and training employment programs (sometimes contracted out)
6. child care arrangements

Which of the political motivations mentioned previously do you see as being responsible for these moves?

Notes

1. The quotation is from Briggs (1965).
2. The quotation is from Altmeyer (1966).
3. The *silent poor* is from Michielse & vanKrieken (1990).
4. The quotation is from Kerbo & Shaffer (1992)
5. The quotation is from Piven (1971).
6. The quotation is from Attlee (1920).
7. The quotation is from *SESI: Procedures and Objectives* (n.d.).
8. *Nondecision making* is from Bachrach & Baratz (1970); *pseudo-democracy* is from Verba (1961).
9. The quotation is from Moynihan (1973).

READ MORE ABOUT IT . . .

For more information on:	See these sources:
Division of social welfare responsibility	Macarov, 1977b
Early history of social welfare	Thoenes, 1966
Henry VIII	deSchweinitz, 1943
Elizabethan Poor Laws	Thoenes, 1966
Farming out	Guest, 1989
Bismarck	Briggs, 1965; Schottland, 1974
Adoption of Social Security	Witte, 1962

For more information on:	See these sources:
The Townsend Plan	Goldston, 1968; Holtzman, 1963; Leuchtenberg, 1963; Manchester, 1973
Strength of the Townsend movement	Altmeyer, 1966; Berkowitz, 1989
Huey Long	Goldston, 1968
Medicare Catastrophic Coverage Act	Reasoner & Mercer, 1991
Influence of the poor	Johnson & Schwartz; 1991
Power of the elite	Kerbo & Shaffer, 1992
Poor relief as a police measure	International Labour Office, 1970
Fear of the masses	Woodroofe, 1962
1932 veterans march	Manchester, 1973
1933 veterans march	Goldston, 1968
Family Assistance Plan	Reischauer, 1989
Fear of the underclass	Sullivan, 1987
Decisionless decisions	Bachrach & Baratz, 1970; DiNitto & Dye, 1987
Social welfare as a by-product	Macarov, 1977c

8. Economics as a Motivator of Social Welfare

Economic motivations for social welfare include the desire to reduce the direct and indirect costs of social problems by alleviating or solving them. Those who suffer from the consequences of social problems may harm the economy by not being productive workers or adequate consumers. Social welfare problems also arise from the economic structure and processes themselves.

All social welfare programs have an economic aspect, because many programs are designed to reduce the costs of social problems and because the programs themselves cost money. In 1989 more than one half of all government spending was for social welfare programs; 49% of federal and 60% of state and local money went for these purposes.[1]

The Cost of Social Problems

Social programs are expensive, but so are social problems. The avowed goal of many social welfare programs is to reduce expenses to society by alleviating or eliminating a problem or its consequences. This is a very compelling motivation for legislatures. Many programs are approved because their designers submit cost-benefit analyses proving that the economic benefits of the program outweigh its costs or because there is a general consensus that the program will reduce the cost of social problems.

For example, counseling services are generally believed to reduce the costs associated with mental illness and marital problems. Probation has been urged over incarceration, because the latter costs more than \$16,000 per year for each inmate—almost 150% more per day than the former.[2] Vocational training programs are funded with the goal of getting or keeping participants off the public welfare rolls by helping them find jobs, thus saving the taxpayer money: "For every federal dollar spent in their rehabilitation, the rehabilitated employed person pays from \$7 to \$10 in federal income taxes each year for the remainder of his working life."[3] The Headstart program is often discussed in terms of preparing young children to succeed at school, and later at work, thus increasing their earnings. Where Congress is concerned, "A general issue is whether the benefits of a program are large enough to warrant the costs."[4] Some programs are approved because they are expected to provide the same benefits as existing programs but at less cost. This is one of the arguments used by those favoring privatization of certain social welfare services.

Although the total cost of social problems, both direct and indirect, is difficult to determine exactly, the cost of some measurable problems is enormous. Take the cost of hospitalized mentally ill persons. In 1981 it cost more than \$35,000 per year to keep a resident patient in a state mental hospital, and at any moment 25% of U.S. hospital beds are likely to be filled by mental patients.[5]

Similarly, although it is very difficult to arrive at a precise cost of crime to society, it has always been described as staggering. Hence, programs to reduce crime and juvenile delinquency, such as neighborhood and community centers, street-corner workers, youth movements, and other leisure-time and character-building efforts are sometimes justified in terms of property damage avoided and crimes not committed. For example, the gross cost of each juvenile arrest in Los Angeles County recently averaged about \$1,754. By comparison, the average cost for damage and loss for each juvenile offense was estimated at only \$756. However, the economic importance of arresting juveniles is argued on the basis that future crimes are also avoided, since there is a high level of recidivism. The total cost of criminal justice— over \$47 billion in 1985—is therefore defended as reducing the losses by more than the costs.[6]

There is a diminishing utility in fighting social problems; that is, greater expenditures do not automatically result in greater and commensurate savings. Again, crime provides an example. Putting an individual guard on every house in the country (and perhaps some guards to guard the guards) would undoubtedly reduce burglaries, but the cost of paying the guards would far outweigh the financial losses from all burglaries. The Clinton administration halted the Bush administration policy of having the Coast Guard stop suspected drug vessels, arguing that the cost was disproportionate to the results. Some have argued that from a purely economic point of view, the losses resulting from crime may actually be a bargain for society. However, this may vary with the kinds of crime and with the public's willingness to accept some level of criminal activity.

The economic value of overcoming racism and sexism has also been argued. Economic losses due to racial discrimination are estimated to cost about 4% a year, whereas gender discrimination is estimated to reduce the gross national product by 3% a year.[7] If the cost of overcoming each of these was shown to be less than the losses they cause, an economic motivation would be provided for antidiscrimination programs.

DIRECT AND INDIRECT COSTS

Although programs that promise to cut the costs of social problems stand a better chance of passage, the savings must be easy to demonstrate and the process must be simple cause and effect. For example, total national health expenditures are expected to reach a trillion dollars in the 1990s and a trillion and a half dollars by the year 2000. In 1992, Medicaid (means-tested health care for the poor) alone cost over $100 billion in state and federal funds.[8]

Today, poor people go to hospitals more often and stay longer—80% more in one study; the average number of days a person is bedridden increases as income comes down; and work-related injuries are more common among the worst paid. Mild retardation is 15 times more likely to occur in impoverished areas, and 20 million Americans are affected by hunger. Comparing upper-income with lower-income neighborhoods, one study found that poor people suffered from 4 to 28 times more health conditions attributable to living conditions than did the nonpoor. Fifty percent of the homeless are in that category because of economic problems.[9]

Thus, to assume arbitrarily that 10% of medical costs are somehow rooted in economic distress—insufficient or improper food, bad sanitary conditions, crowdedness, poor housing, insufficient clothing, untreated minor symptoms, and so forth—is probably a gross underestimate. Relieving this economic distress would save the country, in medical costs alone, 10% of $1 trillion, or $100 billion, every year—the precise cost of Medicaid alone, which is ear-marked for the poor.

Or, as Huff points out, "Sending every American in poverty a check large enough to raise his or her income above the poverty level would cost only $130 billion to $160 billion."[10] This would be outweighed by the savings in Medicaid and general assistance alone, not to mention the savings in other social services now being offered.

However, even if supported by appropriate and incontrovertible evidence, this argument would probably have little influence on legislators and on the general public. The connection between higher incomes for the poor and lower health costs for the government is just not convincing enough to be easily accepted. It also flies in the face of some strongly held beliefs. Moreover, the benefits are not likely to be immediate.

The time factor before changes show results is often formidable. For example, it might take as long as fifty years for an important new idea to find its place in school curricula, just as it took eighty years for the realities of industry to replace the basis of agrarian economics. To implement a decision about new equipment in hospitals generally takes ten years. Senator Daniel Moynihan has commented that it will be at least a generation before we know whether the Family Support Act is working. The peak of health care savings arising from a guaranteed income would probably not show up for a generation or more.[11]

THE STRENGTH OF
ECONOMIC MOTIVATIONS

The economic motivation for social welfare is strong for a number of reasons. Like mother love, saving money is hard to oppose, particularly in societies in which those who approve the programs must also bear the cost. By contrast, political motivations are usually hidden. People who support a program do not usually admit that they want to increase their own political power or that they believe it will co-opt, and thus control, the disaffected. Religious motivations may also be suspect in secular societies and those with church-state separation. And mutual aid, of course, does not require program approval. Thus economic considerations are among the most overt and socially approved motivations for social welfare programs.

Economic considerations are widely used to justify various kinds of welfare programs. For example, the costs of workfare and training programs arising from the 1988 Family Support Act are often justified on the basis that participants' resulting work careers will ease social welfare costs and/or that future taxes paid by graduates will exceed program costs. These were the arguments used by President Clinton in promoting a major overhaul of "welfare as we know it." "The most important unanswered question facing designers of welfare employment programs is whether greater investments in education and training services will result in greater success, particularly for the long-term dependent."[12]

THE COST OF SOCIAL WELFARE

The cost of social welfare itself must also be considered. The Family Assistance Plan was proposed because "it is relatively inexpensive—costing far less than the vast complex of service dispensing programs which we have piled up, one on top of the other, in recent years."[13]

Measures that would reduce the number of people on welfare—whether receiving cash, in-kind benefits, or services—also result in savings. This is referred to as rationing services. Oregon, for example, developed a schedule whereby health assistance to the poor would be rationed. Methods of rationing include delay, queuing, deflection, and dilution. A common method of rationing is to make eligibility for relief more restrictive. Income limitations are often used for this purpose, with a means test to determine eligibility. Another method is to make the means test and other procedures so slow, cumbersome, and demeaning that eligible people are deterred from applying. Still another way is to hedge the law with restrictions. For example, in Israel an unemployed laborer must report to the employment office *every day* to continue being eligible for unemployment compensation. Then there are intentional delays, difficult-to-reach offices, long waiting lines, unattractive surroundings, and unresponsive or surly workers, all of which act to make applying for and receiving social welfare difficult and demeaning.

Another rationing method is not meeting the full needs of clients. As of 1982, only nineteen states paid the full need standard. Furthermore, unemployment compensation replaces only one half to two thirds of recipients' in-work income, and the program covers less than 40% of the unemployed. Income replacement for the elderly amounts to about 66% of work income, and 7% of the elderly need means-tested Supplemental Security Income (SSI) help.[14] Perhaps the most drastic method of rationing is the proposal to limit social welfare to a two-year period, with almost no regard for the cause of the need.

In addition to the direct costs of social problems—property loss, the costs of maintaining institutions and services, payments—there are indirect costs that are hard to quantify. This has been called "buried costs and dispersed benefits."[15] Deterioration of housing leads to tax losses; incarceration of prisoners may lead to child neglect or breakup of families; lack of perceived opportunity may lead to drug abuse. As Harrington points out, "Poverty is expensive to maintain. . . . In some cities a quarter of the annual funds are devoted to taking care of the special fire, police, and health problems created by the slums."[16] It is not surprising, then, that social welfare programs often seek to justify themselves in terms of the money they save rather than the money they spend.

Effects on the Economy: Production

Besides their direct and indirect costs, social problems have other effects on the economy. One is the impact of problem-ridden people on production. The production of goods and services in industrialized countries makes it possible to employ people. Work distributes the resources of society. People who do not or cannot work—or whose work is not sufficiently productive—are seen as a drag on the economy. Hence all social welfare programs include strong pressure to prepare people for, or return them to, productive employment.

The view that social welfare measures are good for the economy dates back to the earliest social welfare legislation. The Statute of Laborers of 1349 was concerned with beggars, not as a problem of destitution but rather, as a seepage from the supply of labor that reduced production. Its modern application has been clearly enunciated:

> From the experience of developed nations it is proved that welfare policies contribute to increased production over time, and also ensure better balance between different sectors of the economy. Price support policies, agricultural subsidies, unemployment insurance are examples. . . . Welfare is not a leakage of national resources but a contribution to productive capacity.[17]

Governmental social welfare is intimately bound up with what is argued to be the core prerequisite of all industrial societies—namely, the development of industry and technology. Similarly, the AFDC program has been defended because one study found that for every dollar spent on recipients, $2.05 in industrial activity was generated. The same has been argued regarding health care: For every dollar not spent on food programs, $3 for health care will be needed in the wake of malnutrition.[18]

This is often the major motivation for social welfare programs in rehabilitation, vocational training or retraining, education, child welfare, community centers, and employment. Kershaw expresses this view clearly: "Increasing welfare payments . . . frequently is the factor that will permit a child to stay in school or a mother to work or become literate, and hence will have a payoff in increased productivity of labor."[19] The "investment in welfare" approach has also been applied to education: "Funds devoted to pre-schools and schools in . . . low-income areas are sound investments and will result in increased employment and productivity and reduced welfare expenditures."[20] Thus social welfare is looked upon as an investment, and its justification becomes the anticipated return in productivity.

TRAINING AND RETRAINING COURSES

A major method of attempting to increase the productivity of welfare recipients is to establish training or retraining programs intended to instill job habits and skills. Mandatory attendance in training programs has a long history. In 1909 a National Employment Authority was proposed in Britain, with the power "to withhold relief from the unemployed who refused to attend industrial training establishments or to order their compulsory commitment to detention colonies."[21] Training and retraining programs have had many problems since their beginnings. The most obvious is the need to train people for jobs that are available, that is, to be reasonably certain that graduates will be able to get jobs in the fields for which they prepare. Unfortunately, most welfare reform programs do not consider the availability of jobs or the structure of the labor market.

Take the case of Ms. Baldwin, discussed in a story in *The New York Times.* While collecting public assistance Ms. Baldwin earned several course certificates for jobs ranging from bank teller, to paralegal, to keypunch operator, beautician, and data processor. She still couldn't find a job.[22] A survey by the General Accounting Office found that opportunities for gainful employment were generally not conducted in planning for vocational education programs.

As a result, course offerings often have no relationship to the current labor market. Beyond specific skills, some argue that current education is teaching attributes not applicable to the workplace. More specifically, it is argued that education is not developing the type of mental discipline needed in industry and commerce.

Matching training and jobs is not an easy undertaking. The job market changes rapidly, so that only very short courses can be easily matched with job opportunities. The skills learned in short courses are mostly for poor-paying, dead-end jobs or the types of jobs that hardly need training courses—night watchmen, motel maids, and so forth. Otherwise, the lag between identifying the need and preparing the graduate may result in "training for incapacity."

In the early days of computers, for example, every operation required at least one punched IBM card and often many more. There seemed to be no limit to the number of punchcard operators who would be needed, and many programs to train them were established. However, in a short time computers moved from punchcards to magnetic tapes, to disks, and to microprocessors.

A further problem is the need for prerequisite basic skills, such as reading and writing at a high school level, which many applicants do not have. Many trainees also need counseling and advice about problems related or unrelated to the course that might cause them to drop out. In many cases, a subsidy payment during the training period is necessary. Finally, even when the trainees graduate and get jobs they were trained to do, they may be dismissed because of personal characteristics: They may have poor health, poor personalities, or poor dispositions; they talk too much or are careless, untidy, intemperate, or unreliable.

Remedial programs can do little to reduce the general level of unemployment in the short run. Most unemployment is caused by job shortages, not lack of motivation or skill. An official 7% of the workforce was unsuccessfully seeking work in 1993, and even if tens of thousands of training graduates succeeded in finding jobs, the unemployment rate would not drop even 1%. Unfortunately, "industry is not altruistic when it comes to employing people it does not require."[23]

Job training programs have limited success historically, and they are very expensive: "Retraining has its price, that of reduced wages, and on the welfare system for additional compensation during the training period and for family support in general."[24] At its peak in 1971, the Emergency Employment Act helped create jobs for one in twenty-five of the unemployed. In 1974 the Job Opportunities Program succeeded in employing 100,000 persons, at a cost of almost $14,000 per person per year, more than double the poverty line at the time—and probably more than many of them later earned. It would have been much cheaper simply to give the money to the unemployed.

However, the desire to increase the country's productive capacity by returning the unemployed to the labor market continues, despite its limitations.

REDUCING THE LABOR FORCE

Returning people to the labor market is not the only way social welfare is used to help the economy. Keeping certain people out of the labor force is also a goal. Mass unemployment, like that experienced during the Great Depression in the United States, made providing jobs an imperative. Therefore, one of the major motivations for the old-age portion of the Social Security Act—Old-Age, Survivors', and Disability Insurance (OASDI)—was undoubtedly a desire to remove millions of older people from the labor force, creating jobs for younger workers. In fact, what began as a program to make retirement possible at a specified age was quickly transformed into forced retirement by restrictive provisions and public custom.

SOCIAL SECURITY AND THE AGED

The situation of the aged in the United States is a good illustration of the strength of economic motivations in social welfare. In 1935, the mandatory age for receiving old-age benefits was set at 65, probably because this was the conventional age used in European programs. At that time, the average life expectancy at birth in the United States was about 55 years. By 1990, life expectancy had risen to 71.5 years for men and 78.3 years for women.[25] Logically, one would expect the mandatory retirement age—or even the age at which pensions begin—to rise proportionately.

In other countries, life expectancy at birth is closely correlated with the date at which old-age pensions begin. Typically, developing countries with short life expectancies, particularly those in Africa, begin their pension plans at age 55, and some even at age 50. Gambia, for example, with an average life expectancy of 41 years, begins old-age grants at age 55, whereas Sweden, with one of the world's highest life expectancies (74 years), begins pensions at age 65. Hong Kong, with a life expectancy of 74.24, begins retirement pensions that are not means-tested at age 70. Generally speaking, as countries become industrialized, life expectancy lengthens, and retirement age creeps up. Countries that base retirement pensions on age 65 for men grew from 26% in 1977 to 31% in 1987.[26]

However, despite rapid increases in life expectancy in the United States, retirement age will be raised very slightly and very slowly—from 65 to 66 in 2009, and to 67 by 2027. This is almost entirely due to liquidity problems.[27]

THE WORKING POOR

The aged are not the only group that social policy attempts to keep out of the labor force. Other policies are designed to keep the working poor in poverty. The reasoning is as follows. An increase in the minimum wage would lift many of the working poor out of their present positions, and because it would not apply to those making more than the minimum, such a move is regularly suggested. But the response is usually no. Opponents say that raising the minimum wage would require employers to pay marginally productive people the same as productive people. This would raise the cost of products and services, contributing to inflation. Some argue that raising the minimum wage would cause management to release the marginally productive workers, thus contributing to unemployment. In short, it is deemed better to allow less productive people to work and earn less, with the difference made up by social welfare, than to have higher unemployment figures. This is a form of underemployment: People who would like to work longer hours or more days are employed only seasonally or part-time. Underemployment helps "mask" the true extent of unemployment.

People working a 40-hour week 52 weeks a year at the present minimum wage of $4.25 per hour will make $8,840 a year. With the official poverty line at almost $14,000 for a family of four, the minimum wage offers no relief to poor families with only one wage earner.

Welfare programs can be used to subsidize the work of those who are paid less than subsistence wages. A historical parallel occurred in 1795 in Berkshire, England. A group of justices and clergymen met in Speenhamland and guaranteed a wage supplement for workers whenever wages dropped below a "floor" based upon the cost of bread and adjusted family size. The experiment was a disaster: Employers promptly dropped wages and the government had to make up the difference to workmen, thereby increasing the owners' profits while not helping the workers. Another parallel is modern Medicaid and Medicare, where government subsidies intended to allow the poor and the aged to obtain medical care are exploited by the care providers for their own profit.

The pressure to keep people out of the labor force is usually stronger during times of and in countries with high unemployment. For example, when Israel was experiencing a labor-short economy, it began retirement pensions at age 70; as unemployment grew, the age was reduced to 65.

Effects on the Economy: Consumption

Using social welfare to increase production is but one side of the coin. The other is the effect of policies on consumption. An economy based on production requires an exactly equal ability to consume. A society suffers if it cannot consume all that it produces or cannot export the surplus. Indeed, it is often said that overproduction, not underproduction, caused the Great Depression in the United States. In this sense, then, people who do not consume enough are also a drag on the economy. An important part of the United States' economic system is based upon advertising, an attempt to induce people to buy. A triumph of advertising and of the consumer psychology it has created is that millions of new automobiles are sold in the United States every year, although they are barely different from previous models. This also shows the need for continued consumption to maintain the economy.

Because poor people do not have much money to spend, their condition depresses the country's prosperity. As it happens, poor people are important consumers: They spend a greater proportion of their income on consumable items than do the more affluent. Food, clothes, transportation, fuel, and so forth make up a large part of the budget of the poor, whereas the more affluent are able to save, invest, buy capital goods, and in general spend on nonconsumable items.

ECONOMIC BASES
FOR IN-KIND PROGRAMS

One way to increase consumption by the poor is to put money into their hands, and this is what most insurance and grant programs do. However, consumption can be forced on the poor, as it were, by giving them all or part of their relief in food or other material items. Food has been distributed directly to the poor for many years through many programs, predating cash relief in the United States, which did not begin under government auspices until the 1930s. Christmas and Thanksgiving baskets are still traditional in some voluntary organizations. Soup kitchens and breadlines continue to operate in some areas and are more widespread in times of economic distress.

During the Great Depression, the government began to buy surplus farm commodities and give them to the poor. To prevent recipients from selling the products rather than eating them, a number of devices were used, including dyeing potatoes a deep blue. Actually distributing food proved inefficient. Currently, many food programs involve selling or giving to the poor stamps that can be redeemed for food. There are four large federal programs—the Food Stamp, Commodity Distribution, Special Milk, and School Lunch Programs—and several smaller and local programs, such as playground lunches and Meals on Wheels for the aged and those with disabilities.

FOOD STAMPS

Food stamps serve both a liberating function—allowing recipients to choose the food and the store they want—and a control function, ensuring that the help given is used for food and nothing else. However, the major purpose of giving food stamps instead of money is to help distribute agricultural surpluses, thus keeping retail prices at a level that benefits farmers. In fact, the Food Stamp Act of 1964, as adopted, begins, "An act to strengthen the agricultural economy." In 1966, the chairman of the Senate Agricultural Committee said, "the Special Milk Program was for the producer, rather than a program to assist children."[28] This motive is also seen in the fact that the Food Stamp Program continues to be administered by the Department of Agriculture, rather than the Department of Health and Human Services. Reports on the efficacy and efficiency of the program are available in publications of the former, and it is this department that reports on the program to Congress. The importance of agricultural and economic considerations is also seen in the restrictions it contains. Food stamps may not be used to purchase imported foods, cigarettes, or alcoholic beverages. They may be used only for products that directly aid the American farmer.

Food stamps are a helpful addition to income for many poor families. On the other hand, the original requirement that stamps be purchased in advance created an insurmountable difficulty for families living from hand to mouth, to the point that this regulation was changed in 1977. There are transportation problems—to get the stamps, to get to a store that will accept stamps (many do not), and to get home with the packages. Some believe the program is stigmatizing, and some store owners have been accused of discriminating against food stamp users by not allowing them "specials" or unusual bargains. The connection between production and consumption is clearly demonstrated by a little-known requirement that food-stamp recipients, with the exception of those in certain categories, must register for work. Partly as a result of such restrictions, only two fifths of poor households received food stamps in 1983.

Although the food stamp program is an excellent case in point, virtually all social welfare programs reflect a central concern with economics.

TRICKLING DOWN

Social welfare affects the economy, but the economy affects social welfare even more profoundly. For example, social-insurance coverage is highly correlated with economic affluence: "The level of economic development has a power role in determining the level of social-insurance development . . . the level of economic development is related to social-insurance program experience."[29] In other words, the more affluent a country, the more likely it is to have good social-insurance coverage.

From this flows the attitude that policy measures leading to a higher GNP are of the most importance and that Social Security and social welfare should be geared to guarantee ever higher GNPs. This has been termed the trickle-down theory, which says, in effect, that the richer the country, the better off the poor will be. Increasing the GNP becomes a mantra of sorts, and social welfare is presumed to occur almost automatically—or, in any event, without too much extra thought or effort. The effects of social welfare and affluence may also be seen as reciprocal—the more social welfare helps the economy, the better the social welfare program will be, which, in turn, will help the economy, and so on.

It may be true that even poor people in affluent countries are better off in terms of absolute goods and services than poor people (and sometimes not-so-poor people) in developing countries. However, this may not be true in terms of relative poverty, nor are distribution policies commensurate with the wealth of the country. For example, Israel's economy cannot begin to compare with that of the United States, yet the average working person in Israel is much better protected by social welfare provisions against the exigencies of life than counterparts in the United States.

Nor does wealth necessarily trickle down. In 1980 the richest fifth of the U.S. population had 44.8% of total after-tax income; the poorest fifth had

5.4%. By 1990, the income of the rich had increased to 49.9%, whereas that of the poor had decreased to 4.3%. The share of household income of the richest fifth of the American population continues to rise. Instead of trickling down from the rich to the poor, income seems to be bubbling up from the poor to the rich.[30]

Social Welfare as
an Economic Side Effect

Just as the political process has side effects that result in social welfare programs, so are there spinoffs from the economic process. Once programs are embedded in the economy, they are never phased out and never disappear. For example, at the beginning, it was assumed that Social Security would eliminate the need for direct assistance to the aged. In his account of the beginnings of Social Security, Altmeyer recalls:

> I well remember the November 27 meeting when the staff exhibited a wall chart which illustrated how the plan would work. It showed two lines: one declining year by year, which represented the declining number of old age assistance recipients, the other rising year by year, which represented the number of old age insurance beneficiaries. The two lines eventually crossed, demonstrating how the old age insurance system would gradually liquidate the old age assistance system.[31]

That was in 1935. In 1992, 1.5 million people were still receiving old-age assistance as part of SSI, a figure that had remained constant for the previous five years.[32]

Welfare programs almost invariably grow over time. Benefits become larger, and more people are covered. A study done by Wilensky, covering sixty-four countries, found a strong correlation between the duration of social welfare programs and their cost and coverage. He argues that both the age of the population (another strong indicator of the amount of coverage) and the age of the program are linked to the affluence of the country. Furthermore, not only is the cost of a program a strong factor in determining whether or not it will be approved, but safeguards against excessive costs become important parts of program planning, arousing more discussion than the benefits the program is designed to impart.[33]

FEDERAL-STATE-LOCAL ARRANGEMENTS

There is another economic aspect to consider. Because of federal-state funding arrangements in the United States, a locality might launch a social welfare program simply in order to qualify for grants. The federal government offers matching funds (and sometimes in amounts more than equal) to persuade or help states mount certain programs. Qualifying for such grants may mean important revenue for a state. Take, for example, a publication once distributed by the State of New York, which reads, in part:

Did You Know?

Hundreds of thousands of New York State residents are eligible for Food Stamps but are not using them. If every eligible person used Food Stamps, it could mean many millions of dollars in new Federal money for the State economy. New Federal money means hundreds of new jobs for New Yorkers. The Food Stamp Program is paid for by Federal funds. No municipal or county taxes pay for the Food Stamp Program.[34]

Another example of social welfare as arising from federal-state financial arrangements is contained in an experiment with simplified applications. The ineligibility rate determined by spot checks of simple declarations of need was no higher than the ineligibility rate resulting from the complicated forms. However, the simple applications were never widely adopted. One reason seems to be that the Social Security amendments of 1962 guarantee that states will be repaid 75% of the cost of social services, with no limit. Thus it was important that state social welfare activities should be defined as "services" rather than as "payments."

When the upper and middle classes are prosperous, they seem to believe that the good economic climate will automatically be reflected in arrangements for the poor—or, conversely, if there are people still poor during prosperity, it is obviously their own fault. However, when the economy is in a recession, the dominant concern is to save money. Larger allotments for poor relief are out of the question; maintaining existing levels is difficult. From this arises one of the Iron Laws of Social Welfare: "When we can afford it, we don't need it. When we need it, we can't afford it."

SUMMARY

The economic motivation for social welfare is to reduce the cost of social problems for the government and to reduce the effects of individuals' problems in the form of lost production and consumption. There is also a social welfare fallout from the economic system itself, and some welfare programs are designed to deal with the consequences of this fallout.

EXERCISES

A. Imagine a situation in which there were no social welfare programs. What would be the effect on:

1. consumption?
2. production?
3. the total economy?

B. Imagine a situation in which everyone is guaranteed enough income to live decently. What would be the effect on:

1. consumption?
2. production?
3. the total economy?

Notes

1. The statistics on spending are from Bixby (1992).

2. Statistics on costs of jail and probation are from Zastrow (1992) and Birenbaum & Sagarin (1972).

3. The quotation is from Black (1965).

4. The quotation is from Congressional Budget Office (1987).

5. The statistics on mental hospital costs are from Callicutt (1987), and Zastrow (1992) provides the estimate of hospital beds filled by the mentally ill.

6. The costs of juvenile crime are from Lipsey (1984), and Sharp et al. (1992) provides the estimated costs of the criminal justice system.

7. The cost of racism is from Joint Economic Committee (1980), and James (1975) estimates the cost of sexism.

8. Sharp et al. (1992) provides the estimate health care costs; Medicaid costs are provided by Colborn (1992a).

9. Statistics are from the following sources: data on hospital stays, from Colborn (1992a); occurrence of mental retardation, from Mandelbaum (1977); on extent of hunger, from Boodman (1992); on poverty and health, from Colborn (1992c); on causes of homelessness, from First & Toomey (1989).

10. The quotation is from Huff (1992).

11. The fifty-year figure is from Marland (1974); the eighty-year figure is from Schneiderman (1992), quoting Ogburn (n.d.); the ten-year figure is from Jolly & Gerbaud (1992); the Moynihan statement is from Offner (1992).

12. The quotation is from Gueron & Long (1990).

13. The quotation is from Moynihan (1973).

14. Statistics are from the following sources: on states meeting need standards, Carrera (1987); on unemployment compensation, Cooke (1988); on unemployment coverage, Blau (1992); on income replacement for the elderly, Hokenstad (1992).

15. The quotation is from Cutler, Bigelow, & McFarland (1992).

16. The quotation is from Harrington (1963).

17. The quotation is from Parmar (1970).

18. The AFDC savings information is from Richan (1987); health care costs are from King (1979).

19. The quotation is from Kershaw (1965).

20. The quotation is from Folsom (1965).

21. The quotation is from Squires (1990).

22. The *New York Times* story is DeParle (1994).

23. The quotation is from Rich (1989).

24. The quotation is from Rich (1989).

25. Life expectancy figures are from *Demographic Yearbook* (1991).

26. Retirement age figures are from U.S. Department of Health and Human Services (1992).

27. Data on retirement ages are from U.S. Department of Health, Education, and Welfare (1977), U.S. Department of Health and Human Services (1987b), and Macarov (1991a).

28. The quotation is from Kotz (1971).

29. The quotation is from Cutright (1965).

30. Statistics on the trickle-down effect are from Stoesz & Karger (1992), Weinberg (1985), and Huff (1992).

31. The quotation is from Altmeyer (1966).

32. Old-age assistance figures are from "Social Security at a Glance" (1992).

33. The study is from Wilensky (1975).

34. The quotation is from the New York State Department of Social Services (1976).

READ MORE ABOUT IT . . .

For more information on:	See these sources:
Cost-benefit analyses	Greenstreet, 1988; Gross, 1978; Palfrey, Phillips, & Thomas, 1991
Estimating cost of social problems	Titmuss, 1974
Cost of crime	Benson & Wolman, 1971; Sharp et al., 1992
Cost of crime as a bargain	Quinney, 1975
Oregon health plan	Stoesz & Karger, 1992
Methods of rationing services	Charles & Webb, 1986
Pressure to work	Macarov, 1980
Industrial development	Sullivan, 1987
Job availability and training	Hagen, 1992
Links between training and jobs	Anthony, 1978; Greve & Gladstone, 1983; Macarov & Fradkin, 1973; Wirtz & Goldstein, 1975
Reasons trainees get fired	McFarland, 1957
Minimum wage	Fisher, 1992; Frank, 1992
Wage supplements	Macarov, 1970b
Consumer psychology	Middleman & Goldberg, 1974
Early in-kind programs	Colcord, 1936
Food Stamp Act and program	Browning, 1986; Select Committee on Nutrition and Human Need, 1975
Restrictions on food stamps	Bell, 1987; Levitan, 1985; Richardson, 1976
Social welfare in Israel	Macarov, 1977b
Social welfare as a by-product	Macarov, 1977b

9. Ideology as a Motivator of Social Welfare

Ideologies are ways of viewing and understanding how the world is structured and what processes should govern behavior in it. Among those ideologies that affect social welfare are those based on altruism and humanitarianism, rather than egoism; individual versus collective responsibility; equity vis-à-vis equality; trust and mistrust; and what constitutes morality.

The word *ideology* (*idéologie*) was first used in France in 1797 to define a school of thought. The word became popularized anew when Marx began to use it in a somewhat different context. Although the concept is difficult to define, there is little disagreement about its importance.

Ideology has been defined as a system of political, economic, and social values and ideas from which objectives are derived. Ideologies not only tell us what is good and what we ought to do, but also explain the way things are and why they are that way. Ideology is also used to explain away inconvenient facts. Facts are not indispensable to central beliefs. They are rationalized if possible; otherwise, they are ignored. Ideologies are both guides and imperatives to action. Furthermore, "What gives ideology its force is its passion . . . the most important latent function of ideology is to tap emotion."[1] In short, the way people view themselves and the world, the things they hold to be good and desirable, and the kind of world they prefer all become components of their ideology. More than just a way of looking at things, ideologies predispose people to assign values and prescribe what is considered appropriate behavior.

Ideologies may include aspirations for all humanity or be confined to the individual's own conduct. They may refer to the totality of life or to a specific

138

area. For example, democracy, communism, and fascism are ideologies containing many facets of political, economic, and social behavior. Thomas Jefferson's ideology of government held that the least government action possible was desirable, whereas Alexander Hamilton's ideology held that government should attempt to do everything that was necessary. Capitalism and socialism are both ideologies of economics. Ideologies are overarching conceptions of what is right, good, proper, and desirable.

Ideologies are culturally determined, and they can be inferred from the behavior of some cultural and national groups. For example, it has been said that the notion of rights is foreign to Japanese ideology: There is only the concept of duties. Social welfare in Yemen has traditionally been the personal responsibility of the privileged Muslim. Israel's political ideology, rooted in the socialist-laborist-humanist matrix of its early years, has resulted in programs that offer average working people more protection against the exigencies of life than those in many other countries. Indian classical tradition emphasizes absence of work (*naiskarmya*) as the ideal situation, which has obvious implications for social welfare programs.

Ideologies give rise to different visions of social welfare, and their impact has been the subject of several analyses. Pragmatists may use the word *ideology* as a subtle way of conveying disapproval. Ideology has also been used ex post facto to explain and justify policy. Atherton points out that the political right's objection to the welfare state is a matter of ideological beliefs.[2]

Ideologies and Values

Although the line between ideologies and values is so thin that it is often hard to discern, it is nevertheless worth drawing. Ideologies postulate how the world should be and/or determine how the world is viewed. They tend to be long-lasting, overarching, and emotion-laden. Within a general ideology, many values may be held. Values are narrower than ideologies. They are determined by law, by professional bodies, or by societal, professional, and individual attitudes. Values can usually be enunciated more easily than an ideology. For example, confidentiality is usually considered a value in social work. It is not an ideology of how the world should be. Self-esteem, when not carried to excess, is usually considered a value for clients, but again it is not an ideology.

CHANGES IN VALUES

People often think of values as deep-seated and long-lasting, resisting change with tenacity. However, an examination of the history of some values, and the experience of others, casts doubts on this. Values are altered in response to shifting demographic patterns and to different beliefs about what is appropriate and reasonable. This can be seen in many areas: child care, care of the aged, privacy, sex, and families.

For example, for many years a basic American value held that parental care is more desirable for children than care in institutions—even in good institutions. Every effort was made to keep children in their homes, and this was one of the most salient reasons underlying the Aid to Dependent Children (ADC) program (later changed to Aid to Families with Dependent Children [AFDC]). As programs that require welfare parents to work became more popular, extensive child care facilities were needed. The desire of many mothers to take jobs outside the home also made such facilities a growth industry. As a result, providing child care outside the home has become not only accepted but prestigious. This social change led to a value change according to which contact with other children, even as early as age 2 or younger, is healthy, and professionally trained personnel provide better care than "amateur" mothers. This has reached the point to where working mothers are now postulated by some as more caring, and more capable of child care, than nonworking mothers.

The reverse value change may be observed regarding the aged and the mentally incompetent. As institutionalization became more and more expensive, the value of community care was promoted. Institutionalized people were sent back into the community as a "therapeutic measure." The value of community care—rarely evaluated empirically—is now held to be self-evident. For example, an official British policy statement says: "The Government believes that for most people community care offers the best form of care available."[3] However, in many countries, including the United States, patients have been released from or diverted from the hospital setting without having suitable alternatives. Some mental health professionals believe that many patients who are released might be better treated in a hospital setting. A more skeptical viewpoint holds that:

Deinstitutionalization is a phenomenon with its basis chiefly in untested assumptions, magical thinking, and anecdotes and legends; moreover, it appears that those responsible for making what mental health policy we do have are among the most faithful believers in those myths.[4]

A more terse statement of skepticism speaks of "returning people to community care within a community that doesn't care" (Sir Alec Dickson, personal communication).

Or, consider the value of privacy. At one time it would have seemed impossible that all of a town's residents would agree to have their names and addresses published in a book, available to anyone who wanted to exploit such information. However, with the invention of the telephone, being omitted from the telephone book became a minor tragedy.

Finally, the concept of marriage as an unbreakable lifetime commitment— "for better or for worse, until death do us part"—is being challenged by the fact that more than one half of the first marriages in the United States today end in divorce, as do 60% of second marriages. Such changes led one researcher to exclaim, "How shallow are our values!"[5]

Although it is both comforting and conventional to think of structures and activities as based on values, very often changes in the former result in new versions of the latter. For example, the official organs of the social work profession long ago established confidentiality of client records as almost inviolable. Confidentiality even extended to clients, who were not permitted to see the records kept by their social worker. In 1980, a court case in England brought a ruling that clients had the right to view the worker's records about themselves. In very short order, client access to records became more than just the client's right. It became a basic social work value, and, with no real evidence, such access was held to improve social work practice.

Social welfare as an institution tends to be based, in large part, on overarching, slowly changing ideologies about how the world is or how it should be. Social work practice is more often based upon values, which may or may not flow from such ideologies, but which are narrower and change more easily with changed circumstances.

Some Specific Ideologies

ALTRUISM AND HUMANITARIANISM

One of the strongest and most widely held motivations for social welfare is the ideology that people should help one another. This is not the same thing as mutual aid, which is predicated upon helping and being helped, and it does not necessarily include a concept of divine commandment. Although the ideology may coincide with political or economic motivations, it may as easily clash with them.

On an individual basis, this might be termed *altruism*—behavior carried out to benefit another without anticipation of external reward. As opposed to egoism, altruism implies an unselfish concern for the welfare of others. On a society-wide basis, this ideology is usually called humanitarianism—having concern for and helping to improve the welfare and happiness of humankind. When this concern becomes part of the ideology of an individual, group, state, or society, it may be reflected in various social welfare activities.

Altruism

There is no consensus on what altruism is or how it arises. Its roots are obscure. Historically, some civilizations seem to have believed that unselfishly helping another person, particularly a stranger, would be foolish, if not unnatural or even dangerous. Altruism would probably have been alien to the Spartans, and wholehearted giving without personal gain would have puzzled an ancient Greek. In modern society, on the other hand, altruism has been termed the foundation of all social relations, and in the early days it was considered of such overwhelming importance and ubiquity that some argued, without proof, that it was based in biology.

There are three generally accepted ideas about the roots of altruism. One is that there is an "altruistic personality"; the second is that there is a tradition of civic stewardship, or a commitment to community; and the third is that altruism results from religious teachings.

A study of altruistic persons concluded that their parents set high standards but disciplined them rarely, explained to them the consequences of their actions for others, and did not use punishment as a cathartic release for themselves. Other investigators find that altruism is more likely to stem from personal security, affirmation, and a strong conviction of self-worth. Like religious motivations, altruism may lead to direct involvement in social welfare, as by personally helping another, or to very indirect methods, such as voting for certain measures.

Humanitarianism

As an ideology, humanitarianism plays a large part in the creation and construction of social welfare programs. In areas such as aging or mental retardation, where the underlying problem cannot be cured or fixed, helping activities may spring from a desire to aid others. For example, we have already seen that two major motivations for OASDI in 1935 were the following:

1. the political fear of unrest and desire for political support by the aged
2. the economic need to remove the aged from the labor force and to increase their consumptive capacity

A third motivation was a deep concern for the welfare of the aged. By and large, the aged were seen as among the "deserving poor": Their condition was not viewed as resulting from their own behavior or deficiency (except, perhaps, by a few dyed-in-the-wool reactionaries who blamed people for not having saved for their old age). They were therefore to be helped. The convergence of all three of these major motivations resulted in the OASDI program.

Opponents of the Social Security Act objected to the government's entering the insurance business and voiced fears about the cost of the program, as well as concern for the "moral fiber" of recipients. Humanitarian considerations combined with the other motivations to ensure passage. However, such humanitarian goals alone would probably not have resulted in passage if no political or economic considerations had been involved. A case in point is the 34 million Americans currently living below the line declared by the American government to be the subsistence level.[6] Humanitarian sentiments alone do not seem to be enough to overcome economic objections and the political powerlessness of the poor.

NONHUMANITARIAN IDEOLOGIES

Other ideologies affect the scope and type of social welfare and even its very existence. Some cultures hold an ideology that the order of things has been foreordained or decreed by God. Not only are people powerless to effect change, but attempts to do so are impious, if not heretical. Another ideology argues that people are basically good, and that in the end, their goodness will triumph and everything will work out all right. In contrast, other societies believe human nature is unequivocally corrupt, and they view people as basically egocentric, antisocial, and malevolent. At present, a popular ideology holds that only greed, in the form of personal or corporate gain, will motivate efficiency and effectiveness in the marketplace, in social welfare, and in society.

Individualism and Collectivism

Ideologies that reflect on the comparative desirability of cooperative and individual endeavor also affect social welfare policies and programs. Where individualism is seen as a virtue, programs that are thought to create, encourage, or leave clients open to charges of dependence might be badly supported. Where cooperation is desirable, programs that put a premium on mutual aid might receive much approval. As Zald says:

> If cultural tradition places a strong emphasis on individual responsibility, then collective solutions are likely to be resisted. On the other hand, a group can have values which stress the importance of collective action as a general rule, and, consequently, welfare problems, too, call forth a collective response.[7]

In Israel, for example, cooperatives and collectives are prominent social features. Almost the entire public health service is sponsored by labor unions, political parties, and other cooperative entities, and the nation's one big labor union has its own widespread social service network. Many African cultures are also said to lean toward cooperation rather than individualism: "I am because I participate" is the way this has been phrased.[8] In China, too, the collective has been held to be more important than the individual.

In the United States, on the other hand, rugged individualism has always been considered an integral part of American ideology. As Kluegel and Smith point out:

> American culture contains a stable, widely held set of beliefs involving the availability of opportunity, individualistic explanations for achievement, and acceptance of unequal distributions of rewards. These beliefs have been labeled the "dominant ideology." . . . The dominant ideology involves three beliefs: First, that opportunity for economic advancement is widespread in America today; second, that individuals are personally responsible for their position; and third, that the overall system of inequality is, therefore, equitable and fair.[9]

This ideology not only may lead to relative poverty and inequality but also justifies these as desirable by-products of freedom and the rule of the marketplace.

Equality and Equity

Competition between ideologies of cooperation and individualism suggests a number of subsidiary questions. Among these is the question of equality versus equity, which can be either "deserved equity" or needs-based distribution. The terms may need some explication. A cooperative venture, with all members sharing alike in the proceeds, is an example of equality. Stockholders, who receive dividends according to the amount they have invested, are an example of deserved equity. A collective, such as the Israeli kibbutz, in which economic needs of all members are satisfied on an individual basis, is an example of pure or need-based equity.

Some social welfare programs, such as state-administered unemployment insurance, are based on the concept of equality. Every recipient—regardless of age, family situation, health, or other individual differences—gets the same amount. Veterans Administration disability compensation is based upon the degree of disability, and everyone with the same amount of disability receives the same compensation, regardless of the individual's situation or needs, as a matter of equality.

Deserved equity is based upon the amount that the recipient has paid in or contributed in some way. Compensation is supposed to be roughly equal to contributions: People should not pay in more than they receive nor should they receive more than they paid in. For example, the upper limit on Social Security premiums is based, at least partly, on the assumption that people should not be forced to contribute to the program more than they are likely to receive. Ozawa puts this somewhat differently: "The U.S. social security system emphasizes the principle of individual equity over the principle of social adequacy. The individual equity system is an activation of individualism and the social adequacy principle, of collectivism."[10]

The results of this kind of pay-in, take-out equity are apparent in the operations of OASDI. People basically receive retirement subsidies based on a percentage of what they earned (and therefore paid in) throughout their working lives. This means that people who held permanent, full-time, high-paying jobs most of their lives will receive the maximum retirement pay. This is sometimes justified on the basis that not only have they paid for it, but people should be able to sustain their lifestyles after retirement.

Conversely, this means that people who have never been able to work except intermittently, perhaps part-time, at low-paying jobs, receive the minimum Social Security payments. One could argue for the reverse: That people who were well-paid all their lives should have saved or invested enough, so they do not need the maximum payments. Following this reasoning, the poor unfortunates who could never get good jobs and led a hand-to-mouth existence should be compensated with generous Social Security payments to enable them to live well at last. Although Social Security payments are somewhat weighted toward the lower end of the scale, especially in terms of a minimum payment, reversing the present schedule does not seem to have many supporters.

Views about deserved equity are more attractive in the abstract than in practice. For example, people who pay into OASDI without reaching the minimum number of quarters worked to be eligible for compensation not only receive no benefits but also do not receive their premiums back. In short, they pay in more than they receive. On the other hand, catastrophic medical insurance is often opposed because some individuals could easily cost the system much more than they would have paid into it.

Another approach to computing equity is to base payment or services on individual or group need, regardless of contributions. This might be called "pure equity." General Assistance, for example, takes into consideration the situation of the recipient and undertakes to meet the client's need, within limits.

The tension between equality and equity affects social policies and programs in areas other than money payments. The momentous legislation and court rulings of the 1960s barring racial discrimination in education, in transportation, in accommodation, and elsewhere were based upon the principle of equality—that all people are equal under the law. Later affirmative action laws and regulations were based on the premise that present and future equality are not enough to compensate for past injustices: Equity demanded more help to enable disempowered groups to reach equality. This is sometimes phrased to suggest that equality of opportunity does not ensure equality of results—hence equity is required.

Mistrust as an Ideology

Mistrust can also be elevated to the level of ideology. This is expressed in the view that people are guided by an "acquisitive instinct," that is, they are out to get all they can by any means.[11] Despite protestations of belief in democracy, and exaltations of mutual aid, much of social welfare—policies, programs, and practices—is based on mistrust. Welfare investigations almost always seek instances of ineligible clients receiving benefits. Very rarely are efforts made to determine if eligible clients are getting all the benefits they are owed.

Mistrust of welfare recipients has its roots in history. Baron von Voght, writing about social welfare in Hamburg in 1796, was skeptical of the poor who declared their income to be only one shilling, sixpence a week: "We knew enough of our poor to suppose that one shilling, sixpence avowed meant earning something more."[12] In modern times, the fear that someone, somewhere, will "rip off" the welfare system results in elaborate rules and stratagems to prevent this. Safeguards against excessive costs become important parts of program planning, often arousing more interest and discussion than the program's benefits.

It is true that people who are being helped do not stand out or make good media copy, whereas "welfare cheats" do. However, the ideology of mistrust has become so pervasive that "welfare" and "cheating" have become almost synonymous to some. Headlines about Medicare, Medicaid, or day care fraud bring to mind cheating clients, rather than the doctors, politicians, and entrepreneurs actually involved. "Welfare reform" has in many cases become a code word for routing out the welfare cheats among clients, not among providers.

Basic mistrust of clients may be linked to the difficult and complex regulations and arrangements regarding benefits referred previously to as "rationing." These include offices placed in inconvenient locations; equally inconvenient hours of operation; uncomfortable physical arrangements; demands for written evidence of various sorts; referral from one office or worker to another; long waits; and multifarious forms. All of these are intended to discourage clients whose needs or motivations are not great enough.

THE NEWBURGH EXPERIMENT

Mistrust of clients seems widespread and deep-seated. Like many such beliefs, it is not easily influenced by statistics, facts, or experience. A case in point is the city of Newburgh, New York, where the popular image of relief recipients in 1961 was of unemployed African American men living off their women's welfare checks. To cope with the perceived situation, the city enacted measures to limit the time AFDC families could receive relief and to require all able-bodied men to "work off" their relief checks. Relief checks had to be picked up at the police station. The city threatened to remove children from "unsuitable" homes. Later it became clear that most relief recipients were white and that the city was spending less on relief than it had allocated. Only one able-bodied "relief chiseler" was found on the welfare rolls.

Welfare payments for the support of dependent children sometimes lead to so much distrust that the restrictions and stigma attached to getting help may perpetuate a life in poverty for the very children who are in need.

TRUST AND MISTRUST IN HISTORY

Although the ideology of mistrust is not unusual, it has not always existed. In ancient days the Talmud said, "Better that a thousand guilty go free than that one innocent should suffer." At a much later time—1655—a church historian put the same idea in different words:

> Better it is, two drones should be fed, than one bee famished. We see the heavens themselves, in dispensing their rain, often water many stinking bogs and noisome lakes . . . only because much good ground lies inseparably intermingled with them; so that the bad with the good must be watered, or the bad with the good parched away.[13]

Perhaps these exhortations to trust others demonstrate a long history of mistrust. More than a century later, the same lesson was offered: "The mass of worthy, honest, and economical poor should not be treated as thieves and paupers, because large numbers of these last classes attempt to defraud us, or because a few of them may possibly succeed in doing so."[14] These pleas are just as relevant today.

Many unintended consequences flow from social welfare based on mistrust. For example, hospital care is subsidized at a higher level than home care, a situation reflecting remnants of an attitude that if people are not willing to be hospitalized, they can't be really sick, or that financial help to stay at home while sick can be more easily diverted to other purposes. As a result, hospitals have been known to accept and keep people, rather than treating them as outpatients, because this increases hospital income. In effect, the providers rather than the recipients are given both opportunity and incentive to cheat.

The ideologies of humanitarianism and mistrust are intrinsically incompatible. One way to resolve the incompatibility is to limit mistrust to a specific group. This has been called the ideology of the elite, which holds that most people are basically honest, hardworking, and trustworthy, but the poor—or, more specifically, welfare recipients—can't plan, think, or be trusted. Thus, the larger society must guard itself against them. This view postulates a culture of poverty that is different from the majority culture, one in which poverty is equated with laziness. In short, mistrust leads to welfare policies at variance with those that an ideology of trust would institute.

Other ideologies, large and small, affect social welfare. In some cases—for instance, Sweden—a classless society, or a society with less social stratification, is an ideological goal. Then social welfare is seen as a method to redistribute incomes more equally. In many African countries, national development is an overwhelmingly strong factor in ideology, at least government ideology. Social welfare is viewed as an important instrument toward this end. In Israel, absorbing immigrants is seen as an almost sacred duty, an outlook that permeates social welfare policies and programs. In other countries, population control is the overwhelming goal, and social welfare is used as one instrumentality.

Morality as an Ideology

A vision of what constitutes moral behavior and attitudes operates in many social welfare programs. An ideology based on morality holds that all who need help should receive it, but their eligibility or the amount of aid they receive should depend on their attitudes or behavior. For example, lazy people should be kept alive (although this is by no means universally agreed upon), but they should not be helped as much as industrious people who are simply unfortunate. Under this ideology, substance abusers, unwed mothers, and others whose condition is presumably the result of their own conduct are not entitled to the same level of help. This has been referred to as "the politics of conduct"—that is, the use of conduct to determine benefits.[15]

A historical instance of the strength of moral views occurred during the Irish famine. With 8 million people starving, the ruling British were concerned that proposed relief measures would reward the Irish for what the British saw as their improvidence (which was and is seen as ipso facto immoral). Hence the British did nothing while millions starved to death.

USE OF SOCIAL WELFARE
TO PROMOTE MORALITY

The moral aspects of some social welfare programs are clearly evident in decisions such as the one in New Jersey that penalized mothers on welfare for having more children—and, conversely, for undergoing abortions. Many states require clients to attend educational programs as a condition for continuing payments. Virginia, Maryland, and Wisconsin punish parents whose children do not attend school regularly or who neglect preventive health care. Some proposals would limit payments to unmarried mothers or deny additional benefits for children born to women on welfare. Proposals to withhold payments from the unemployed who will not undertake training courses date back at least to 1909. Although these provisions may have financial and other aspects, the morality factor supports and sometimes overwhelms them.

The moral aspects of social welfare policy are also evident in proposals to withhold help from chemically dependent people; from persons who "waste" their grants; and, in some cases, from gay and lesbian clients. Some view social welfare as immoral, if not in itself, at least in some of its particulars. Elsewhere, the belief that some welfare recipients are given more money in grants than others get in wages arouses great moral indignation. Regardless of whether wages are sometimes woefully inadequate, or whether needs are clear and pressing, some ideologies cannot accept that nonworking people should ever get more than workers.

The interplay of several ideologies is seen in the assumption of female moral superiority during the nineteenth century—an ideology that was a central component of daily life. Containing elements of both sexism and morality, it led to cadres of female social workers, part of whose duty was uplifting the morals of clients. Indeed, some early social workers and social work organizations seemed to include influencing the morality of clients as part of their charge, if not its major thrust.[16] Evangelical Christianity, with its emphasis on personal salvation, is seen by some as having spawned a social work emphasizing the rescue of the immoral or prevention of immorality.

SUMMARY

Individual and collective views about what constitutes a desirable social order operate to bring about different versions of social welfare. Visions of the world based on "rugged individualism" result in different services than views based on "collective responsibility." Assuming that society is—or should be—based on altruism also leads to programs different from those based on the assumption of egoism or greed. Programs based on trust are different from those rooted in mistrust, which can be extended only to certain people or groups, or only to those dependent on welfare. Similarly, an ideology defining what is moral shapes social welfare in discernible ways.

EXERCISES

A. You are the head of an agency with a budget of $100,000 for client needs. Your client file consists of ten families whose needs are so great that it would take $10,000 worth of services to help them; and 100 families whose needs can be met with about $1,000 each. How would you allocate your resources? On the basis of what considerations would you make your decision? What role do the concepts of equality and equity have in your decision?

1. Take care of the ten families whose needs are so much greater.
2. Take care of the majority of the clients, that is, those with $1,000 in needs.
3. Take care of some of the former and some of the latter.
4. Make some other decision.

B. A client asks for an increased grant in order to buy liquor. He/she explains, "My life is so difficult that the only way I can get by is to get so drunk that nothing bothers me."

1. Would you approve the request for more money?
2. Why, or why not?
3. What else would you do, if anything?

Notes

1. The quotation is from Bell (1960).
2. Atherton (1990) provides assertion.
3. The quotation is from Secretaries of State (1989).
4. The quotation is from Johnson (1990).
5. The divorce rate is from Glick (1984), and the quotation is from Saint George (1970).
6. Figure on people below poverty level is from Colborn (1992b).
7. The quotation is from Zald (1965).
8. The quotation is from the United Nations (1965).
9. The quotation is from Kluegel & Smith (1986).
10. The quotation is from Ozawa (1989).
11. The phrase is from Tawney (1948).
12. Baron von Voght is quoted by deSchweinitz (1943).
13. The quotation is from deSchweinitz (1943).
14. The quotation is from Colcord (1936).
15. The phrase is from Hill (1992).
16. In the literature of and about the early days of social work, the phrase *moral treatment* is often used. This should not be confused with morality as such. Moral treatment meant humane rather than punitive treatment of the client.

READ MORE ABOUT IT . . .

For more information on:	*See these sources:*
Characteristics of ideology	Bluhm, 1974; Drucker, 1974; MacIver, 1948; Schorr, 1965b
Japanese ideology	United Nations Technical Assistance Program, 1963
Yemen ideology	Arab Information Center, 1965
Israeli ideology	Macarov, 1977b
Indian ideology	Saha, 1990
Impact of ideology on social welfare	Kluegel & Smith, 1986; Lee & Raban, 1983; Marmor, Mashaw, & Harvey, 1990
Ideology to justify policy	Cates, 1983

For more information on:	*See these sources:*
Values as changing	Berrick, 1991; Schindler-Rainman, 1992
Values and AFDC	Berrick, 1991
Working vs. nonworking mothers	Raichele, 1980
Release of hospital patients	Holmes & Hokenstad, 1991
Privacy and phone books	Brody, Cornoni-Huntley, & Patrick, 1981
Confidentiality and social work	Macarov, 1987a; Macarov & Rothman, 1977; Saltzman & Proch, 1990
Clients' right to see records	Munday, 1987; Shemmings, 1991
Definitions of altruism	Macaulay & Berkowitz, 1970; Stein, 1966
Definition of humanitarianism	Stein, 1966
Nonaltruistic civilizations	Story, 1992
Altruism in ancient Greece	Palmer, 1970
Biological basis for altruism	Brosse, 1950
Roots of altruism	Joseph, 1989
Studies of altruistic people	Oliner & Oliner, 1988; Titmuss, 1971; Wuthnow & Hodgkinson, 1990
Ideology of human nature	Macarov, 1968; Saha, 1992
Individualism as virtue	Gurin & Gurin, 1976
Israeli collectives	Macarov, 1987b
Chinese collective	Dixon, 1992
Individualist ideology	Mishra, 1990
Aspects of equity	Kluegel & Smith, 1986

For more information on:	See these sources:
Need-based equity	Near, 1992
The Newburgh experiment	Abramovitz, 1988
Effects of mistrust	Karger & Stoesz, 1989; Kluegel & Smith, 1986
Ideology of the elite	Thoenes, 1966
Culture of poverty	Macarov, 1970b; Kluegel & Smith, 1986
Sweden ideology	Persson, 1990
Immigrants in Israel	Macarov, 1970b
Irish famine	Marcus, 1965
Examples of moral aspects of welfare programs	*The New York Times* (July 21, 1992, p. B1); *The Washington Post* (July 21, 1992, p. D4); Abramovitz, 1992; Squires, 1990
Female moral superiority	Ginzberg, 1990
Morality and social work	Johnson, 1990
Impact of evangelical Christianity	Sullivan, 1987

10. Isms as Ideologies: Racism, Sexism, Ageism, and Xenophobia

An ideology that holds a group or groups inferior to others—or that believes some groups are destined to and/or should be superior to others—can become a motivation to extend or withhold social welfare benefits. Race, national origin, religion, ethnic roots, age, gender, and length of time in a locality may all serve to influence the amount and nature of social welfare benefits available.

Racism, sexism, ageism, and xenophobia—individually and in varying combinations—may affect different groups of people. The common denominator of these "isms" is the stereotyping of a group, assigning the same attributes to all of its members. The stereotype serves as a basis for discrimination, and the results of the discrimination often "prove" that the stereotype was true. This is a classical "self-fulfilling prophecy"—a belief that brings about its own proof. For example, prejudice may deny a group opportunities, and their subsequent failure is seen as proof that they did not deserve to be given opportunities.

Garrison and Jones distinguish between two kinds of prejudice.[1] In *pathological* prejudice, an individual displaces his or her own conflicts and frustrations upon some convenient scapegoat. What they term *normal* prejudice is found among individuals growing up in a culture in which there are derogatory ideas and attitudes toward certain individuals or groups. Normal prejudice can be further divided. In *minimal* prejudice, one group considers another group inferior in degree but not in nature. With changing environment (education and training), the inferior group can rise to the level of the superior group. In *maximal* prejudice, a group regards another group as inherently inferior, so that it becomes both inevitable and desirable that the superior group will dominate the other.

There are usually both economic and social bases for discrimination, as well as cynicism in its usage. Still, some people sincerely believe that the stereotyped attributes exist. They usually have no problem providing an example or two, which they then project onto the entire group. Social welfare policies that ignore or deny the supposed attributes of the stereotyped group may create opposition or dissension among such people.

Some people suffer negative discrimination resulting from more than one of these "isms." Racial, ethnic, gender, and age categories can coexist and overlap. Social workers must treat clients as individuals. Elderly Black farm women, for example, suffer multiple injustices—by being aged, non-white, women, and rural.

Racism

Racism, racial prejudice, and racial discrimination—which are not the same things—have existed in America since the colonial times. When the first European explorers viewed Native Americans as primitive, uncultured savages, they were engaging in prejudice, which is pre-judging others (hence, pre-judice) in a negative manner. To assume that Europeans (later "Anglo-Saxons") were superior to all other groups, nations, or "races," and that the others should become like Europeans, was racism. Acts that harmed Native Americans because of their identity—such as taking their territory or forcibly removing them to other areas—constituted discrimination.

RACISM, PREJUDICE, AND DISCRIMINATION

At least theoretically, it is possible to be racist without being prejudiced or practicing discrimination. Ringer poses the conceptual structure as "weness" and "theyness." We are what we are, and they are different. In its theoretical form, this does not necessarily imply that we are better than they are—only different. Goldsen, for example, speaks of a racial problem in Puerto Rico, although there is no discrimination in the American sense.[2]

Believing that white civilization has accomplished achievements that other races have not—whether or not the belief is justified—may lead to pity for the others or a desire to help them, not just to prejudice or discrimination. Indeed, affirmative action can be viewed as a desire to bring those who face racial discrimination in employment to the level of those who started the discriminating.

Also, a person may be prejudiced without being racist or committing acts of discrimination. A famous piece of research done during the days of rampant anti-Oriental prejudice in the 1930s asked hotels and restaurants across the United States whether they would accommodate a traveling Chinese couple. Most said no. But when a Chinese couple appeared, most of the establishments served them without question—even those who had said they would not.[3]

Finally, one can discriminate against others without being racist or prejudiced. During the period of severe restrictions against African Americans in the South, some employers were neither prejudiced nor racists. However, they knew that serving African Americans in their establishments would not only violate local laws but would result in loss of all their white patrons. As a result, they practiced discrimination without being racist or prejudiced.

The term *racism* came into prominence when people began to distinguish between human races on the basis of physiological characteristics—skin color, facial features, hair, and so forth. Later research showed the difficulty of isolating such characteristics in any absolute way. Few people are racially pure. Even more important was a growing awareness of the role of cultural characteristics in shaping behavior. Thus racism merged with ethnicity as a way of defining others. In the early 1900s, the arrival of masses of new immigrants to the United States gave rise to manifestations of xenophobia. Xenophobia emerges periodically when economic conditions are adverse for the native born or when large groups of immigrants press for admission.

Any discussion of prejudice and/or discrimination in the United States can refer to races, ethnic groups, new immigrants, sexes, religions (including cults and sects), sexual preferences, different classes in society, ideological groups such as right-to-life and pro-choice proponents, and any combination of the above. For purposes of convenience, this chapter will use the word *racism* as a general description, except when more precision is required.

Racism arises from many motivations and takes different disguises. Morner, for example, mentions the sexual aspect of racism (which is not the same as sexism).[4] Fear or envy of the assumed sexual prowess of certain groups, or the belief that they prefer sex partners from another group, may lead to racist attitudes and/or actions. Native Americans hid their women not from each other, but from Spanish explorers; such actions can be interpreted as a kind of racism with sexual overtones.

ECONOMIC, RELIGIOUS, AND POLITICAL USES OF RACISM

Racism obviously can also be linked to economic purposes, such as acquiring cheap labor or preserving good jobs for "one's own." Religion, too, can serve as a wellspring of racial prejudice. Despite occasional questions as to the skin color of Abraham, Moses, and other founders of Judaism, the idea of Black Jews was an oxymoron until the (re)discovery of Ethiopian Jews (although Yemenite Jews and many from North Africa were clearly not white in the European American sense). African Americans once were barred from the Mormon Church, and they are still barred from its priesthood. Finally, the political uses of racism were blatant in the poll tax, literacy requirements, and knowledge tests that were once part of voter registration, all procedures designed to screen out African Americans. Conversely, during Reconstruction in the South, newly freed voters were avidly sought by politicians, usually Northerners called carpetbaggers, who wanted to get elected. In Boston, almost all elected officials were Irish—another political exploitation of ethnicity.

Although the focus of this book is on the United States, it should be mentioned that prejudice, racism, and discrimination are not exclusively American traits. Writing in the 1840s, Gilliam noted that the typical Mexican "believes that his people are the most learned and pious in the world; hence his prejudice to foreigners."[5] Although the most blatant and visible racism in the United States has long been directed at African Americans, the increasing number of Hispanics, Asians, and members of other groups has led to a mixing of ethnic origins and a fusion of racism and xenophobia, with skin color and/or "race" no longer the only or even the most important variable.

In the 203 years since the U.S. census began using racial categories, twenty-six different designations have been used. In 1990, interviewees were offered the choices of Black, White, American Indian/Alaskan Native, Asian/Pacific Islander, and Other. About 10 million of them answered "other." About 28% of those answering an open-ended ancestry question listed two or more ethnic groups in their lineage.[6]

Between 1900 and 1930 more than a million Mexican immigrants came to the United States—this was nearly 10% of the total population of Mexico at the time. In the 1940s, one of the most vivid displays of prejudice against Mexican Americans took place as the so-called Zoot Suit Riots flared. Since 1965, the Latino and Latina population of the United States has grown at three times the rate of the national average. The Hispanic population of the United States is now about 8% (18.8 million), and it is projected that Latinos will surpass African Americans as the largest ethnic minority in the next thirty to forty years. New York City has the largest Puerto Rican population of any city in the world, and the largest population of African descent outside of Africa.[7]

Since World War II, the flow of immigrants from Asia has increased greatly. Since 1975, more than 800,000 Southeast Asian refugees have come into the United States, and the foreign-born population of the United States increased by 46% during the years 1970-1980.[8]

U.S. history includes discriminatory laws and prejudiced attitudes against many immigrant groups, including Mexicans, Chinese, and Japanese, as well as against religious groups such as Mormons, Amish, Hutterians, and Jews. Although the experience of African Americans and that of immigrants have many similarities, they are not identical. Racism against African Americans has been more widespread, more deeply rooted, of longer duration, and of greater severity than prejudice against any other group. Individual expressions of racism may be attacked in a number of ways, with varying degrees of success. A vast literature describes efforts to overcome racist attitudes, ranging from intergroup activities through individual therapy to legal retribution. In social welfare policy, *institutionalized* racism is the prime factor.

INSTITUTIONALIZED RACISM

Institutional racism is a societal structure that systematically discriminates against certain groups. Although racial discrimination is not explicitly written into social welfare laws or regulations, administration of the programs, particularly on a local level, often reflects the endemic racism of American society. The social welfare system is not immune to racism, and programs and services are delivered in a white cultural mode based on policies developed from a middle-class bias. These policies serve to maintain the position of minority groups. When the image of recipients changes from the white deserving poor to African American—and therefore presumably undeserving—poor, programs are slashed, grants are cut, and services become punitive, as in the case of AFDC.

The discrimination that pervades American society also shows up in the welfare system. For example, if certain groups are largely confined by the socioeconomic system to low-paying, temporary jobs, the welfare benefits they acquire from work-linked social insurance programs will be equally sparse. Accordingly, the average monthly OASDI payment in 1990 was $592 for whites and $495 for African Americans.[9] Disability payments were $616 to whites and $537 to African Americans.

As any number of writers have observed, racism against African Americans was both the cause and the consequence of the institution of slavery. The legal emancipation brought about by the Civil War did little to improve the socioeconomic position of most former slaves. In some cases it declined, particularly as policies became the legal responsibility of the various states. Nearly a century later, despite bright hopes that World War II would result in better interracial relationships, the situation of African Americans was little improved.

During the 1960s, widespread dissent concerning the Vietnam War, among other things, contributed to greater demands for a voice in determining policies and an end to various kinds of discrimination. The student movement, the women's movement, and the gay and lesbian movement all made their voices heard and their presence felt. However, the "Black Revolt" (generally subsumed under the rubric "Civil Rights Movement") achieved the greatest judicial and legislative gains. During the two-year period from June 1963 to August 1965, more legislation was introduced, debated, and enacted than in the previous two decades.[10]

MARTIN LUTHER KING JR.

African American leaders, sometimes aided and abetted by white associates, created organizations and initiated activities to bring the civil rights agenda into reality. None became as well known and/or influential as the movement's charismatic leader, Dr. Martin Luther King Jr., who was dedicated to nonviolent social protest. He had an unparalleled ability to inspire people, to organize them, and to lead them in dramatic gestures such as the march from Selma to Birmingham and the march on Washington, D. C., where Dr. King delivered his famous "I have a dream" speech. He also was able to reach out to other groups for support: Jewish groups, among others, marched with, trained, and contributed to African American groups.

Dr. King's efforts were aided and supported by sympathetic administrations under presidents Kennedy and Johnson. However, the results were achieved primarily through the judicial system, followed by legislation. Changes in the South, where the major efforts had been expended, were rapid and dramatic in the areas of voting rights and integration of schools and commercial establishments. Among other mandated changes were demands that a certain percentage of jobs go to members of minority groups—a requirement generally referred to as affirmative action. With the passage of time, this became one of the most controversial reforms, because it set up a direct conflict between equality and equity. The program was called "reverse discrimination," among other things, and challenged on various levels.

With the advent of the Reagan-Bush administrations and the transfer of the equal rights struggle from the South to the ghetto areas of large cities, the drive for equal rights was virtually dismantled. Another factor may have been the tragic killing of Dr. King. Riots in the ghettos of Watts, Roxbury, and similar places have provided evidence of continuing racial problems. Since the 1960s no plan has been proposed and no policy developed that would provide substantial access to white housing, schools, and job opportunities for African Americans confined to urban ghettos. No president since Johnson has even made a major speech on the issues. Instead, the situation seems to have been reversed. Instead of calling for measures to overcome the plight of the African American inner-city ghetto, political leaders are blaming welfare programs for causing dependency and reducing motivation to work.

RESULTS OF RACISM

Of the 34 million poor people in the United States, 23 million are white and 9 million are African American. However, African Americans are three times as likely to experience poverty. About 34% of African Americans are poor, compared to 12% of whites and 28% of Hispanics. Of the families headed by females, 27% of those headed by whites are in poverty, compared to 52% for African Americans and 53% for Hispanics. About 20% of the population under age 18—but nearly half of African American children— live in poverty. Although African Americans make up only 12% of the U.S. population, they account for 44% of all AFDC recipients, 27% of SSI recipients, and 35% of all food stamp recipients.[11]

This becomes a closed circle. As society excludes African Americans, Hispanics, and others from good jobs, their welfare needs grow. As their welfare needs grow, they are viewed as lazy, irresponsible, dependent, and so forth. Because of these perceptions, they are not considered for good jobs. Breaking this cycle will require significant legislative and judicial actions.

Sexism

The ideology that "It's a man's world," and should remain so, is responsible for sex discrimination in society. Social welfare provisions have always had a sexist orientation, with the most obvious bias against equality for women. The basic conception of OASDI (or OASI in its original form) was the outdated norm of a husband in the workforce and wife at home. The system favors the woman who has remained at home and, through a long-term marriage, has been supported by her husband. In short, Social Security is built on the assumption of a work pattern that most clearly matches that of the adult able-bodied male. Public pensions are determined by men, with men in mind. The model is that of men who started working at age 18, worked full time for forty-seven years, and for the same employer after age 35, and who retire at age 65 after receiving all the raises and perquisites to which they were entitled.

In Europe, even more than in the United States, having a dependent spouse results in higher benefits. In many countries, all women who remain at home are automatically dependents. That status, with its attendant rights, is rarely granted to the husband of a female employee. This difference in treatment reduces the value of the wife's contribution. In most schemes, entitlements are not the same for widowers as for widows—rarely does a wife's pension entitlement revert to the widower.

When regulations do not discriminate against women, social welfare agencies exercise control over them in subtle and informal ways. Many benefits are based upon work records. Because of their shorter working career, preponderance of part-time work, and lower earnings, women's benefits tend to be lower than men's. This is not a function of their education or experience; it is more attributable to labor market discrimination.

Even when both spouses are working in a family business, the woman is usually insured only through her husband's activity. Thus, when she is unable to work because of maternity, illness, or accident, she is not entitled to payments.

Nor does she acquire any personal entitlement to old-age benefits. Also, U.S. Social Security does not include maternity insurance, a feature of programs in many other countries.

PROGRESS AGAINST SEXISM

The past twenty years have brought about a reinterpretation of what is proper for men and for women with respect to their roles in society. For example, using "earnings sharing" to compute Social Security income more accurately reflects women's contributions to the family income. In 1978 the U.S. Supreme Court ruled that women could not be required to pay higher premiums than men in supplementary insurance plans on the basis that they tended to outlive men; nor, by implication, could they be required to pay more for health insurance on the basis of sex. Furthermore, in approving reforms in 1983 that provide for a gradual increase in the retirement age from 65 to 67 by the year 2027, Congress included no provisions referring specifically to women. This might mean that retirement ages for women will not be raised or, alternatively, that there will be no difference in male and female retirement ages. Either result would be a mixed blessing: If retirement age is the same, women will have to work as long as men to be eligible for Social Security. If women's retirement age remains at the present level, "One might ask whether a lower retirement age really is an advantage for women. The effect is to shorten their working lives and, since they often receive lower wages than men, earlier retirement is more in the nature of a handicap."[12]

Restrictions on the use of Medicaid funds for abortions limit women's use of the program, but there are no similar restrictions on situations that apply only to men, such as prostatitis.

SEXISM AGAINST MALES

Sexism does not always run in one direction. The prevailing view in the nineteenth century was that the evils of society were created by men, and that it was women's task to provide a remedy: "To female moral reformers, however, one evil dominated—indeed, created—all others: men."[13] Women were stereotyped as more caring, more tender, more understanding, and more capable of relating to children. This view may partly account for the preponderance of women in nursing, social work, and teaching; 67% of social workers are women, as are 95% of nurses and 85% of elementary school teachers.[14]

Although there are certainly other reasons why males are underrepresented in these professions, the stereotype of the "macho" male still causes some people to look askance at, and even put subtle obstacles in the way of the man who wants to become a teacher, a nurse, and in some cases, a social worker.

More serious is the fact that the original Social Security Act provided for payment of benefits to divorced wives who were elderly or had disabilities, but benefits were not provided for similarly situated men. In Finland, widows benefit from a clause that eases their transition period by a less stringent interpretation of the law, but widowers are not mentioned. In the United States, husbands and widowers are now eligible under provisions that formerly applied only to wives and widows. Furthermore, the law now provides benefits for fathers who care for children of their retired, disabled, or deceased divorced wives. In Finland, a pension is paid to persons, both male and female, who choose not to take up paid employment in order to stay home taking care of children, the elderly, or sick or disabled relatives, and fathers are entitled to six days paid "father's leave" on the birth of a child. Complete equality between the sexes concerning premiums, payments, and regulations has not yet been achieved. As has been noted, gender is a category that will not go away.[15]

Ageism

Despite the fact that many aged people in the United States live in poverty, and that, conversely, many poor people are old, most social welfare programs have a bias in favor of the elderly. The aged are almost automatically included in the "deserving poor," even when they do not receive as much as they seem to deserve.

FORCED RETIREMENT

One real disability inflicted on the elderly by the social welfare system is the requirement to stop working at a given age. In the United States, full Social Security pensions are available to men at age 65, and reduced pension can be taken at age 62. There is no *requirement* to take up such pensions nor to stop working. Social Security payments are simply reduced in the face of continued paid employment. However, the establishment of age 65 as pensionable age for men was almost immediately seized upon by employers as the age at which they could easily retire workers. Only in 1978 did it become illegal to fire workers because of age alone. Although some people undoubtedly prefer to continue working, the number who retire, and even retire early, has not been appreciably affected by that law.[16]

INCOME REDUCTION OF THE ELDERLY

In 1980, single retired persons in the United States received 52% of the minimum wage and 41% of the average wage. The income replacement rate for the elderly has risen to 66% in 1992, representing a cut of a third in preretirement income. Some people argue that this income reduction is reasonable, because older people have fewer expenses than younger ones. However, the assumption that on the day that people become 65 their needs are substantially reduced has no basis in either logic or experience.[17]

Reducing Social Security payments because of continuing paid employment can also be viewed as an age-related inequity. Private pension plans rarely limit the earning capacity of pensioners. For example, Army retirees continue to receive their full pensions regardless of whether they work or have income after retirement, as do government employees. Both of these are paid by the government. In this light, government restrictions on postretirement Social Security income can be viewed as negative discrimination.

INCREASING LIFE EXPECTANCY

The problem of ageism will probably continue to expand, quantitatively at least, as the number and proportion of the aged in society increase. The accelerating increase in population is not solely the result of a growing or even a high birthrate. It is more closely linked to increasing longevity.

In 1550 B.C., for example, life expectancy at birth in Egypt was only 15 years, primarily due to the high rate of infant deaths. In 1700, life expectancy at birth in Europe was 33 years; in 1950, it was 66 years; and in 1990, it was 74.4 years.[18]

At the start of the twentieth century, average life expectancy throughout the world was 48 years. Between 1985 and 1990, it reached 63.9 years, and it is expected to be 75.7 years by the year 2000. Between 1955 and 1990, life expectancy throughout the world has increased by 16.4 years, or 34.5%. In 1990, life expectancy for men was 61.8 years, and for women, 65.9 years. It has been predicted that by the year 2000 the average life span for men will be 65, and for women, 75.8. By the year 2025 these figures will be 71.6 for men and 79 for women. Continuing increases in life expectancy are theoretically possible, with most experts holding that the maximum age attainable is 115 to 120 years, although they do not predict when this will come about.[19]

The observed and expected lengthening of life expectancy is not simply a statistical artifact based upon lowered infant mortality. When life expectancy at age 30 is examined (thus neutralizing the effect of infant death rates), continual lengthening of life expectancy remains a fact. In 1930, life expectancy in the United States at age 30 was 36 more years for women and 34 more for men; in 1985, these expectancies were 50 and 45 more years, respectively.[20]

This growth in longevity is partly due to the reduction in the number and severity of calamities that once reduced the population. Antibiotics and other new drugs have controlled many diseases. Pneumonia, for example, was once referred to as the "old person's friend" because death from pneumonia was common among the aged, and considered relatively painless. Pneumonia is now rather easily cured in most cases. Other diseases, such as smallpox, have been virtually eliminated through public health measures. In fact, it has been estimated that one third of the people born since 1950 are alive today only because of modern drugs. Also contributing to longevity are advances in nutrition; remedial medicine; sanitation; sounder construction of buildings, bridges, dams, and so forth; and more reliable forecasting of hurricanes, tornadoes, snowstorms, and, quite recently, earthquakes and volcanic eruptions.

GROWTH OF THE OLDER SECTOR

Primarily as a result of these increases in longevity, there has been phenomenal growth in the number of older people and in their proportion of the population. Within the category of *aged, aging,* or *elderly,* there are subcategories, sometimes called the young aged, the frail elderly, the very old, and so forth. One semi-humorous categorization speaks of the aged as the go-go, the go-slow, the slow-slow, and the no-go. Whatever these groups are called, their high growth rates are clear.

In the United States, the *proportion* of those over age 65 rose from 4% in 1900 to 11% in 1984, and it is estimated that by the year 2030, the proportion of elderly people will be 21.2%. There are now about ten times as many people age 65 or older as there were at the beginning of this century. Between 1980 and 2030 the under-60 age group is expected to grow by 25%, but the over-60 group will at least double. In 1900, one person in sixteen was over age 60; now one in six is; and in 2030, it will be one in four. In 1988 the U.S. Census Bureau predicted that by the year 2050, the 65-plus population would total 68.5 million, compared with the then-current 32 million. So rapid is the growth of this group that five years later that estimate was increased to 78.9 million—a 15% rise.[21]

Even more striking is the expected growth in the very old group—those 85 or older. In 1940, the 85-plus group represented 0.3% of the American population. By 1982 this had become 1.1%, and by the year 2000, the oldest group will top 2% of all Americans, numbering 5.1 million persons. By 2040 this group will number 13 million. Furthermore, by the year 2000 more than 100,000 Americans will be 100 years old or over.[22]

Women tend to outlive men in all developed countries. Among those over age 65 in the United States as this century ends, there will be 150 women for every 100 men, and among those over 84, there will be 254 women for every 100 men. Fifty percent of all American women over 65 are widows, and nearly 80% of all married women will become widows and probably will survive sixteen years after that.[23]

This expected selective growth has many implications for future social welfare policies concerning Social Security, finances in general, health care, family structure, housing, and much more. For example, about half the Americans who survive to age 65 are likely to live in a nursing home or require extensive home services, with all that this means for health demands, finances, housing, and so forth. Finland provides another interesting case. Survivors' pensions in Finland are discontinued if a widow or widower without children remarries before age 50, but the pension is restored if the new marriage ends within five years. An extreme and violently debated proposal would eliminate life-extending care for most people over the age of 75.

Although research indicates that social workers prefer working with groups other than the aged, in 1987 26% of members of the National Association of Social Workers—almost 30,000 of them—were working with older people. This figure is expected to increase to 40,000 or 50,000 by the year 2000.[24]

Xenophobia

In places where rapid population growth is seen as a major cause of physical, social, and economic problems, population control is understandably an important goal of national policy. The methods vary. Some countries depend on or encourage emigration, to reduce population and for other reasons. India derives a large part of its foreign-currency reserve from money sent home to family members by Indians abroad, and such remittances are also an important part of Lebanon's economy. Other countries view emigration with disfavor. In 1990, thirty-five countries indicated that emigration was too high.

As for immigration, only 6 of 169 countries felt that immigration was too low, whereas 37 felt that it was too high. Many countries prohibit or limit immigration for population-control reasons. Forty-two percent of developed countries want to reduce immigration, and only 5% want to increase it. Moreover, despite publicity about refugees flooding into the developed countries, almost five times more move from one developing country to another developing country.[25]

The arrival of immigrant and the persistence of visible minorities may create xenophobic reactions. In the United States, the predominantly white Christian Western ideology may view non-white, non-Christian, non-Western immigrants as inferior and/or as a threat to the majority culture.

IMMIGRATION AND EMIGRATION
IN THE UNITED STATES

Immigration and emigration as factors in population growth or control are of no great public interest in the United States, but the impact of immigrants is another matter. In some states and regions, legal and illegal immigration are of great concern because the sheer numbers of immigrants may threaten to outstrip the resources allocated to welfare and education. In 1989, the United States granted immigrant rights to over a million persons, and it continues to receive a net immigration of about 900,000 per year. Between 25% and 60% of immigrants to the United States later leave, suggesting that their integration is temporary, at best. Interestingly, since 1930 the majority of immigrants—in the world, and not just in the United States—have been women. These facts would seem to require a well-thought-out immigration policy, with significant welfare implications.[26]

However, the U.S. government as such has no policy for the absorption of new immigrants, and "no public consensus exists on whether and how to assist immigrants and refugees."[27] Other countries have departments of immigration and absorption, or they fund absorption activities directly. In the United States, such activities are left almost entirely to voluntary organizations, including churches and church-affiliated bodies or groups such as the National Association for New Americans or the Hebrew Immigrants Aid Association.

ILLEGAL IMMIGRANTS

Public feelings about illegal immigration run higher. Estimates of the number of undocumented immigrants in the United States in 1989 run from 3 to 6 million, and 1.7 to 2.9 million, with the number rising.[28] This tide does not seem to have been stemmed by passage in 1986 of the Immigration Reform and Control Act, which led to over 3 million applications from undocumented immigrants who had been in the United States since before 1982.

THREE VIEWS OF ABSORPTION

Three classic views of absorption are often found in the United States. The ideology of assimilation holds that the culture or civilization of the majority is desirable and that other groups must change to become like the existing majority group. Mutual assimilation, or the "melting pot," holds that each group must hold onto part of its heritage, while another part is absorbed by, and becomes integral to, the larger society. Thus, from an amalgam of all groups, a new entity arises. This ideology never envisioned the merging of religions. Hence, the theory of the "triple melting pot"—Catholics, Protestants, and Jews—provides for each religion to merge national origins, skin color, and cultural differences within their individual groups.

Finally, cultural pluralism holds that each group should maintain the essential parts of its own culture while sharing in an overall framework. Variation of this theory include exclusive multiculturalism—each ethnic group remains an island unconnected with other islands—and pluralistic multiculturalism—whereby many ethnic groups relate to and interact with each other.

The Civil Rights Movement (sometimes referred to as the Black Revolt) of the 1960s, U.S. Supreme Court decisions, new laws and regulations, and changing public attitudes have led away from the pure assimilation model. However, various groups favor the melting pot or cultural pluralism goals. In the United States, it is common to give rhetorical support to the melting pot and practical support to assimilation. However, the assumption that ethnicity is a temporary phenomenon in a strategy of long-term assimilation has been shaken. Hansen, an early student of American assimilation, postulated that, "What the grandparents want to forget, the grandchildren want to remember."[29] That is, new immigrants are anxious to become and to be perceived as like the majority of Americans, so they reject anything tying them to their original culture. Their children, still insecure of their status, maintain this attitude. However, the third generation, according to Hansen, is secure enough of their Americanism that they can begin to search out their ancestral roots without embarrassment or fear. This refers only to the more exotic aspects—songs, dances, food, costumes—of the old culture, not its values and ideology. Without official and structural encouragement and support, Hansen predicted that the fourth generation would no longer be interested in such things.

However, the fourth and succeeding generations of some immigrant groups are proving more tenacious in their attachment to ethnicity than Hansen foresaw. A growing move toward cultural pluralism expresses itself not only in education conducted in foreign languages, but in a resurgence of ethnic pride, in the maintenance and rehabilitation of ethnic neighborhoods, and in the recognition of ethnic groups as political forces of importance.

Welfarism as Ideology

Social welfare is influenced not only by independent ideological stances but also by its own ideology. Some view social welfare as residual—that is, as a "last resort" service when the family, mutual aid, the church, and the marketplace have failed. This attitude is sometimes called *subsidiarity,* meaning help given at the lowest level possible. Others view social welfare as a structural component of society, part of its institutionalized ongoing activities. The residual view represents social welfare as a privilege to be earned or as an undeserved charity, whereas the structural view conceives of social welfare as the deserved right of everyone in society. The latter view has been elucidated by Smith, who points out that no constitutional or legal right guarantees decent housing, sufficient food, or other necessities in American society. An agency can be sued for not fulfilling its obligations, but the government or its agents cannot be sued simply because someone lacks the necessities of life. Smith argues, therefore, for a social welfare based upon the right to life: Benefits should not be based on what people are or have done, how they behave or what they believe; rather, benefits should be offered to them simply because they are alive. This, too, is an ideology, although one held by very few people.[30]

Another ideology holds that gross inequality in the distribution of income is undesirable—because it is dysfunctional for the society, inimical to individuals, or simply immoral. The use of social work programs to achieve a more nearly equal distribution is one conception of social welfare. Whether the redistribution is achieved by direct means (such as children's allowances, a guaranteed minimum income, and larger welfare payments) or indirectly (through improved education, affirmative action, or otherwise), the use of social welfare as an instrument for redistribution is a serious concern to some planners and policy makers. However, the dominant ideology accepts an unequal distribution of rewards not only as inevitable but as desirable.

Some "radical" social workers believe that social welfare policies and programs are being used to maintain the capitalist system and that this should be resisted. They argue:

> We have to break with the professional doctrine that the institutions in which social workers are employed have benign motives; that the purpose of hospitals is to provide health care for the sick; that the purpose of welfare agencies is to provide assistance for the impoverished; that the purpose of child care agencies is to protect children.[31]

Competing Ideologies

Different ideological positions, or even elements of single ideologies, may clash. The ideology that all people are equal conflicts with the belief that to deserve help, people must behave in ways seen as moral. Humanitarianism confronts mistrust. Jeffersonian "least government" clashes with Hamiltonian "strong government." Not surprisingly, then, social welfare programs based on their proponents' ideologies may also conflict with one another. For example, proposals to reduce unemployment may clash with plans to raise the minimum age for OASDI—and thus encourage older people to continue working—or to make it easier for women, wives, and mothers to work. Similarly, proposals for a children's allowance are resisted on the basis that such a program will encourage out-of-wedlock births.

There are also antiideologies. Characterizing a social welfare policy or program as communistic or socialistic is often enough to ensure its defeat.

This helps explain why national health insurance, often called "socialized medicine" by its opponents, is so long in coming. A U.S. congressman once said, "The word 'social worker' is not a good word. People connect social worker with socialization, and socialized medicine, and socialism. I have suggested that we ought to get rid of that term."[32]

Institutionalization of Ideologies

Ideologies that lead to social welfare can become institutionalized. That is, they spawn social systems that develop lives of their own. Examples are the growth of voluntary organizations and of both laws and organizations whose major concerns are philanthropy.

VOLUNTARY ORGANIZATIONS

Voluntary organizations are often organized around the interests of one person or a small group. Examples of small-group initiatives are parents whose children are exceptional in one way or another; people whose loved ones are suffering from a disease such as leukemia or Alzheimer's disease; advocates for groups such as Native Americans, Vietnamese orphans, or the homeless, or for causes such as preventing child abuse, abuse of women, and the like. People with similar interests sometimes get together to do something about their concerns.

The goal may be to comfort and/or help one another, to spur research, or to seek government intervention. Almost invariably, such voluntary organizations need money, and fund-raising becomes one of their important activities. With fund-raising comes licensing, legal controls, and accountability. Lack of accountability may lead to excessive administrative and fund-raising costs: Some organizations consider 5% the acceptable limit for fund-raising costs, whereas others operate with a 2% limit. Organizations with no accountability have been known to pay more than 50% of proceeds to the fund-raisers and others.

ORGANIZED PHILANTHROPY

Organized philanthropy has become big business in many countries. Fund-raisers have their own professional association, code of ethics, continuing education seminars, and employment services. Federation officials are also organized into a number of associations, and some universities offer extension courses for them. A good part of education for community organization in social work uses federation bodies and offices of various kinds as field-work settings.

In 1987, Americans gave $93 billion to philanthropic endeavors. But the nonprofit sector does not depend purely on contributions. In 1984 an estimated 40% of nonprofit income came from government sources. There are an estimated 6 million volunteer organizations in the United States. If volunteers are included, 10% of all U.S. employees work in the nonprofit sector, including one of every ten service workers and one of every six professional workers. One ninth of all property is owned by voluntary organizations.[33]

FOUNDATIONS

Although philanthropic foundations are often viewed as a feature of the modern world, these are ancient institutions. In the fourteenth and fifteenth centuries, bequests and large gifts by individual benefactors were not uncommon. At the time of the Reformation, there were at least 460 charitable foundations in England. Some had exotic beginnings. One was founded to purchase faggots to burn heretics, and another was started in order to deport foreign bullfighters. The giant foundations that exist today were begun at the turn of the century.

A considerable influence on this development was an article titled "Wealth," written by Andrew Carnegie. He called upon the rich to administer their wealth as a public trust because, "having proved themselves in the struggle for commercial success, they were particularly fitting agents of the public trust."[34] Carnegie contributed much of his money to build libraries, parks, concert halls, museums, and educational institutions with a practical slant.

John D. Rockefeller Sr., carried the idea further, establishing trusts and engaging personnel whose life work it would be to "manage benevolence properly and effectively." Rockefeller may have been motivated by the desire to improve his image from that of the "most execrated name in American life"[35] or simply to annoy his family. Henry Ford may have established his foundation as an attempt to keep the motor company within the family, but he and Rockefeller established immense nonprofit charitable foundations.

The spread of foundations has been aided by tax laws that exempt most philanthropic contributions from income taxes and make the property of such bodies tax-exempt. In 1987 there were 4,367 foundations in the United States, not including corporate or company-sponsored foundations. Corporate philanthropic contributions grew from $30 million in 1936 to $4.6 billion in 1986, tripling in the last decade alone. In 1969 the annual income of the Ford Foundation exceeded that of the world's largest bank, and the income of the 596 largest tax-exempt foundations was more than twice the total net earnings of the nation's fifty largest commercial banks.[36]

The institutionalization of philanthropy—whether in the historical mold of the Charity Organization Society, a social services exchange to compare information about recipients, or the huge modern foundations and organizations—serves to rationalize services, to increase professionalization, to make possible long-range planning, and to increase accountability. However, institutionalization may also result in a type of paternalism: The umbrella organization gives or withholds according to the deference of applicants to its wishes. For example, it may require hymns to be sung or prayers to be said before it offers food, or funds may be available only for narrowly defined purposes—for example, the higher education of deaf African American orphans.

GOAL DISPLACEMENT
AND SUBSTITUTION

Goal displacement occurs when the activities required to keep the organization going become more important than its stated goal. Givers and volunteers, professionals and other staff, may form interest groups more concerned with preserving and building the organization itself than in serving its initial purpose. People may become very active in soliciting members, fund-raising, presenting programs, and other aspects of the organization, with little knowledge about or concern for its goals.

Goal substitution is a somewhat different process. When the stated goal of an organization is reached, a new goal may be chosen, either because the work continues to be meaningful to members or because it seems a waste to disband such a successful instrument. An example is the Infantile Paralysis Foundation. Its effective March of Dimes program, spurred by President Franklin D. Roosevelt's personal interest, contributed greatly to the successful fight against polio. Rather than disband the organization, a new goal was sought and found in the fight against birth defects.

SUMMARY

Despite notable gains by both women and African Americans, sexism and racism continue to influence the extension or withholding of welfare benefits. These prejudices can be combined with others to create discriminatory policies and practices. In turn, these conspire to perpetuate rather than alleviate the conditions or problems that welfare policies are presumably intended to address.

Ideologies change, albeit very slowly, but there is little reason to believe that societies of the future will be less humanitarian, or that individuals will be less altruistic, than those of today. On the other hand, racism, sexism, ageism and xenophobia have proved tenacious, despite undoubted successes against them. Overcoming the effects of these attitudes in social welfare policies and programs will not be an easy task.

EXERCISES

A. On racism and sexism:

1. An African American male client wants his OASDI pension increased to the level of the average white male, retroactive to his retirement ten years ago. He says that he has been discriminated against in employment all his life and that this will be in the nature of affirmative action. If you had a limited amount of discretionary funds at your disposal, how would you respond? Why?

2. An African American female client wants her OASDI survivor's pension increased to the level of the average white female

survivor, retroactive to her husband's death ten years ago. How
would you respond? Why?

3. An African American female client wants her OASDI pension
   increased to the level of the average African American male,
   retroactive to her retirement ten years ago. How would you
   respond? Why?

4. An African American female client wants her OASDI pension
   increased to the level of the average white male, retroactive to
   her retirement ten years ago. How would you respond? Why?

5. A white female client wants her OASDI pension increased to the
   level of the average male. How would you respond? Why?

6. A male white client wants his OASDI pension, which is minimal,
   increased to the level of the average female, which is higher.
   How would you respond? Why?

B.   On assimilation, melting pot, and cultural pluralism theories:

By agreement between the two countries, the entire population of
the island of Agrid, threatened by rising waters caused by a new dam,
have been airlifted to your area. They number 168,000—80,000 men,
20,000 women, and 68,000 children. The Agridis are a green-skinned
people, tall and stately. The men wear only loincloths and the women
wear very short grass skirts. They chew a native bark called mastika,
which they spit out when done and which stains everything it touches,
including their tongues and lips, with an indelible blue dye. Non-
Agridis who can bring themselves to try mastika are ecstatic over the
taste.

Agridi men not only are permitted three wives but are required to
choose three mates, due to the imbalance in the sexes. However, the
men and women do not have to marry formally, and they can swap
among themselves as they wish. The children are a communal concern
of the entire group.

Both the men and the women are extremely hard workers and
astonishingly creative in finding easier ways to do their work. In the
spare time thus created, they drink morin, an addictive aphrodisiac,
and play chromo for high stakes, often losing all their wages on one
hand.

They worship Stella, Gardo, and Plimp, and once a month they sacrifice a dog, a cat, and a rabbit to these gods.

1. Which attributes of the Agridis do you think should be changed for their assimilation into American society?
2. Which attributes would you like to see contributed to American society?
3. Which attributes should the Agridis be encouraged to maintain?

C. Can you identify an organization in your community whose goal is no longer pressing, but whose activities have continued or grown? Can you identify an organization in your community whose goal has been reached, but which changed its goal rather than disband?

Notes

1. The distinction is made in Garrison & Jones (1969).
2. Remarks are in Ringer (1983) and Goldsen (1950).
3. This research is described in LaPiere (1934).
4. Sexual motivations are mentioned by Morner (1970).
5. Gilliam is quoted in Leary (1970).
6. The census responses are from Barringer (1993).
7. Statistics are from the following sources: on Mexican immigrants, from McWilliams (1970); on Latinos and Latinas, from Simon (1992); on growth of the Latin population, from Petrovich (1989); on African Americans in New York, from Fitzpatrick (1971).
8. Statistics are from the following sources: on Southeast Asian refugees, from Kelly (1992); on the increase in foreign-born, from Drachman & Halberstadt (1992).
9. Differential payments are documented by U.S. Department of Health and Human Services (1991).
10. The reform agenda of 1963-1965 is described in Orfield (1985).
11. Comparative poverty figures are from DiNitto & Dye (1987).
12. The quotation is from Brocas, Cailloux, & Oget (1990).
13. The quotation is from Ginzberg (1990).
14. The statistics on women are from Zastrow (1992).
15. The gender statement is from Tannen (1991).
16. Lack of effect of retirement law is from Hurwitz (1987).
17. Information is from the following sources: retirement income as percentage of minimum wage, Macarov (1980); cuts in retirement income, Hokenstad (1992); lack of need argument, Habib & Lerman (1976).
18. Life expectancies in ancient Egypt are from Sheldon (1978); other figures are from United Nations (1992e).

19. Statistics are from the following sources: life expectancy in 1900, Cetron & O'Toole (1982); life expectancy in 1985-1990, United Nations (1992e); life expectancy in 2000, Cetron & Davies (1991); the rest of the figures in this paragraph, United Nations (1992e); the 115-120 year prediction is from U.S. Department of Health and Human Services (n.d.).

20. Life expectancy at age 30 in 1900 is from *Demographic Yearbook* (1989); in 1985, from U.S. Department of Commerce (1987).

21. Statistics are from the following sources: proportions of elderly, American Association of Retired Persons (1985); the "ten times" figure, Zastrow (1992); between 1980 and 2030, and ratios, Fowles (1983); the change in census predictions, "Census Bureau Ups" (1993).

22. The 13 million prediction is from U.S. Department of Health and Human Services (1987a); all other figures are from Zastrow (1992).

23. The ratios of women to men are from Hartman (1990); widowhood is discussed by Kamm (1991).

24. Preferences of social workers are from Macarov (1987c); numbers of social workers working with the aged are from Peterson (1990).

25. The survey results are presented in United Nations (1992e).

26. Statistics are from the following sources: on official U.S. immigration, United Nations (1992e); on net immigration, Ludington (1993); on the number of immigrants leaving and preponderance of women, Yans-McLaughlin (1990).

27. The quotation is from Ross-Sheriff (1990).

28. Estimates of illegal immigration are from Ross-Sheriff (1990) and United Nations (1992e).

29. The quotation and subsequent discussion are from Hansen (1964).

30. These views are from Smith (1955).

31. The quotation is from Cloward & Piven (1975).

32. The quotation is from Fogarty (1962).

33. Statistics are from the following sources: total contributions, from Joseph (1989); nonprofit government income, from Salaman (1987); number of volunteer organizations, from Commission on Private Philanthropy (1975); proportion of nonprofit workers, from Barretta-Herman (1992); proportion of property held, from Commission on Private Philanthropy (1975).

34. Carnegie's article is quoted in Commission on Private Philanthropy (1975).

35. *Managing benevolence* is from Horowitz & Kolodny (1969), and *execrated name* is from Norton (1989).

36. Statistics are from the following sources: number of foundations, from Weber (1988); the growth of contributions, from Smith (1989); the income of the Ford Foundation, from Horowitz & Kolodny (1969).

READ MORE ABOUT IT...

For more information on:	*See these sources:*
Distinctions between minimal and maximal prejudice	Raiklin, 1990; Schermerhorn, 1970
Multiple forms of discrimination	Carlton-LaNey, 1992; Sands & Nuccio, 1992
Distinctions between racism, racial prejudice, and racial discrimination	Johnson & Schwartz, 1991
Distinctions between racism and ethnicity	Ringer & Lawless, 1989
Zoot Suit Riots	Adler, 1970; Scott, 1970
Racism against Blacks	Ringer & Lawless, 1989
Racism in social welfare	Johnson & Schwartz, 1991; LaPiere, 1934
Cooperation of African Americans and Jews	Ringer & Lawless, 1989
Presidential inattention to civil rights	Orfield, 1985
Welfare linked to dependency	Murray, 1984
Sexism in social welfare	Abramovitz, 1993; Carabine, 1992; Gottlieb, 1987; Payne, 1991
Basic concept of OASDI	Burkhauser, 1978
Pensions	Brocas, Cailloux, & Oget, 1990; Myles, 1989
Women's lower earnings	Terrell, 1992
Women in family businesses	Burkhauser, 1978
Male and female roles	Vianello et al., 1990
Earnings sharing	Gottlieb, 1987

For more information on:	*See these sources:*
Court ruling on insurance	Brocas et al., 1990
Medicaid restrictions	Gelb & Palley, 1982
Nonsexist Finnish laws	United Nations, 1992d
Benefits to U.S. men	Jehle, 1991
Impact of modern drugs	Sheldon, 1978
Implications of aging population	Kane & Kane, 1991; Macarov, 1991a;
Finland survivors' pensions	United Nations, 1992d
Eliminating life-extending care	Callahan, 1991
Views about absorbing immigrants	Price, 1969
Triple melting pot	Herzberg, 1955; Spickard, 1989
Cultural pluralism	Rubin, 1992
The fourth generation	Kivisto & Blanck, 1990; McAll, 1990
Ethnic neighborhoods	Vigilante, 1976
Unequal distribution of rewards	Kluegel & Smith, 1986
Early philanthropic foundations	deSchweinitz, 1943; Norton, 1989
Andrew Carnegie	Commission on Private Philanthropy, 1975
John D. Rockefeller Sr.	Commission on Private Philanthropy, 1975; Horowitz & Kolodny, 1969; Norton, 1989
Henry Ford	Norton, 1989
Goal displacement	Etzioni, 1964

PART III

Influences on Social Welfare

Actions rarely proceed directly and in their intended form from motivations. Many factors intervene: situations, structures, events, attitudes, and processes. Also, the beliefs of the motivated person, as well as those of society, determine whether and in what manner motivations lead to action and how motivations themselves change.

The major motivations for social welfare discussed in the previous section influence one another, and they are also acted upon by deeply held societal attitudes. The ultimate shape of social welfare policies and programs is determined, in large part, by the interplay of motivations and attitudes in the face of reality. Described here are Martin Luther's views about the proper activities of people, Social Darwinism's concept of who deserves to survive, and Adam Smith's laissez-faire economics. This does not, obviously, exhaust the attitudes that permeate society or even those most closely related to social welfare. However, they are among the ideas that have had the clearest and most immediate impact on the thinking that shapes social welfare.

11. The Influence of Martin Luther on Work and Welfare

Luther's influence on social welfare was to lessen the emphasis on good works (that is, charity) as a method of salvation, in favor of faith alone. In addition, his doctrine that working serves God brought about a link between work and welfare that exhibited itself in the doctrine of "less eligibility." Luther's ideas inspired the distinction between the deserving and the undeserving poor and gave rise in modern times to work tests, workhouses, relief work, employment training programs, and work as the basis for benefits in social insurance programs.

When Martin Luther nailed his ninety-five theses to the church door in Wittenberg in 1517, he set in motion two sets of ideas that have influenced social welfare to this day. The first was emphasis on faith rather than on good works. One of Luther's motives for breaking with Catholicism was his disgust with the system for obtaining absolution for sins by undertaking good works. By Luther's time, the system had degenerated so much that indulgences could be purchased in advance for sins not yet committed. Indeed, sinners could "shop around" for the priest who gave the greatest bargains. Furthermore, the money thus collected did not necessarily go to the poor and needy: It might be used to pay the priest's personal debts.

This led Luther to deny the efficacy of good works to earn grace or to guarantee salvation. Luther insisted that faith alone had merit, and he repeatedly attacked as pagan and corrupt the Catholic Church's emphasis on good works as a road to heaven. The effect of this thinking on later attitudes toward

183

charity has been described as "anti-social welfare stands."[1] Nevertheless, Protestantism served as a powerful factor in the establishment of voluntary social welfare organizations and in the emergence of labor unions.

The Protestant Ethic

A second influence of Luther's Reformation has been more widespread, leaving a deeper and more pervasive mark on social welfare policies and programs. This is the attitude toward work that is often referred to as the Protestant ethic. Luther viewed work of any kind as service to God, and he endowed work with religious dignity by defining it as a vocation, or a calling. In his view, people serve God best by doing most perfectly the work of their own vocation. Conversely, people who do not work, or will not work to the full extent of their ability, are sinners.

John Calvin took this conviction a step further: Not only is work a religious duty, but people are called upon to work without desire for the fruits of their labor, simply because to work is to carry out the will of God. Such work will establish God's kingdom on earth, and this is both its value and its goal. Thus, it does not matter whether people become rich or earn too little to meet their subsistence needs; whether their work is satisfying or stultifying, socially useful or harmful, degrading or elevating: God-fearing people work.

By giving work a religious cast, the Protestant Ethic deepened the roots of work in many Western societies and intensified their fervor for work. Luther's stance and influence added impetus to the creation of a work-centered society. The religious motivation for work, along with the manpower needs of the Industrial Revolution, the economic philosophy called mercantilism, new inventions, and changing forms of government, combined to make work the central factor of people's lives and of socioeconomic structures. The Protestant ethic placed a religiotheoretic base under the demands of industrialization.

THE MEANING OF WORK

Luther's influence and the changing nature of work in industrializing societies have combined to influence many aspects of modern life. Work is seen as both necessary and desirable for the individual and for society.

Political, social, and economic programs are all based upon the assumption that people need and want to work and that society needs all the work that everyone capable of laboring can produce. On an individual basis, people are judged not only by the work that they do but also by the manner in which they perform. People who do not or cannot work are viewed as somehow outside the mainstream of life. Work structures time, determines attitudes, shapes images of self and others, and permeates every aspect of life, including schools, the family, religion, and even the prison system. Work not only provides income but also gives structure to the day, week, year, and lifetime. It provides a means of identification, determines companions, provides a sense of belonging, and offers almost indefinable psychic rewards.

NON-WORK-BASED CIVILIZATIONS

The overwhelming emphasis on work in Western civilization was not inevitable. The ancient Greeks saw many kinds of work as inherently degrading, fit to be done only by slaves. Their rejection of such work, far from being sterile or destructive, resulted in the beginnings of literature, mathematics, theater, art, and democratic government. In the Yoga tradition of Hinduism, the devotee is advised to work for Krishna, not for any benefit inherent in work, but simply to avoid idleness. Work must not be done for profit, which buys things that gratify one's senses, because gratification of the senses leads away from oneness with Krishna: "A real Yoga does not desire such fruits. He has no desire other than Krishna, and Krishna is already there."[2] On the other hand, the classical tradition of India emphasizes absence of work (*naiskarmya*) as an ideal worth striving for, and those who manage to attain this state command popular respect. Japan seems to be moving from a period in which life took its major meaning from a person's work to a time where concern is also given to the larger aspects of life.

In preindustrial societies, work is usually done only to satisfy current needs. In such cultures farmers grow only what they and their families need for immediate consumption. Without transportation facilities, means of storage, or credit, farmers are not likely to produce a surplus, which will only take up space and eventually rot. If work has no religious or value connotation, it makes little sense for the farmer to engage in useless or unproductive labor. Instead, the free time may be taken up by other activities, recreational, aesthetic, or spiritual. For this reason, some preindustrial societies celebrate a hundred or more holidays a year. This practice is often reinforced even in industrialized countries where most people practice Catholicism, with its assortment of work-dismissing, leisure-providing feast days. A Brazilian senator, musing on this, once told this author that if it were possible, Brazilians could occupy themselves full time with three things—church, carnival, and football. In fact, without a religious motivation, "people who are clear-sighted, undeluded, and sober-minded will not go on working once their reasonable needs are satisfied . . . the readiness to work springs from trivial, questionable motives."[3]

THE PROTESTANT WORK
ETHIC IN THE INDUSTRIAL WEST

In industrializing and industrialized countries where Protestantism is strong, the Protestant ethic and the reliance on faith rather than good works tend to be mutually reinforcing. Work becomes more than an income-producing activity: People should want to "get ahead," should want to make money, and should work. Hunnicutt says:

> Something like a Theology of Work has ensued; Americans now tend to answer traditional religious questions (Who am I? Where am I going? What do I need to do to get out of the mess I am in?) in terms of work instead of traditional religions. The new work ethic is not Protestant; there is little or no God-talk associated with it. It is a distinctively modern and secular work ethic/religion.[4]

There is no doubt that people in the industrialized West are socialized not only to work but to see work as a positive value. It begins in nursery school with rhymes, such as: "See-saw, Marjorie Daw, Jack shall have a new master. He shall get but a penny a day, because he can't work any faster." Children learn the same lesson from Aesop's fables (the grasshopper and the ant), biblical admonitions, and illustrated books that show the admired father (and nowadays perhaps the mother) coming home from work. Doing schoolwork and homework, they pass through an educational system whose primary purpose is to prepare graduates for the world of work. The socialization process is aided by the church, the media, and role models. In fact, so widespread and universal is the emphasis on work that it is not always called the Protestant ethic, because it permeates non-Protestant societies just as deeply. Instead, it is simply called the work ethic.

Effects on Social Welfare

Few areas of social welfare in the industrialized world have not been influenced by the Protestant ethic. Accusing those who do not work of sinfulness or immorality sharpened the distinction between the deserving and the undeserving poor. It led to tests of an applicant's willingness to work, even in cases in which no work is offered or available. It helped transform alms-houses into workhouses, and added consideration of "potential" assets, in the form of possible employability, to the actual assets examined by means tests. Finally, the Protestant ethic led to relief work, in contradistinction to direct relief.

THE DESERVING AND THE UNDESERVING

The distinction between those who deserve help and those who do not has many connotations. One criterion is the ability of the recipient to use the help—or, more accurately, to use the help properly or well. Those who are found unable to use help may get none. In social work terms, they are sometimes labeled resistant, unsuitable for service, or unable to arrive at (or maintain) the contract. In Britain, persons who cannot find employment during a specified period of time are labeled "unemployable" and dropped from the unemployment rolls. In the parlance of community organizations and inter-national aid, the recipient must not only need the aid but be able to use it wisely. The dilemma arises when inability to use aid wisely creates need. Helping only those who can use help wisely results in "creaming"—dealing with the easiest situations and ignoring or neglecting the more difficult.

This distinction has been made in many social welfare programs. Great care is taken to distinguish the able, deserving client temporarily in crisis from the chronically disabled or disadvantaged client who will need ongoing support. Investments are more acceptable than expenses, so help given able clients usually exceeds that given the disabled or disadvantaged. Studies show that social workers prefer working with adolescents or families, whose problems can presumably be "solved," rather than with the aged, whose con-dition can only continue to worsen. Deserving clients thus become defined as those who can be helped to leave the rolls. This is why work relief is usually more liberal in payments and less restrictive concerning eligibility than poor relief.

THE ROOTS OF LAZINESS

Another perspective suggests that the needy are unfit and therefore to a certain extent blameless. This contrasts dramatically with the idea that those who do not work are immoral, and the differences have implications for policies and programs. If laziness is a sickness rather than a moral defect, the lazy are the victims of pathology and must be treated rather than punished.

LAZINESS AS PATHOLOGY

Since the 1800s, it has been considered appropriate by some to treat paupers as pathological. This position, which leads to holding the economic sector blameless, can be described as follows. If the pathological are not held responsible for their own situation, obviously they cannot be expected to treat themselves. Someone else must do so. Seeing the needy as unfit or pathological leads to paternalism. Decisions and actions must be taken on behalf of the unfit. It is not only possible but necessary to interfere in their lives, because patients are not supposed to know what is good for them. Society has not only the right but the responsibility to cure the pathological, even against their will, and even if the cure is both painful and uncertain.

LAZINESS AS DEVIANCE

However, if not working is defined as deviance rather than pathology, it can be viewed as both purposeful and reprehensible. Deviants are responsible for their own situation and therefore deserve punishment for willfully violating the norms of society. Hence the poor are exhorted to conform to middle-class standards of dress, conduct, speech, thrift, and other virtues. Like any deviants, they are considered unsuitable for normal company and kept at arm's length, which makes it unlikely that the poor will participate effectively and significantly in social welfare programs. Defining poverty as deviance, with refusal to work as the cause, dates back to the Puritans' dictum that those who will not work should not be permitted to eat—an attitude still conspicuously part of the public discourse today.

WORK TESTS

When work is available, the willingness of the deserving poor to work can easily be tested. But even when the agency can neither provide work nor refer the client to a job, motivation to work is seen as important, and methods are devised to test it. In colonial America, a woodyard was usually maintained for these purposes. Applicants who would not lift the axe were ipso facto unworthy. Sometimes applicants were required to move a pile of rocks from one side of a yard to the other and back again. The work test was originally designed to determine suitability for relief. It began to change into make-work or relief work when specific standards were established, such as three hours of work in the woodyard entitling the applicant to three meals and lodging. Work tests for women included sewing garments; some of these were given to relief clients, but others were torn up. Work tests were employed in shelters for the homeless with a deterrent motive—to keep the undeserving out.

These early work tests required applicants to demonstrate some ability to do a job, as well as a general willingness to work. Motivation remains the primary aspect of today's work tests. For example, recipients of unemployment compensation must prove that they are, in truth, seeking work, and they are urged, or in some cases required, to re-register at specific intervals, and in person. This requirement exists today in Israel: Laborers must report in person daily to be eligible for unemployment compensation.

WORKHOUSES

The almshouse was initially intended to take care of the helpless—the aged, the chronically ill, those with disabilities, and those who for any other reason could not take care of themselves at home. In time, the almshouse became a dumping ground for dependents of any age, of either sex, and with every kind of disability.

The idea behind sending the able-bodied poor to workhouses was that if they could learn to support themselves, the wealth of the nation would increase. Even if the program should fall short of all that was expected of it, the poor (particularly, poor children) would acquire skills and habits of industry. The city, state, or country would profit through the increasing number of efficient workers.

Workhouses, as a rule, were less successful than almshouses in achieving their aims, but given the prevailing belief in the justice and efficacy of work, almshouses were gradually transformed into workhouses "in which work is provided for every degree of ability in the pauper; and thus the able poor [are] made to provide, partially at least for their own support, and also to the support, or at least the comfort of the impotent poor."[5] As the work element became more important, it became more and more like relief work or, synonymously, work relief. For example, supervising almshouse workers who did farm work often cost more than hiring farmhands to do the work. As work relief became more prominent, workhouses began to diminish in number and importance. Workhouses are a thing of the past today, on both sides of the Atlantic, but recipients of social welfare are often kept on the equivalent of desert islands in the midst of cities—islands called ghettos, low-cost housing projects, and the like.

WORK RELIEF

Work relief is a method of making relief payments through the mechanism of work. It differs from public works in that work relief is mostly concerned with relief, rather than with employment or with getting certain public jobs done, such as cleaning public areas or running recreation and tutorial programs. In work relief, workers are selected according to their need and projects are managed to maximize employment. Workers are paid on the basis of need rather than work performed. Work relief often involves a means test, and the number of hours that can be worked or the amount earned are sometimes limited.

In public works programs, on the other hand, workers are selected for competence, projects are chosen for intrinsic value, and pay is based on what private employers pay for similar work. The growing service sector of the economy has led to another distinction: between public service jobs and public works projects.

Work relief was originally designed as a test of the unemployed person's willingness to work. The test of motivation evolved into a schedule of amounts of work that would merit amounts of help, and the requirement of work for help became the norm. Public works were used as a means of relief for the unemployed in the 1850s, but the depression of the 1890s resulted in extensive use of work relief, which at that time was quite honestly called "made work."[6] The rationale for work relief was very positive: to save able-bodied workers who were unemployed from becoming destitute and to spare them the humiliation accompanying application for relief. As noted, work relief usually pays more than does outright relief not connected to work.

During the Great Depression of the 1930s, work relief came into its own in the United States. The number of able-bodied people out of work far outstripped the available work, including public works projects. Indeed, public works projects were drastically curtailed as states and communities were unable to finance them. The choice was between direct relief—payments in cash and in kind—and work relief—with payments made as salaries. Those unable to work had to be given direct relief, but for the employable, work relief was instituted.

THE WORKS PROGRESS
ADMINISTRATION (WPA)

Franklin D. Roosevelt was quite clear that Americans would rather work than "go on the dole," and most Americans agreed with him, including those in need. This led to the creation of one of the New Deal's most important, if some- what temporary, institutions, the Works Progress Administration (WPA). The WPA paid salaries that were not technically "adequate" but nevertheless kept people from starving. Instead of basing salaries on individual need, the WPA paid standard salaries to all workers, with some differences between the states. Workers were picked for ability to work, and many, especially artists, musicians, writers, and other skilled people, were allowed to work in their chosen fields. Much of the WPA work met the standard established by the American Association of Social Workers: The work was productive in itself, not just a way to avoid idleness.

The amount of work accomplished under the WPA is staggering:

- 600,000 miles of highways, roads, and streets were constructed or improved.
- 116,000 bridges and viaducts were built or rebuilt.
- More than 110,000 public buildings were built or renovated.
- Nearly 80 million books were repaired.
- More than half a billion school lunches were served.

Plays written on WPA commission are still being performed, and murals in post offices and other public buildings owe their existence to the WPA. After the Depression, work relief returned to a low standard:

Wages . . . dropped to a starvation level, and are paid on the . . . "budget deficiency basis." There is no test of "employability" and little attempt to fit the skill or experience of the worker to the demands of the job. The system has taken on many characteristics of the poor relief work-test in which the needy person is required to prove his "worthiness" to receive relief.[7]

Despite the success of the WPA, many of the experiences were perceived as negative.

THE COSTS OF WORK RELIEF

Take, for example, the question of costs. Intuitively, if people capable of work are being given relief, any work they do in return would seem to be an asset, even if their efficiency is low. In fact, work relief involves many nonlabor costs—for tools, transportation, supervision, recording, bookkeeping, insurance, and so forth. Just as farm labor was done more cheaply by farmhands than by almshouse residents, work relief during the Depression was more expensive than direct relief would have been. Whether the work accomplished was worth the extra costs is debatable, but it would have been cheaper to give out checks.

COMPETITION WITH THE PRIVATE SECTOR

A second problem is competition with the private sector. Every job given out through work relief represents work that could have been done through the regular job market. The manufacture of goods competes in work relief programs directly with manufacturers, wholesalers, and retailers. The challenge facing work relief sponsors was to produce goods that were not useless but that had no normal commercial demand—a formidable challenge. This proved almost impossible. In practice, few relief jobs did not compete in one way or another with private business. Business owners were not the only people to complain. Unions wanted their members to have the jobs created under work relief. They also saw the low salaries being paid to those on work relief as undermining the salaries they had fought hard to win. Giving work, even relief work, to nonunion people while union members were idle was another source of contention.

Finding jobs for everyone who wanted them proved difficult. An estimated ½ to 1 million people certified for WPA employment were without assignment most of the time, and another 2 million were eligible but not certified. Of those who worked, 77% were employed in public construction and maintenance work.[8] Devising other types of work for unskilled workers while not competing with private industry proved exceedingly dif- ficult. For example, housing projects were intended to employ 25% of the people on work relief, but an average of less than 1% were actually used this way.

THE EFFECTS OF MAKE-WORK

These problems with work relief were relatively minor compared to the erroneous expectation that working for relief would allow the unemployed to maintain work habits, skills, and, most important, their morale. In practice, very little skilled work could be provided. Most relief work was unskilled make-work, and it was perceived as such by those who did it and by others. The image of the WPA worker in American folklore is of the leaf raker leaning on his rake while gossiping with his fellows. The classic story is of the worker who complained about lack of a rake. Told that without the rake he would not be expected to do anything, he continued to complain—because everyone else had a rake on which to lean. Relief work might give the un-employed some of the benefits of working—structure to the day, companion-ship, and relief from boredom—but whether morale is maintained under such circumstances is at least open to question. Charnow says,

> As a matter of fact, the extent to which work relief has preserved these values has depended upon conditions which varied with the type of program and with individual workers [and with] needs tests, makeshift projects, poor planning and supervision, assignment of skilled workers to unskilled work, low effi-ciency, irregular hours, lax discipline, [and] unstable financing . . . injurious rather than desirable work habits and attitudes were likely to develop. . . . Com-munity attitudes became . . . derisive as the program assumed a semi-permanent character.[9]

Not only did the workers become disillusioned: The view of work relief as a method of exacting a moral duty from recipients of public support faded as costs mounted, taxes increased, and the workers seemed to be developing an attitude that the government was obliged to provide work. The lessons of history must be learned again and again. As the Depression and its massive work-relief programs cease to be a living memory, the demand is again heard that people receiving welfare should be required to give some work in return, even if only symbolically.

Paying a person the monetary equivalent of wages to do nothing shocks Anglo-American sensibilities. The act of handing . . . dollars to healthy men and women generates a collective insanity among the nonwelfare population that precludes serious debate. Perhaps an ugly worm in all of us wants to control the behavior of other humans.[10]

Even during relative prosperity, the demand that people work continues:

It is a notorious fact that a picture of men at ease and in the middle of plenty most often makes people contemplating it both nervous and abusive. . . . the anti-utopians appear to be saying that the world must have pain, deprivation and impairment in it. . . . It may be good for themselves and surely could not be too bad for others.[11]

Work and Welfare

There is an asymmetric relationship between work and welfare. When employment policies are debated, the effects they will have on the welfare population are a minor consideration. If this were not so, the minimum wage would be adjusted so that no working person's income fell below the poverty line. However, when welfare policies are debated, the effects on recipients' employment patterns are a major consideration. An important underlying concern of all income-maintenance programs and many service programs is the presumed effect on the recipients' incentive to work.

COVERAGE

Work shapes welfare through four mechanisms: coverage, vestedness, regulations, and the wage stop. Most programs extend coverage only to those who work. Of 139 countries reporting old-age, survivors, and disability insurance programs in 1991, 119 (88%) have programs linked with work. Of the sixty-three family or children's allowance programs reported, forty-five (67%) were for workers' families only. Unemployment compensation and payments for work injury almost invariably require a record of prior employment, and even sickness and/or maternity benefits are available only to workers in 89% of the cases.[12]

The term *unemployment insurance* suggests that everyone who works will be compensated if they become unemployed. However, due to differing definitions, regulations, and interpretations, only 40% of the unemployed in the United States are covered by unemployment compensation programs.[13]

VESTEDNESS

Vestedness is another mechanism by which work shapes welfare programs. This means that eligibility for benefits usually requires a minimum prior period of employment. For example, the qualifying period of work for old-age programs varies throughout the world from five to forty-five years, averaging around fifteen years. Although technically covered, people who have not worked long enough do not receive the programs' benefits. In the United States and other countries, they are not even refunded the premiums they paid. People who are in and out of the labor force for various reasons may pay premiums while they work, but they may not work long enough to receive benefits.

REGULATIONS

Other administrative regulations also play their part in linking welfare to work. Payments are usually based upon a percentage of salaries. In many countries, the length of time that payments continue is determined by how long the recipient has worked. During the last century, someone who had worked a year or more in England and was injured on the job became the responsibility of the parish. As a result, people were customarily hired for only eleven months to save the taxpayers' money. The waiting period for unemployment compensation is usually longer than for other programs—in some states as long as seven weeks—and it is often not compensated at all. Applicants may be required to bring documents attesting that they sought other work. As with other methods of rationing services, offices may be difficult to reach and unpleasant, and personnel may seem unaccommodating.

THE WAGE STOP

The wage stop is used to ensure that no one can receive from welfare as much, or even close to as much, as they would receive if they were working. The earliest attempts at organized welfare in Europe emphasized that measures must be taken to prevent "Any man from securing a shilling which he was able to earn himself."[14] In 1834, this became one of the foundations of social welfare in Britain: "His situation on the whole shall not be made really or apparently so eligible as the situation of the independent laborer of the lowest class."

The inclusion of the word "apparently" is indicative of the force, or the fear, of public opinion, which might mistakenly judge the pauper's situation as being the equivalent of the nonpaupers' and react accordingly. A frequently told anecdote from American history records the reaction of Governor Huey Long after he was informed that federal law required the payment of "prevailing wages" to participants in federally financed employment programs: Long defined prevailing wages as the "lowest wages you can prevail upon a person to take." This fear that the situation of the poor might approximate that of others now marks most social welfare programs. Its apparent violation creates some of the deepest and most emotional antiwelfare expressions.

Methods for determining an individual's earning capacity vary with program and place. One way is to base payments on the last salary, paying a proportion. Another, used by U.S. Social Security for old-age payments, is to average the individual's lifetime earnings, based on representative periods. It is also possible to determine the average wage for a country or a region, or for an occupation or a group of occupations (for example, white-collar work). How well these averages reflect different salaries for different age groups, fringe benefits, and so forth is part of the problem of reaching an equitable determination.

The wage stop operates to limit payments to a percentage of the prevailing wage in a clearly discernible and almost universal manner. In the United States, unemployment insurance payments compensate for only 35% of the wages lost, and payments as high as average weekly salaries are virtually nonexistent. Unemployment compensation throughout the world is only 40% to 75% of average earnings. Old-age pensions paid to single persons are about 41% of the average wage or 30% of recent earnings. Local relief payments are almost invariably limited to a small proportion of the average or the lowest salary, and the proportion is growing smaller.[15]

Such payments are based on the principle of less eligibility, rather than on need. There is no reason to believe that people who become unemployed thereby reduce their living expenses by one quarter, or that the needs of a single person fall by 70% on the day that he becomes 65, or she reaches 62.

The principle of less eligibility virtually guarantees the continuation of poverty, because a fraction of the average or lowest wage, or of payments made in uninflated currencies twenty or thirty years ago, is in many cases below the poverty line.

KEEPING PEOPLE AT WORK

In view of the overwhelming importance attached to work in modern society, the ultimate goal of many social welfare policies and programs is to prepare people for, or return them to, the labor force. Vocational guidance, counseling, training, retraining, and rehabilitation programs are all established to help people find their way into productive employment. Some programs go further, in an attempt to help the participant remain on the job, by dealing with problems that arise either on the job or in other areas. Rapidly changing employment conditions may require mobility from job to job, or from occupation to occupation. The American worker in the twenty-first century may have ten to twelve jobs over a working life, with multiple entries and exits from the labor force.[16] Recognizing this, Great Britain passed the Employment and Training Act in 1973, which gives workers over 19 the right to one year's training every five years at a tax-free stipend equal to 60% to 90% of their income.

WORK AS THERAPY

Work is often assumed to have therapeutic qualities. Because working is normative in most societies, those who cannot work, for any reason, tend to feel diminished, damaged, stigmatized, and outside the mainstream. One of the aims of social welfare is to help people enter or return to employment. Besides the economic benefits this may provide, important therapeutic effects of a job are becoming like everyone else, acquiring self-esteem, avoiding stigma, and strengthening positive self-image. For this reason, work activities are included in many programs to help those with physical or mental disabilities and others. The supposedly therapeutic qualities of work lead to work programs within institutions—prisons, reform schools, hospitals for the mentally ill, and so forth—as well as in noninstitutional settings such as sheltered workshops for the aged, those with disabilities, and others.

SHELTERED WORKSHOPS

Certain dilemmas are inherent in the use of sheltered workshops. One of these is that in attempting to rehabilitate clients for the larger society, the workshop becomes a subculture of deviant people, bringing with it ridicule and subnormal role expectations. For some participants, being able to work only in a sheltered setting symbolizes their failure and hopelessness. Another problem arises from the fact that although the workshop may not be intended for "real" work, the need for production often begins to dominate the scene. This may lead to screening out the least productive—who may need the workshop most. The emphasis on production may also lead the workshop to market its products, putting social welfare in competition with private business and the unions again. The operating workshop must be able to keep participants busy. Therefore, it may accept contract work at prices that substantially reduce the project's income or that result in very low wages to the workers if it is a profit-sharing institution. Workshops have the notorious reputation of paying substandard wages.

Because sheltered workshops may have several different aims, it is difficult to evaluate their success. The goals of the staff—often therapeutic, recreational, or rehabilitative—seem to differ from those of participants, which often include acquiring some additional income. In one study, the most frequent suggestion for change was to increase wages, but sponsors often refuse to recognize this motivation, perhaps because they deem it unworthy.

WORK AS INSTILLING MORALITY

If work is seen as moral in its own right, then a natural conclusion makes work a means of instilling moral discipline. In the early days of industrialization, moral guidance and physical training were among the remedies proposed for the unemployable. So deeply rooted were feelings about nonworkers that some proposed sending to detention colonies those who would not attend training courses. Work is also seen as morally required in institutions for criminals or juvenile delinquents, where it is viewed as a highly effective means of reforming the individual wrongdoer.

INCENTIVES TO WORK

Few beliefs are as widely held and deeply felt as the tenet that people will not work if they can achieve the same income, or even nearly the same income, some other way. Social welfare payments are based on this belief, even though it is supported by little empirical evidence and entails many contradictions and paradoxes. The literature on work motivation and incentives is enormous. Since Adam Smith published *The Wealth of Nations* more than two hundred years ago, devoting part of it to "The Causes of the Improvement in the Productive Powers of Labour," investigation of ways to increase productivity has never ceased. Increasing evidence shows that individual work patterns are more or less stable over a lifetime, affected only slightly, or for short periods, by the conditions or the content of work. The range of possible patterns is from "workaholics" through what Sigmund Freud called a "natural human aversion to work," to the patterns of those who believe with Sumner that work kills.[17] Little research has been done as yet on the reasons for these different approaches to work.

By the same token, few empirical studies have been done specifically about attitudes of poor people toward work. One exception was Goodwin's study of four thousand people, comparing attitudes of welfare families and participants in federal work-training programs with those of middle-class families with steady employment. His findings:

> Evidence from this study unambiguously supports the following conclusion: poor people—males and females, blacks and whites, youths and adults—identify their self-esteem with work as strongly as do the nonpoor. They express as much willingness to take job training if unable to earn a living and to work even if they were to have an adequate income. They have, moreover, as high life aspirations as do the nonpoor and want the same things, among them a good education and a nice place to live. This study reveals no differences between poor and nonpoor when it comes to life goals and wanting to work.[18]

Another study, conducted on a wide scale and continuing for three years, actually made payments to the members of an experimental group, bringing them to 50%, 75%, 100%, and 125% of the poverty line, and comparing their consequent labor patterns with those of a control group.[19] The study reached 1,357 families in four cities. The major finding is that there was only a small (5% to 6%) reduction in average hours worked by the male heads of families who received payments, and this occurred entirely among white men.

GUARANTEEING A MINIMUM INCOME

In 1962, Milton Friedman proposed a reverse income tax (alternatively termed a negative income tax) to replace all existing welfare programs. In

1963, Schwartz proposed a "family security benefit." Various forms of guaranteed income have been advanced since then, including President Nixon's Family Assistance Plan. All of these plans are intended to place an income floor beneath the population, guaranteeing that no one will have less than a predetermined minimum. Supporters from the conservative side favor wiping out today's crazy quilt of programs, with different conditions of eligibility, different payments, and overlaps and gaps. They also favor less government control by giving cash rather than goods or services and a reduction in the number of social welfare service employees. Supporters from the liberal wing want to do away with means tests and categories of recipients and to make sure that everyone is above the poverty line, regardless of location, occupation, work linkage, race, and other distinctions.

All of these proposals provoke two important questions: Would everyone making a salary below the poverty line stop working, and would many others, slightly or even far above that line, prefer less income with no work? In short, do people dislike working, or their work, so much that they would stop if they could?

WORK AND SATISFACTION

Most surveys that ask questions more penetrating than "Are you happy at work?" conclude that there is widespread dissatisfaction with and at work. Furthermore, although retirees are not representative of the entire labor force, their behavior is instructive. Under Social Security regulations since 1961, males may retire with full pension (based on their past earnings) at age 65. However, they may elect to retire at age 62, receiving 80% of their entitled pension. In 1970, about 36% of male workers took advantage of the opportunity to retire early; in 1990, this had grown to about 65% of all retirees, and 90% of new retirees. In other words, two thirds of male workers (and the number is growing) have elected to give up three years' salary, the opportunity of increasing their eventual pensions by paying three more years of premiums, and 20% of their actual pension receipts for the rest of their lives, for the right to stop working.[20]

In the Netherlands, early retirement pensions were established in the early 1980s. A before-and-after comparison is instructive. In 1972, 75% of Dutch males between 55 and 65 years were working; in 1991, this had fallen to 35%. In Finland, where men may retire at age 58, so many availed themselves of the opportunity raising the retirement age has been proposed. In addition, U.S. legislation that effectively raised the involuntary retirement age from 65 to 70 has had no appreciable effect on the number of men retiring and retiring early—hardly an indication of satisfaction and happiness at work.[21]

Because of general agreement that payments near wage levels would create a work disincentive, income-guarantee proposals have work-incentive programs built into them. Under such provisions, the basic payment would be a portion of the guarantee. Only a percentage of any additional money recipients made would be counted in computing the income that determined their entitlement. The percentage would increase as income from work increased, but an absolute amount would still be added to their income until the predetermined minimum, or "break-even" point, was reached. This plan provides an advantage to those who earn wages while receiving guaranteed income. To create these incentives, beginning payments must be lower than the poverty line. Thus, people who cannot work—the aged, children, people with disabilities, and mothers of small children—would not be raised out of poverty by such programs, although some might receive more than they do now, and with less hassle.

Various plans differ on the amount of the basic guarantee, the rates and progression of diminishing payments, and the maximum attainment or break-even point. None of the proposals have been accepted, primarily for fear that an adequate income floor would disincline people to work. The belief that people should work, and the fear that they will not, operates to emasculate programs designed originally to eliminate poverty, help the unemployable, and protect the population against some of the more severe exigencies of modern life. The voice of Luther continues to resound through social welfare policy and will probably be heard in the land for many a year.

SUMMARY

The emphasis on work as a religious duty, espoused by Martin Luther, has resulted in social welfare programs that discriminate between those who work, those who cannot work, and those who can but are not working.

EXERCISES

A. A healthy young white male has a record of working only long enough to be eligible for unemployment compensation, then causing himself to be fired and asking for financial assistance when unemployment payments run out. He explains that he just doesn't like to work. How would you deal with his request?

B. A healthy young white male with a similar record explains that he is writing a novel and that working takes time away from his essential interest. How would you deal with his request?

C. A healthy young white male with a similar record explains that he is taking care of an invalid mother and working keeps him from giving her the care she needs. How would you deal with his request?

D. A healthy young white male with a similar record explains that he is a heroin user and works only long enough to make enough to buy heroin. How would you deal with his request?

E. If everyone were assured a basic income sufficient to provide the necessities of life and a bit more, how do you think this would affect:
1. the society as a whole?
2. various groups within society?
3. families?
4. individuals?
5. the economy?
6. the work world?
7. social welfare?

Notes

1. The phrase is from Gutman (1976).
2. The quotation is from Prabhupada (1972).
3. The quotation is from Hoffer (1969).

4. The quotation is from Hunnicutt (1990).

5. The quotation is from Axinn & Levin (1975).

6. The term *made work* is from Feder (1936).

7. The quotation is from Brown (1940).

8. The number of applicants and types of jobs are from Charnow (1943).

9. The quotation is from Charnow (1943).

10. The quotation is from Graham (1970).

11. The quotation is from Kateb (1963).

12. Statistics are from U.S. Department of Health and Human Services (1992).

13. Extent of unemployment coverage is from Blau (1992).

14. This quotation and the next are from deSchweinitz (1943).

15. Statistics are from the following sources: U.S. unemployment, from Abramovitz (1992); international unemployment, from U.S. Department of Health and Human Services (1992); old-age pensions, from Ball (1978).

16. The prediction is from Schneiderman (1992).

17. The quotation is from Freud (1958); Sumner (1963) is the work cited.

18. The quotation is from Goodwin (1972).

19. The study is reported in Pechman & Timpane (1975).

20. The early retiree figures are from *Social Security Bulletin* (1991; *54*[6], 10), U.S. Department of Health and Human Services (1991), and Hurwitz (1987).

21. The Dutch statistics are from Van Praag & Van Beek (1991); the Finnish data are from U.S. Department of Health and Human Services (1992); effect of the new law is from Hurwitz (1987).

READ MORE ABOUT IT...

For more information on:	See these sources:
Luther's motivations	Erikson, 1958
Role of good works	Nisbet, 1932
Mercantilism	Macarov, 1977c
The importance of work	Macarov, 1982, 1985
Work in India	Prabhupada, 1972; Saha, 1990
Work in Japan	Yakabe, 1974
Work in preindustrial societies	Buckingham, 1961
Influence of Catholicism	Nisbet, 1932
Importance of getting ahead	Whyte, 1955
Socialization for work	Macarov, 1988c
Client preferences of social workers	Macarov, 1987c; Macarov & Meller, 1985, 1986a, 1986b; Norman, 1982
Work relief vs. poor relief	Charnow, 1943
Laziness as sickness	Gilbert, 1973; Graham, 1970
Early work tests	Feder, 1936
Unemployment registration	Howard, 1943
Unemployment in Israel	Macarov, 1987b
Almshouse as dumping ground	Woodroofe, 1962
The idea behind workhouses	deSchweinitz, 1943; Frederico, 1973
Distinction between work relief and public works	Colcord, 1936
Distinction between public service and public works jobs	Leahy, 1976

For more information on:	See these sources:
Extent of WPA work	Howard, 1943
Costs and problems of work relief	Charnow, 1943
Competition with private business	Feder, 1936
Qualifying periods	U.S. Department of Health and Human Services, 1992
11-month contracts	Hardy, 1869
Waiting periods	Griffiths, 1974
Work and welfare limits	Macarov, 1980
Follow-up programs	Meiss, 1991
British Employment and Training Act	Striner, 1975
Workshops as subcultures	Friedman, 1974
Wages at sheltered workshops	Reingold, Wolk, & Schwartz, 1972
Remedies for unemployable	Squires, 1990
Work as way to reform wrongdoers	Martin, 1966
Work patterns	Macarov, 1982
Workaholics	Machlowitz, 1981
Research on attitudes toward work	Macarov, 1988c
Family Assistance Plan	Moynihan, 1973
Work and satisfaction	Macarov, 1982, 1988a

12. The Influence of Charles Darwin and Adam Smith on the Development of Social Welfare

Charles Darwin's theory of the biological *survival of the fittest* has been vulgarized into societal and individualized versions, which serve as philosophical bases for conservative attitudes that every person is responsible for his or her own position and that the successful have proved their superiority by their very success. Smith's conception of an "invisible hand" regulating market activities militated against social welfare as a disturbing influence in the free market.

Biological Darwinism

In the fifty years before Charles Darwin published *On the Origin of Species* in 1859, the problems of variation, adaptation, heredity, and environment had been receiving considerable attention from scientists, but no one had developed a comprehensive theory as widely accepted as evolution came to be. While Darwin was engaging in a systematic inquiry about the differences between species, he happened to read Thomas Malthus's famous essay on population. He was at once struck by the fact that under circumstances of insufficient sustenance for all, "favorable variations would tend to be preserved and unfavorable ones to be destroyed."[1] From this grew the concept that later came to be generally termed *survival of the fittest*.

Although Darwin knew nothing of the principles of Mendelian genetics, he based his theory of natural selection on the universal somatic variations

206

among organisms. His theory dealt with species rather than individuals, and with somatic (that is, genetically determined) differences rather than with those that are attributable to nurture, environment, or socialization. In short, Darwin dealt with the biological world, in which genetic mutations favorable to survival eventually result in a changed species—provided the mutation is transmitted to enough offspring.

A major challenge to Darwin's theory and to its underlying genetic principles came from the Soviet biologist Trofim Denisovich Lysenko. Lysenko contended that environmental conditions could be manipulated in such a way that plants would change while growing, and thus produce a new species. For example, by subjecting wheat to heat at certain periods, it could be made to produce rye, and cuckoos could be hatched from warblers' eggs. Lysenko claimed to have caused environmentally induced changes to continue genetically, through breeding. The Chevalier de Lamarck, in France, had argued many years earlier that acquired characteristics could be inherited, but his ideas had been discredited. Lysenko's theory was highly compatible with communist ideology under Stalin, because it suggested that the Soviet socio-economic system could produce a new type of citizen who would transmit his or her characteristics biologically, eliminating the need for continuing educational or socialization efforts. As a consequence, Lysenko and his theory were elevated to high positions in the Soviet Union, and all question— let alone dissent—was suppressed until after Stalin's death. Then Lysenko and his theories were repudiated by Khrushchev, himself once a farmer.

Darwin's theory of genetically transmitted mutations and subsequent development of new species had little direct impact on social welfare. For one thing, evolutionary change was felt to occur over time periods difficult for the ordinary mind to grasp, and second, conscious intervention in the evolutionary process was seen as impossible.

Social Darwinism

The major impact of Darwinian theory on social welfare came about not as the result of a massive perversion like Lysenko's but, rather, through a vulgarization of Darwin's thesis, which came to be called Social Darwinism. Social Darwinism is distinct from biological Darwinism in that it attempts to apply Darwin's theory of natural selection and the struggle for existence to the evolution of human society. That is, it moves Darwin's theory from the evolution of biological species to social individuals and, more recently, to social institutions. Social Darwinism concerned itself less with the evolutionary process of individuals and institutions than with the end result—that the fittest had survived.

> The most popular catchwords of Darwinism, "struggle for existence" and "survival of the fittest," when applied to the life of man in society, suggested that nature would provide that the best competitors in a competitive situation would win, and that this process would lead to a continuing improvement.[2]

Clark holds that Darwin's theory exalted competition, power, and violence over convention, ethics, and religion, and that it declared, in effect, that the end justifies the means. It had both societal and individual implications. As applied to society:

> Biological Darwinism asserted that all species of organic life had evolved and were evolving by a process of the survival of the fittest. According to . . . "Social Darwinism," society, too, was an organism that evolved by the survival of the fittest. Existing institutions were therefore the "fittest" way of doing things, and businessmen who bested their competitors had thereby proved themselves "the fittest to enjoy wealth and power."[3]

The inference that successful businesspeople were responsible for their own status and that the unsuccessful were, so to speak, getting what they deserved, was a very congenial doctrine for the successful, and it became the common ground between early charity organizers and pragmatic men of affairs. Echoes of this theory continue to be heard among those who view the "bottom line" as the ultimate test of business organizations and even societal institutions. In this view, organizations that show a profit are ipso facto both successful and desirable, without regard to how the profit is produced, and those that cannot show a profit thereby indicate their unfitness to survive.

On an individual level, Herbert Spencer, philosopher, writer, and teacher, was one of the earliest proponents of Social Darwinism. Although he was English, he was enormously influential in the United States from about 1870 to 1890. From the very beginning, Spencer carried Social Darwinism, as applied to individuals and human groups, to its logical conclusion:

> He who loses his life because of his stupidity, vice, or idleness is in the same class as the victims of weak viscera or malformed limbs. Under nature's laws

all alike are put on trial. If they are sufficiently complete to live, they do live, and it is well they should live. If they are not sufficiently complete to live, they die, and it is best they should die.[4]

SOCIAL DARWINISM AND BIG BUSINESS

No philosophy or theory could have been so well suited to the American upper classes in the days of the robber barons. It mattered not how a man became rich or powerful; his having done so proved that he was entitled to his wealth and power, for he was one of the fit. The cries of those whom he hurt, and the outrage of those who observed his methods, were merely fulminations of the jealous unfit not worthy of consideration. Thus John D. Rockefeller could say to a Sunday school:

The growth of a large business is merely a survival of the fittest. . . . The American Beauty rose can be produced in the splendor and fragrance which bring cheer to its beholder only by sacrificing the early buds which grow up around it. This is not an evil tendency in business. It is merely the working-out of a law of nature and a law of God.[5]

The United States did not lack for its own prophets of Social Darwinism. William Graham Sumner, one of the most articulate and influential, had no patience with those who would lavish compensations upon the virtueless:

"The strong" and "the weak" are terms which admit of no definition unless they are made equivalent to the industrious and the idle, the frugal and the extravagant . . . if we do not like the survival of the fittest, we have only one possible alternative, and that is the survival of the unfittest. The former is the law of civilization; the latter is the law of anti-civilization . . . a plan for nourishing the unfittest and yet advancing in civilization, no man will ever find.[6]

Social Darwinism, as it has evolved, differs from classical Darwinism, and even from early Social Darwinism, in a number of ways. In some versions, it does not admit the existence of mutations—that is, breaks with the past or with tradition. Instead, it holds that individuals and groups, and even entire social classes, must move upward step by step: specifically, that the "virtues" of the elite class can be attained only by first achieving the virtues of the lower classes and continuing to develop. In the developmental view, immigrant groups, too, were presumed to be moving along a continuum from peasant village to modern urban culture. If a group did not emerge as successful in comparison with other groups, the defect was obviously inherent in the group. The success of immigrant groups was sometimes put in terms of the group's assimilability—the more difficult to assimilate, to become like Americans (that is, White Anglo-Saxon Protestants), the more negative the group image. The major thrust of the developmental viewpoint is that efforts to reform society, or even social welfare, are doomed to failure because only slow evolutionary change in people can bring about changes in society.

Social Darwinism quickly became a rationalization for racism and/or prejudice against ethnic groups of various kinds. The inferiority of some groups was proved by the very fact that their economic status was low, or their educational attainments inferior, or their social status undesirable. This aspect of Social Darwinism resulted in the displacement of "equality" as the basic American social goal by "equality of opportunity." As equality obviously had not been achieved, it was dismissed as anti-evolutionary and, therefore, unnatural. Instead, the United States offers everyone equality of opportunity. If some cannot take advantage of such opportunity, it can be only because of their own deficiencies—or, more bluntly, their inferiority.

Kluegel and Smith put this clearly:

> The major premise in the argument is that opportunity for economic advancement based on hard work is plentiful. From this premise two deductions follow. Individuals are personally responsible for their own economic fate: Where one ends up in the distribution of economic rewards depends upon the effort one puts into acquiring and applying the necessary skills and attitudes, and upon the native talent with which one begins.[7]

Sometimes the superiority-inferiority dichotomy is expressed in terms of class, but class consciousness has been relatively ephemeral in the United States as compared to consciousness of race, color, or creed. It was to the latter kinds of minorities that the inferiority postulated by Social Darwinism was imputed. Social Darwinism thus offered special opportunities to those who sought scientific bolstering of their prejudices, and the opportunities were fully exploited to reduce African Americans and some "non-Anglo-Saxon" immigrants to a position of permanent inferiority.

BLAMING THE VICTIM

The early Social Darwinist view that the defects causing personal and group failure were inherent and inherited soon came to be identified with prejudice and racism. A later, more genteel variation of the theory came into prominence:

> The idea that problem families cause their problems rather than merely experiencing them has become the commonsense folklore of social work agencies and social workers. Social work attitudes may have shifted from a perspective which held that "indigence was simply the punishment meted out to the improvident by their own lack of industry and efficiency . . . poverty was the obvious consequence of sloth and sinfulness," but often seems to have become stuck at a point which suggests family pathology as responsible for poverty, loose morals, drunkenness, delinquency, criminality and child neglect.[8]

This new version of Social Darwinism has been termed *blaming the victim*.[9]

In its several variants—developmentalism, equality of opportunity, and blaming the victim—the net effect of Social Darwinism is to rationalize away the inequalities of society on the grounds that some people are smarter, stronger, more moral, or even more finely tuned in their ego defenses than others and, conversely, that the cognitive capacity, moral development, and psychodynamic organization of the needy, the lower class, or the unsuccessful are inferior. In this way, hunger can be explained away on the grounds that parents are ignorant of what constitutes a balanced diet, or child neglect on the basis of parents who were themselves neglected or abused.

By defining need as individual deficiency, rather than as institutional or resource deficiency, poverty comes to be viewed as a normal state for large segments of the population, and most people come to agree that relative poverty and inequality are necessary, if not desirable, by-products of the prevailing system. When social workers accept Social Darwinism, implicitly or explicitly, they view the existing situation as inevitable. What results is a concept of social welfare as enabling and strengthening people who are deprived or have disabilities so they can cope with their situation within the current reality; that is, it confirms the existing economic and social system.

Social Darwinism has also been charged with offering a theoretical basis for elevating selfishness to a science. As such, it is diametrically opposed to mutual aid, a fact that caused Kropotkin to remark that evolutionists might admit the importance of mutual aid among animals, but like Spencer, they refused to admit it for humans.

As a method of analyzing society, Social Darwinism was less useful than it was as a rationalization for the status quo, and it soon lost the interest and support of intellectuals. Thorstein Veblen turned from individual behavior to that of institutions and saw the social institution, rather than the individual, as the subject of selection, or survival of the fittest. Consensus on the success of institutions is more difficult to achieve than on the individual's success. Because it is harder to link inherent defects to unsuccessful institutions, the very continuation of institutions, rather than their success, becomes the criterion for "fitness." Social Darwinism thereby becomes an ultraconservative tautology: Whatever *is* has proved its fitness by continuing to exist; whatever exists is fittest to exist. Everything, therefore, is as it should be, and nothing should be changed. In this manner, Social Darwinism leads to the practice of defending the status quo.

Effects on Social Welfare

Social Darwinism was seen as the working out of natural law as immutable as the laws of evolution, and any attempt to alter or disturb its workings by aiding the unfit (that is, the needy) was worse than futile. It was also immoral—an attempt to thwart the will of God or nature. In addition, helping the unfit must be at the expense of the fit—a further immorality. Spencer's categorical repudiation of state interference with the "natural," unimpeded growth of society led him to oppose all state aid to the poor. As he said, "The whole effort of nature is to get rid of such, to clear the world of them, and make room for better."[10] Sumner spoke more directly to social welfare:

> The next time that you are tempted to subscribe a dollar to a charity, I do not tell you not to do it, because after you have fairly considered the matter, you may think it right to do it, but I do ask you to stop and remember . . . that if you put your dollar in the savings bank it will go to swell the capital of the country which is available for division amongst those who, while they earn it, will reproduce it with increase.[11]

Mostly as a result of the influence of Spencer and Sumner, the Charity Organization Society movement accepted Social Darwinism as a theoretical base for its activities. The theory strengthened the belief that the cause of social problems lay in the individuals afflicted with them, rather than in the rest of society. Such individuals were thus seen as living outside the mainstream of the country's activities and development. Unfit to survive, they were nevertheless kept alive by humanitarian charity. Far from contributing to the development of mankind and society, they were deadweight—a drag on the movement to ultimate perfection.

Pity for those afflicted with problems was replaced with blame, leading to the creation of an outcast class viewed and treated not with indifference but with contempt. Those who have "made it" are sure they have done so through their inherent fitness, motivation, and efforts, and any lingering doubts are exorcised by comparison with the purported unfit, unmotivated, and inactive. As Tawney pointed out long ago: "The demonstration that distress is a proof of demerit has always been popular with the prosperous."[12]

When the fit or successful feel this way about the unfit and unsuccessful, their attitude becomes a major influence in the formulation of social welfare policies and programs. Regulations that once denied the vote to paupers, nonowners of property, or nontaxpayers have been revoked, but the question of whether the mentally ill should be allowed to have children, or even get married, is still subject to passionate debate in some places. Similarly, laws to help the poor must be gingerly proposed and enacted, lest the agency or the government be accused of pampering the poor. Help given to the ill, the aged, and those with disabilities is usually less than sufficient to make a decent life possible, because they are no longer in a position to contribute to societal development.

The force of Social Darwinism is emphasized by the fact that although the major thesis of biological Darwinism—evolution—has come to be generally accepted throughout the world, the survival of the fittest as applied to individuals and institutions can no longer be logically argued. With the discovery of new medicines such as antibiotics, with the invention of life-sustaining devices such as kidney dialysis machines, and with the replacement of organs and limbs (sometimes with mechanical devices), toughness and durability in the individual have been replaced by "medicated survival," more or less independent of any inherent quality of the individual. Similarly, it is difficult to argue that organizational survival has any basis in fitness, except in the most self-interested sense, in light of government-approved protective tariffs, monopolies, and cartels; international consortia and conglomerates; and government subsidies and cost overruns—to say nothing of the public relations triumph of image over reality. As Tawney put it:

Few tricks of the unsophisticated intellect are more curious than the naive psychology of the businessman, who ascribes his achievements to his own unaided efforts, in bland unconsciousness of a social order without whose continuous support and vigilant protection he would be as a lamb bleating in the desert.[13]

Social Darwinism is an ex post facto theory—that is, it does not attempt to predict which individuals or groups will succeed (except, perhaps, as used by the Nazis). Instead, it evaluates success and declares the successful to be the most fit—an example of a theory not supported by facts that has become a free-standing belief system, with little relationship to reality or logic. Speaking of the blaming-the-victim brand of Social Darwinism, Ryan says:

> It is central in the mainstream of contemporary American social thought, and its ideas pervade our most crucial assumptions so thoroughly that they are hardly noticed. Moreover, the fruits of this ideology appear to be fraught with altruism and humanitarianism, so it is hard to believe that it has principally functioned to block social change.[14]

Not only does Social Darwinism block social change; it is also at the root of some opposition to social welfare. Such opponents argue that social welfare activities somehow maintain the unfit at the expense of the fit, that they defend the "rights" of those who should have no rights and thus undermine the rights of those who strengthen society and support the development of a new and better way of life.

Social welfare has been singularly ineffective in breaking down the self-fulfilling prophecy that is Social Darwinism's contribution to society: The needy are unfit to survive; we therefore make it difficult for them to survive; their difficulty in surviving proves that they are unfit.

Laissez-faire Economics

The approach of Social Darwinists to individuals and institutions and the Protestant ethic of work have been heavily reinforced by Adam Smith's conception of the role (or lack of role) of government in the economy.

THE INDUSTRIAL REVOLUTION

The advent of the Industrial Revolution both used and strengthened the Protestant ethic. At first, the Protestant emphasis on work had been observed mainly in agriculture and small handicrafts, but the time came when many people had no work. Some places had too little arable land for too many family members; primogeniture, the medieval custom in which the eldest son inherited and the younger joined the army or the clergy, was dying out. Hence the Elizabethan Poor Laws emphasized keeping people in their hometowns, putting vagrants to work, and making work for those who had none.

With the establishment of factories, a wage economy began to take the place of the agricultural barter economy. Because wages were easily convertible into goods, acquiring mere sustenance was no longer a goal that limited work hours and effort. People could convert more work into more possessions. A religious belief that work was a duty owed to God was admirably suited to the new economy. Factories needed workers and workers needed jobs, not just to make money but also to be moral, religious, law-abiding people. Factory owners thus did people a favor by allowing them to work, and workers were expected to be grateful for the opportunity. The growth of labor unions many years later was not resisted only by employers who did not want to pay higher wages and to offer better conditions. Many people saw attempts to organize workers as questioning or putting conditions on God's design for man: This was not only ingratitude but was almost blasphemy.

The new economic system resulted in a shift away from the limited production of high-priced objects for the few to large-scale production of low-priced goods for the many. The economic circle went from salaries to purchases to production to jobs to salaries. With this change in the economic situation, a new economic theory was required to explain and predict the behavior of the market. That theory was supplied by Adam Smith.

LAISSEZ-FAIRE

Smith was a man of enormous knowledge and wide-ranging interests. Although he was basically an economist, his *The Wealth of Nations* is encyclopedic in its subject matter. Among other things, Smith commented on the tremendous increase in production that division of labor and specialization bring in their wake, using a pin factory as his model. Later, Max Weber attributed these same aspects to bureaucracy, and Smith's ideas also gave birth to the scientific-management principle of Frederick W. Taylor. Smith's economic theory has been termed that of "laissez-faire"—in effect, "hands off." Basically, Smith held that if people sought to make the most of their own economic condition, everyone would benefit. With everyone competing against everyone else, the most efficient enterprise would survive, and society would profit by a supply of the best merchandise at the cheapest prices. The inefficient would, of course, go into some other enterprise, where they could become the most efficient. Smith's classic example has to do with manufacturing gloves and shoes:

> Suppose we have one hundred manufacturers of gloves. The self-interest of each one will cause him to wish to raise his price above his cost of production and thereby to realize an extra profit. But he cannot. If he raises his price, his competitors will step in and take his market away from him by underselling him. . . . Let us suppose that consumers decide they want more gloves than are being turned out, and fewer shoes. . . . Glove prices will tend to rise as consumers try to buy more of them than there are ready at hand, and shoe prices will tend to fall . . . but as glove prices rise, profits in the glove industry will rise, too; and . . . profits in shoe manufacturing will slump. . . . Workers will be released from the shoe business. . . . they will move to the glove business. . . . glove production will rise and shoe production will fall.
>   And this is exactly what society wanted in the first place. As more gloves come on the market to meet demand, glove prices will fall back into line. As fewer shoes are produced, shoe prices will again rise up to normal. . . . Society will have changed . . . production to fit its new desires. Yet no one has issued a dictum, and no planning authority has established schedules of output. Self-interest and competition . . . have accomplished the transition.[15]

According to Smith, supply and demand will regulate not only prices and goods but also the incomes of those who produce the goods. The important thing is that no one should interfere in any way with the free operation of supply and demand, self-interest, and competition. This is the source of the term *laissez-faire*. The competitive network, left without interference, becomes an "invisible hand," ensuring everyone's benefit.

"THE ECONOMIC MAN"

Smith has become one of the classical economists in the modern pantheon. Classical economics assumes perfect knowledge and rational behavior. It assumes that economic theorists know all the pertinent facts and that people will behave in what is, to them, a rational manner—that is, people will respond automatically to financial considerations. From laissez-faire economics, the concept of "the economic man" flowed naturally.

The economic man invariably responds to rational stimuli, and only rational stimuli; these are, in the nature of things, economic. Hence, in Smith's view, workers—pursuing their own interests—will take the job offering the highest salary. Considerations of enjoyment, working conditions, work companions, distance from home, or career opportunities are not assumed to affect economic considerations, nor are apathy and lethargy. This image of the economic man is specifically disavowed in contemporary economic theory, but it still influences many of those who determine or discuss social welfare and economic policy. It finds expression in such policies as the wage stop and in the belief that women have children only in order to collect welfare benefits. In fact, the economic man has become not only a description, but a moral value. When unemployed persons refuse to undertake demeaning, difficult, dangerous work, even though it pays slightly more than their unemployment compensation, a common reaction is outrage at such a repudiation of purely economic considerations.

SOCIAL WELFARE AS UPSETTING THE MARKET

Because the invisible hand that regulates the market is the economic man's competition with everyone else, people who do not choose to compete, or do not maximize their economic conditions, upset the market. So do agencies or institutions that enable them to drop out of competition. Such people should be penalized, and such institutions should be minimized. The social welfare system is a prime offender, because it enables recipients to exist outside of the market system, giving them other choices. It interferes with the supply of labor and allows people to purchase items with resources other than their own labor. In short, whereas the Protestant ethic said that God requires people to work, laissez-faire adds that a just and balanced economic system also requires that everyone who is capable not only works but works as hard as possible.

In social welfare terms, the influence of Adam Smith reinforces Social Darwinism, which casts the needy in the role of the unfit, and the Protestant ethic, which makes them seem immoral. Laissez-faire theory makes them deviant: Because they are presumably uninterested in competing with others in the open market, they disrupt the economic picture.

SOCIAL WELFARE AND THE MARKET

The fact that social welfare operates outside the market economy not only causes problems for its clients but also results in difficulties for social welfare programs and for the entire social welfare institution. In a culture that measures most things in economic terms, social welfare is hard to understand and even harder to evaluate. P. F. Drucker, for example, holds that social welfare cannot succeed because it does not have a "bottom line" of profit or loss against which it can evaluate its success—and success can be properly evaluated only in financial terms. Without such an evaluative device, success can be judged only in terms of continuing or extending activities, which means, in turn, continuing or increasing social welfare budgets. Hence, social welfare agencies are accused of undertaking the activities that will ensure their budgets, rather than those that are in the best interests of their clients.

The acknowledged difficulty of evaluating social welfare programs and activities is made doubly difficult when an evaluation has to be couched in terms meaningful to economists, financiers, and businessmen, who tend to make social policy. This is even more of a problem for services that do not result in reduced costs to society. For example, whereas preventive medical services for the aged can be linked to reduced hospitalization and institutionalization costs, recreation services for these people do not have the same result. The need to quantify what are essentially qualitative services results in distortions of services, as well as of bookkeeping. As Etzioni points out, emphasis on measurement leads to undertaking the most easily measurable activities, which are not necessarily the most desirable.

"EVERYONE SHOULD PAY SOMETHING"

Regarding the economic system as the norm to which social welfare should aspire has another influence: the insistence upon fees. The question of whether to charge fees for services has many facets, including eligibility, means tests, and revenues. One assumption is that it is morally good and even therapeutic for clients to pay for services. In private psychotherapeutic settings, discussing the cost of treatment is considered part of the contract between practitioner and client. The manner in which the client relates to money, the need to discuss it, and the arrangements for payment are all used for both evaluative and treatment purposes. Indeed, even when private practitioners deal with people of very limited means, perhaps as a public service, a symbolic fee is often insisted upon.

This attitude is also evident in many community centers and settlement houses, where everyone pays something, even if only symbolically. The stated rationale for this attitude is that it is good for people to have to pay. Examined more deeply, the assumption is that people who pay behave differently, appreciate the service more, and therefore use the service better. It is interesting that this belief, like many others, rests upon little, if any, evidence. There is no proof that symbolic payment for services affects behavior or even attitudes. To the contrary, payments, no matter how small, may act as a selective device barring certain participants, and any apparent differences in behavior may arise from differences in clientele.

COST-FREE SOCIAL WELFARE

Smith's laissez-faire philosophy not only resulted in questions about welfare's being outside the market system but also caused welfare to be seen as an economic activity itself, subject to the rules of the marketplace. Thus insurance-type programs are expected to operate with actuarial soundness, and fears that the Social Security system will "go bankrupt" are widely heard, despite the fact that there is no need, outside of marketing practice, for income to match payments. Similarly, administrators of insurance-type programs view participants as "investors" who must receive a reasonable return. The wage stop limits the amount of payments, but there must be a limit to premiums as well. The rationale for limiting the income that is taxed for Social Security in the United States is that people who make more than the set amount would not recover their premiums in benefits—a poor investment from their point of view. However, Social Security beneficiaries receive back an average of 2.5 times the value of their original payments into the program.[16]

The most ubiquitous and influential impact on social welfare flowing from Adam Smith's theories is the recent move toward privatization of social welfare services. As in most cases, motivations for this change are mixed, including:

- the economic cost of social welfare as reflected in national budgets
- the ideology of "least government"
- the rather amorphous but strong popular opposition to "bureaucracy"
- the desire for renewal of mutual support, especially within families

Perhaps the most important motivation is the belief that private business, operating for profit, can perform social welfare functions more efficiently, or more effectively, or both, compared to government or even to voluntary efforts.

Social Darwinism and laissez-faire economics are complementary, each strengthening the other. This can be recapitulated: If nothing is allowed to interfere with the survival of the fittest in the marketplace, the result will be successful—that is, profitable—enterprises that achieve their success by offering the best services at the lowest price. The only condition is that nothing—including social welfare—support the unfit or interfere in the free market.

SUMMARY

Social Darwinism postulated that the weak or less fortunate, the less successful or competitive, were less fit and, by implication, less deserving. Laissez-faire economics postulated the notion of economic man: that people would always act in their own best economic interests. Both theories, although no longer in vogue, continue to influence the development of social welfare. In particular, they tend to exaggerate the extent to which welfare may aid in the survival of the "unfit" or in distorting the market by supporting the uncompetitive.

EXERCISES

A. Survival of the fittest:

1. Do only the "fittest" individuals, corporations, and societal structures survive?
2. What help do they need or get?
3. Can the "unfit" individual, corporation, and societal structure survive?
4. What help do they need or get?
5. What do you consider to be the essential differences between a corporation being given a tax break (worth money) and an individual being given general assistance? How does your view compare to that of society in general?

B.   Jamie Smith was born to a poor family, and his father died while Jamie was young. Jamie struggled to overcome the difficulties of his life and graduated high school, although with very low marks. During the recession he was rarely able to get a good job, and he refused to take many jobs that he felt were beneath him. He was on and off unemployment compensation and social welfare throughout his life, to the point that he stopped looking for work and lived on social welfare payments. When he reached retirement age, he found that his Social Security payment was the minimum amount, and he became depressed as he looked back at his life. At that point a bachelor uncle whom he didn't remember died and left him a sizable inheritance. Having few needs, he gave lavishly to philanthropic causes, and, liking to be with young people, he supported several young men and women who loafed around his house with all their needs met. He died con- sidering his life a failure.

1. How would a strong believer in the Protestant work ethic react to Jamie's story?
2. How would a biological Darwinist react to Jamie's story?
3. How would a Social Darwinist react to Jamie's story?
4. How would a believer in laissez-faire economics react to Jamie's story?

Notes

1. The quotation is from Darwin (1888).
2. The quotation is from Clark (1984).
3. The quotation is from Goldman (n.d.).
4. The Spencer quotation is from Hofstadter (1944).
5. Rockefeller's quotation is from Hofstadter (1944).
6. The Sumner quotation is from Hofstadter (1944).
7. The quotation is from Kluegel & Smith (1986).
8. The quotation is from Sullivan (1987).
9. The phrase is from Ryan (1974).
10. Spencer's quotation is from Hofstadter (1944).
11. The quotation is from Sumner (1963).
12. The quotation is from Tawney (1958).
13. The quotation is from Tawney (1958).
14. The quotation is from Ryan (1974).

15. The quotation is from Heilbroner (1953).
16. The 2.5 figure is from Longman (1990).

READ MORE ABOUT IT . . .

For more information on:	*See these sources:*
Survival of the fittest	Spencer, 1852
Lysenko	Joravsky, 1970
Social Darwinism	Clark, 1984
Social Darwinism as congenial to the successful	Wuthnow & Hodgkinson, 1990
Developmental view of Darwinism	Lerner, 1971
Rationalization of racism	Goldman, n.d.
The need for poverty	Mishra, 1990
Social Darwinism maintains the existing system	Nanavatty, 1992
Thorstein Veblen	Persons, 1959
Adam Smith's theory	Smith, 1937
Weber's application to bureaucracy	Weber, 1952
Drucker on social welfare	Drucker, 1973
Influence of measurement on welfare	Etzioni, 1964

PART IV

Issues in Social Welfare

This part outlines four major current issues in social welfare—poverty, unemployment, changes in the welfare state, and welfare reform. All of these are results of the interaction between the various motivations and influences outlined in the previous chapters. Readers can trace these factors as they surface in the various problem areas to gain greater understanding of the reasons for the continued existence of these problems.

13. Persisting Poverty

Despite differences in political systems, changes in economic climates, and the growth of social welfare in both amounts expended and efforts made, the poverty rate remains between 10% and 15% in most Western industrialized countries. Poverty may be defined in relative, normative, or absolute terms, and its existence may be rationalized by scapegoating the poor—that is, by blaming them for their own situation.

Given the many positive motivations for social welfare and the multiplicity of programs to redistribute income or to help those in need, the extent and the depth of poverty throughout the world is appalling. This is true not only in Third World countries but also in the United States. As Burghardt and Fabricant point out:

> If ever there were a country where there should be no poor, it is the United States of America. With a Gross National Product in the trillions, 70% of the largest economic corporations in the world, and its overabundance of foodstuffs found in warehouses throughout its agricultural heartland, America is indeed rich.

In March 1993, an article in *The New York Times* said that despite the purported economic recovery, more than 10% of Americans were relying on food stamps, the greatest proportion since food stamps were first issued in 1964.[1]

Like a fata morgana, the eradication of poverty in the United States always seems just within reach, only to recede. In 1929 President Hoover said:

We in America today are nearer to the final triumph over poverty than ever before in the history of our land. The poor house is vanishing from among us. We shall soon with the help of God be in the sight of the day when poverty will be banished from this nation.[2]

A few months later the Great Depression began, throwing millions into poverty.

Defining Poverty

Like so many other important concepts, poverty can be defined in various ways. Even Congress recognizes that what constitutes poverty is a subjective judgment, defined relative to societal norms, and that there is no objective method of defining need standards and resource requirements. For example, twelve different measures of poverty were applied to children in 1982, with results showing that anywhere from 19.4% to 27.6% of them were poor. The official rate was 21.9%. In general, poverty, like other forms of need, can be defined in relative, normative, or absolute terms.[3]

RELATIVE POVERTY

Relative poverty is based upon subjective criteria—whether one *feels* poor or deprived, or whether people feel others to be deprived. The oft-heard argument that Indian peasants who earned even a meager American salary would be considered millionaires in their homeland ignores the relative aspect: Americans do not have to descend to an Indian farmer's standard of living to feel or to be seen as poor.

Relative poverty changes with the times—once an indoor toilet instead of an outhouse was seen as an evidence of prosperity. Early social workers judged need by the presence or absence of a rug; later, an electric refrigerator; still later, a television set; then whether the set was black-and-white or color; and, finally, by ownership of a car. Each of these possessions, once an extravagant luxury, came to be seen as necessary to normal life. The standard of living of all Americans has risen enormously in the last century; those who do not share proportionately in that rise are, in relative terms, poor.

There are other relative ways of defining the poor: for example, by comparing income levels by thirds, fifths, tenths, or other fractions of the population, or by comparing incomes to average, median, or minimal salaries. Among those who use a relative measure of poverty in the United States, 50% of the national median income is considered poverty and 40% is considered severe poverty.[4]

NORMATIVE POVERTY

According to various normative definitions, certain groups are assumed, ipso facto, to be poor. The unemployed are usually defined as poor, even though most of the unemployed are not poor—and most of the poor are not unemployed. The aged are also often regarded in the public mind as poor, although only 12.4% of them were living in poverty in 1991.[5] Residents of institutions, the mentally ill, those with physical disabilities, residents of the inner city, and immigrants—particularly illegal immigrants—are individually and collectively often seen as poor. There are poor people in each of these groups, but the popular stereotype that all members are poor, or that poverty in the United States consists solely or mainly of such groups, is an artifact based on normative definitions.

ABSOLUTE POVERTY

Absolute definitions of poverty are the most difficult to defend, and Congress has denied the existence of an objective criterion. Still, counting the poor in the United States is based upon an absolute definition, which is food consumption. As Orshansky noted, "There is no generally accepted standard of adequacy of essentials of living except food."[6] Consequently, in the 1960s she took two food budgets, one published by the U.S. Department of Agriculture and one by the U.S. Department of Labor, and translated the minimum food requirements they contained into dollars and cents—that is, how much would it cost to buy a balanced diet of the given number of calories.

On the basis of surveys showing that food costs, particularly among poor people, were about a third of total living costs, she multiplied the cost of food by three. She then assumed a family of four, multiplying by that factor, and multiplied the result by the 365 days of the year, arriving at what has subsequently become the official poverty line of the United States. According to the current formula, the poverty line is reported as about $6,620 for a single person and $14,000 for a family of four.

The Department of Labor food budget was intended to be used for a few days only during a temporary emergency—presumably a catastrophe or a layoff from work. It allowed for about 2,300 calories per day. With many subsequent refinements and alterations, this remains the basis for counting the poor in the United States. Orshansky's formula is, in great part, the same one used previously by Rowntree and by Beveridge in England during the 1940s. However, Rowntree postulated that 3,500 calories a day were required by a male laborer. Both Rowntree and Beveridge acknowledged that the poverty lines they had drawn were not sufficient to meet human social needs. It is therefore not surprising that of seven European countries, plus Australia, Canada, and the United States, the latter has the lowest poverty line, because it is based on an emergency situation. If the U.S. consumption figure were raised to a more rational level, the proportion of poor people among the elderly alone would rise by at least 50%.[7]

USES OF THE POVERTY LINE

The poverty line was not established to determine the size of welfare payments. Instead, it is used primarily for counting the poor. Although the same organizations that establish the poverty level often determine benefit levels, rarely does the first determine the second. State needs standards range from a low of $112 to a high of $673 per month for a family of four, but very few states pay the full need standard. In 1988 only 20% of Social Security benefits went to recipients with incomes less than twice the poverty line, and most of the more than $100 billion collected every year by private nonprofit organizations is spent on activities that only remotely affect lower-income Americans. In total, Americans spend more than $1 trillion every year on welfare, but less than 10% of that is specifically earmarked for low-income people. This does not mean that over the long run no progress has been made: At the turn of the century, about 40% of wage earners did not make enough to achieve a minimal standard of living. With the addition of the nonworking poor, the proportion of the poor was much greater then.[8]

Regardless of how poverty is defined, more than 10% to 15% of the U.S. population remains below the official poverty line. About 36.9 million Americans are living below the poverty line, the highest number since 1964. About 21.9% of American children and one child in four under 6 years of age live in a poverty household. The situation is not improving. The number of the poor has risen every year since 1992. Theisen says that:

> There is a growing similarity between poverty in the United States and in Third World nations. A growing underclass of Americans have poor education and poor

medical care. Almost 40 million people live in poverty. Most of them are single women with children, minorities, and rural people.[9]

Who Are the Poor?

The poor make up a heterogeneous and constantly changing group. In Britain during the early 1970s, pensioners formed the largest portion of the poor, but as high levels of unemployment continued, the unemployed, and particularly the long-term unemployed, became a larger group.

In the United States, there are also poor people among the unemployed, many whose poverty arises from unemployment. During the recession of 1982 only 45% of the unemployed received benefits, compared with 75% in 1975. By the end of 1984, coverage had dropped to about 25% of the unemployed—the lowest figure on record since unemployment insurance began. From 1984 to 1990, unemployment compensation covered less than 40% of the unemployed. However, working is no certain ticket up from poverty. A wage earner working full time at the minimum wage of $4.25 per hour would leave a family of four $1,000 below the poverty line. A person making twice the poverty line and working 30 hours a week would not earn enough to keep a family of four above the poverty line.[10]

LOW-PAID WORKERS

One of the most rapidly growing groups in poverty are low-paid workers. The average American's real wages have declined since 1980, and for the poor and near-poor, the drop has been even more severe. It has been estimated that between 40% and 43% of poor adults have jobs, and 9% of them work full-time. One in five Americans cannot get work that will keep them above the poverty line. The working poor include 2 million full-time and 6.5 million part-time workers. The proportion of full-time workers who were paid too little to raise a family of four to the poverty line increased by half between 1979 and 1990 and is growing. Twelve percent of full-time year-round workers were paid low wages in 1979; by 1990, this had risen to 18%. That amounts to 14.4 million people—a greater number than any year since the Census Bureau started recording this figure in 1964. Increasingly, the poor tend to be working; fewer rely on welfare for long periods, and fewer are heavily dependent on government support, yet more remain poor for longer periods of time.[11]

People will work for such low wages in part because welfare payments are pegged even lower. This is the way society demands that workers "price themselves into the market"—that is, accept low wages on penalty of even lower benefits. As Squires points out, never in history has a supply of labor existed, untapped, ready and willing to be exploited for production. Rather, people had to be, figuratively speaking, pushed into the factory—and they still do.[12]

The growth of the working poor indicates that policies designed to help the undeserving (that is, nonworking) poor are rapidly becoming outdated. For example, the Supplemental Security Income (SSI) program is only for the old, disabled, and blind—not for working but underpaid family heads. AFDC payments do not usually approach the poverty line, and they are reduced as recipients begin to work. Not a single state provides enough cash income to bring a mother with one or two children up to the poverty line—as low as that is. In 1988 the average monthly payment per person in all states was $127 a month, and for a family of three, the average grant was $371 a month, or $4,452 per year, which is one half of the poverty level for a family of three. Some of the homeless work but cannot afford to buy or rent housing on their salaries.[13]

The working poor are a challenge for both social policy and social work:

> A new model of social work practice may be necessary to train practitioners to work with the working poor. Social workers may need to seek new ways to work with clients who struggle continually to achieve economic security. Perhaps social workers should advocate for new forms of family income assistance rather than assume that self-sufficiency can be achieved in the world of work.[14]

Other groups contribute significant numbers to the poverty population, and among these are the elderly, the fastest-growing age group in the U.S. population.

THE AGED POOR

In many countries elderly people have a higher poverty rate than any other group and make up a large part of the poverty class. They constitute 57% of the poor in England, 40% in Australia, and 36% in Israel. Although indexing

of Social Security payments in the United States has kept the elderly closer
to the majority of the population in terms of income, one survey found that
22.5% of those over 60 were below or close to the poverty line; another study
puts this at 37%—compared with 18.7% of the nonelderly. Elderly households in the United States are about 65% as large as nonelderly households,
but the median household income of the elderly is less than half that of the
nonelderly. In 1983, almost 43% of households headed by older persons in
the United States had total incomes below $10,000, compared to only 17%
of nonelderly households.[15]

Although income reduction is generally part of retirement in Western
countries, the poverty and near-poverty of many elderly is often rationalized.
They are said to be still working or to have other (sufficient) income, or to have
reduced financial needs. The first of these assumptions ignores both the
limitation on additional earnings imposed by Social Security and the well-
documented difficulty that persons over 60 have in finding employment. As for
the second, in 1993, 40% of working people were not covered by any pension
plan other than Social Security, and only 34% of all aged persons received
private and/or government pensions. Today the income replacement rate for
the elderly is 66%, and projections are that in the year 2000 Social Security
payments will pay 54% of the preretirement year's wage to low earners, 42%
to average earners, and 28% to maximum earners.[16]

Those who say the financial needs of the elderly are smaller do not account
for the fact that the medical expenses alone of each elderly person average
six times more than those faced by young adults. The total health care costs
of the elderly are now $50 billion a year, and they are expected to grow to
$200 billion by the year 2000. The high rates of divorce and single-parent
families put additional strains on aged parents, many of whom continue to
support their children and grandchildren, especially widowed daughters. One
in five elderly households have no net assets, and one in seven have no health
insurance.[17]

As a result, reaching retirement age means financial readjustments for
most people and wrenching changes for some of them. The future financial
outlook for the elderly is not reassuring, because no current pension plan
(governmental, business, union, or private) is actuarially based on the expectation of great numbers of people living for twenty-five to thirty-five years
past retirement age. Although the financial structure of U.S. Social Security
has been revised in an effort to provide liquidity during the next few decades,

continued lengthening of life expectancy may soon make these revisions obsolete. As Habib notes, the literature on the economics of aging has barely begun to come to terms with the implications of this phenomenon. Attempts to adjust pension programs to increasing life expectancies will place an ever-increasing burden on the younger, working population—a burden that may be resisted. The shrinking ratio of working to nonworking people may become one of the most difficult problems social and economic planners will face in the coming years.[18]

POOR CHILDREN

Another large group living below the poverty line is children. This is mostly as a consequence of their families being poor. Between one in four and one in five American children live in poverty. This rate is twice the poverty rate for those over 65 and the highest for any age cohort in the population. Although a married or cohabiting couple may be able to manage on one or two incomes, poverty grows with family size, and single parents with children obviously have even more financial difficulty. Over 30% of all two-income households would be earning less than the official poverty level if they depended on one income only, and single-parent families outnumber married couple families by three to one in inner cities.[19]

Children's poverty is not confined to lack of money. For example, nearly one third of all children living in poverty in the United States get no medical assistance because their families are ineligible for Medicaid. Families with children make up 34% of the urban homeless. Many programs are designed to help poor and/or disadvantaged children, ranging from educational enrichment programs such as Headstart to direct means-tested grants such as AFDC. Children in poverty, particularly those in single-parent families, have become the focus of much attention and activity, to the point that some believe that American policy makers are obsessed with the problem of single-parent families with children and that all poverty is being defined in these terms. Many of these efforts are insufficient to overcome children's poverty. For example, the median AFDC grant is 41% of the poverty line—even when combined with food stamps it reaches only 72%. Thus, despite the many efforts to aid children and to alleviate family poverty, the surest way of becoming poor in the United States remains to be born into a poor family.[20]

THE FEMINIZATION OF POVERTY

Within the groups of the unemployed, the working poor, children, and other poor sections of the population is the subset of women. In addition to discriminatory practices in society, in social welfare policies, and in the world of work, the situation of women as mothers and as primary caregivers to infants operates in American society to feminize poverty. When poverty is discussed in terms of the number under the poverty line, it tends to depersonalize the poor, who become statistics. However, many people are subjected to what has been called "face-grinding, belly-gripping" poverty. Dear raises the question of how people survive on so little income.

> Some welfare mothers ransack supermarket garbage bins (called "garbaging") . . . to get enough food for their children. Others sell their blood plasma twice a week for about $10 a pint to gain desperately needed additional income. Still others pilfer Good Will drop-off bins to get clothing for themselves and their children. . . . Some mothers, in absolute desperation, resort to prostitution to get money.[21]

The Politics of Conduct

The continuing existence of poverty in what is admittedly one of the most prosperous nations on earth leads to a number of ways of justifying, rationalizing, or denying the problem. One method is to invoke Social Darwinism and declare that the poor are responsible for their own situation. The word *lazy* seems too pejorative, so the poor are labeled *dependent,* the implication being that they are comfortable, happy, and deliberately exploitative in their dependence on others, or on society as a whole. Katz takes this further and holds that *dependency* has become the modern word for pauperism.[22] The stereotypical view is to link poverty and laziness. In this view, the "cure" for poverty is to make people responsible and to motivate them, enabling them to deal with their own problems, usually by increasing the capacity of families to care for themselves through jobs. In short, this view holds that the root of poverty is in the individual, not in society, and policies designed to encourage, cajole, or coerce people to change their behaviors are the indicated course of action. This has been termed the *politics of conduct—* making people change the way they act to be eligible for help.[23]

SCAPEGOATING THE POOR

Another method of dealing with the embarrassing phenomenon of poverty is to see the poor as an "out-group," with their own culture, values, morals, and so forth. Because they are not part of mainstream American culture, they have no legitimate claim on its bounty. A very early proponent of the existence of a culture of poverty was Oscar Lewis, and although much controversy surrounded this thesis, it persists. In fact, although the underclass is not defined as a class in the socioeconomic hierarchy, it is nevertheless seen as a subset of the poor whose poverty is attributable to their behavior. Seen in this way, policies are designed to affect the entire group or subgroups within the subset—teenage mothers, Black inner city males, fatherless children, and so forth.

Concomitant with the view of the poor as a subset, or a distinct culture, is the phenomenon of scapegoating. It is not enough to view the group as different; they must be punished for being so. The origin and meaning of the term *scapegoat* are found in the Bible: The High Priest placed upon the head of a goat the sins of the people and sent it off to die in the wilderness. By transferring to the goat the sins of the people and punishing it, he relieved the people of their feelings of guilt. Scapegoating, in its classical sense, occurs when an individual or group feels guilty of holding unacceptable views. The guilt and the feelings are denied or repressed, and the individual or group often becomes vehement in advocating existing norms. Indeed, the more guilt, the more vehemence. ("Methinks the lady doth protest too much.")

Many people question the need for and desirability or usefulness of their work—even if their questions are unspoken or all but unconscious. However, they publicly share the prevailing societal norms concerning working, being productive, and being useful. They need a scapegoat, and they find one in the poor. The poor are fantasized as happy connivers who live without work, enjoying guiltless leisure, sexual freedom, immunity from laws and morals, exemption from obligations, and total lack of concern about the future. Thus a culture of poverty is not only established but made the scapegoat for the more affluent. This image of the culture of poverty matches nothing that has ever been learned about real poor people. Indeed, it is a tragically distorted picture of the tense, bitter, anxious, humiliated people who cannot afford meals for their children. However, this has no effect on the process of scapegoating. Once assigned these reprehensible characteristics, the poor can—nay, must— be punished, changed, and isolated because of them. Scapegoats can do nothing to change their roles, because the reason for their punishment lies in the feelings of others, not in their own behavior.

STRUCTURAL POVERTY

A third way of explaining poverty is to emphasize the lack of opportunities available to poor people. This provides a structural explanation, rather than an individual or group diagnosis. For example, "Improvement in the life chances of poor people cannot occur unless labor markets offer much more abundant and attractive job prospects . . . to ordinary, unremarkable citizens." Others are more blunt: "The problem is lack of jobs in the ghetto."[24] Social welfare programs designed to answer the needs of the working population in times of distress cannot adequately deal with the situation of the nonworking poor. The problems of the poor are more complex and far-reaching than the problems of those who are ordinarily in the workforce. Even trying to insert them into the labor market has little chance of success, because "most welfare reform programs do not consider the availability of jobs or the structure of the labor market."[25]

Solutions to the problem of poverty are obviously connected with the way one views or defines the situation and its causes. These range from personal counseling, job motivation and training, salary subsidies, service corps and community service ideas, to various kinds of income maintenance plans. One proposed solution suggests that sending every American in poverty a check large enough to raise his or her income above the poverty level would cost only $130 billion to $160 billion. Others argue that the national failure to deal adequately with poverty arises from inability or unwillingness to realize that it cannot be remedied by cash payments or work requirements.[26]

Given its long history, and the fact that it has remained at substantially the same level for decades despite numerous policies and programs aimed at alleviating or eradicating it, poverty is one of the most intractable problems faced by social welfare planners. It is one example of how the complex interplay between motivations and other influences operates to determine the outcome of social welfare policies.

SUMMARY

Although poverty may be defined in relative, normative, or absolute terms, its continued existence in the face of decades—if not centuries—of efforts to eradicate it, indicates the tenaciousness of the problem. Subgroups among the poverty-stricken include the working poor and many of the aged, children, and women. Because societies cannot solve the problem of poverty, they often rationalize that poor people are responsible for their own situations and that efforts to eradicate the problem are useless.

EXERCISE

The poverty line is roughly $14,000 a year for a family of four. To get the poverty line for an individual in such a family, divide by four. Then, to get the daily allowance for food, divide by 365 days of the year; divide the result by three (food costs are considered a third of the total); and divide that by three meals a day.

If this were your permanent allowance for food, what sort of foods would you eat, and how much?

Plan a menu for a week, within these limitations, costing out every ingredient.

How do you think this would affect your body? Your abilities? Your attitude? Your social life?

Notes

1. The quotation is from Burghardt & Fabricant (1987), and the food stamp figures are from "Hunger Amid the Plenty" (1993).

2. The quotation is from Lens (1969).

3. The measures of poverty are from "Measuring Poverty" (1985).

4. The relative measures are by Mollison (1991).

5. The numbers of poor aged are from "Ranks of Poor" (1992).

6. The quotation is from Orshansky (1965b), and the formula that follows is from Orshansky (1965a). The current poverty line is from U.S. Department of Health and Human Services (1991) and Frank (1992).

7. The 50% rise is projected by Schulz (1992).

8. The needs standards are from Carrera (1987); expenditures for low income people are from Huff (1992); the 40% figure is from Atherton (1992).

9. Numbers of the poor, and of poor children, are from Atherton (1992), Frank (1992), and Pear (1993); the 1964 comparison is from *The New York Times* (July 21, 1992; p. B1); increases in poverty are from Pear (1993); the 1983 comparison is from *The New York Times* (March 7, 1993; p. IE5). The quotation is from Theisen (n.d.).

10. Statistics are from the following sources: percentage receiving unemployment benefits, Mishra (1990); 40% unemployment coverage, Blau (1992); the minimum wage calculation, Frank (1992); the thirty-hour week figure, Pear (1993).

11. Statistics are from the following sources: on wages of low-paid workers, Huff (1992); Frank (1992) and Schneiderman (1992), respectively, calculate that 40% and 43% of poor adults have jobs; on full- vs. part-time work, Atherton (1992); on increase in working poor, *NASW News* (1992; 37[7], 11); on increases and change in situation of poor workers, Mollison (1991).

12. The phrase *pricing themselves into the market* is from Mishra (1990); Squires (1990) describes being pushed into the factory.

13. Average payments are from Dear (1989).

14. The quotation is from Nichols-Casebolt & McClure (1989).

15. Statistics are from the following sources: on international elderly, Macarov (1982); on elderly poverty, Fowles (1983) and Silverstone & Burack-Weiss (1983); on nonelderly poverty, Fowles (1983); the 43% to 17% comparison of household income is from *American Association of Retired Persons Bulletin* (1985; 26[6]).

16. Statistics are from the following sources: 40% with no pension plan, *International Herald Tribune* (June 19-20, 1993; p. 3); 34% with no pension income, Chen (1985); today's replacement rate, from Hokenstad (1992); and projected rates, from Chen (1985).

17. Statistics are from the following sources: medical expenses, Zastrow (1992); total health care costs, Rich (1989); parents as supporters of widows, Bankoff (1983); assets and health insurance, the *International Herald Tribune* (June 19-20, 1993; p. 3).

18. The assertion is from Habib (1985); the shrinking ratio is from Hardcastle (1978).

19. Schneiderman (1992) provides data on children in poverty and on two-income households; data on single-parent families are from Hill (1992).

20. Statistics are from the following sources: children without medical care, Mishra (1990); homeless children, "Security for America's Children" (1992); inadequacy of AFDC grants, Schneiderman (1992). The comment about policymakers' obsession is from Hill (1992).

21. The quotation is from Dear (1989).

22. The assertion is in Katz (1986).

23. *The politics of conduct* is from Hill (1992).

24. The first quotation is from Murray (1988), and the second is from Kasarda (1989).

25. The quotation is from Hagen (1992).

26. Huff (1992) proposes sending everyone a check, and Atherton (1990) decries cash payments and work requirements.

READ MORE ABOUT IT . . .

For more information on:	See these sources:
Definitions of poverty	Doron, 1990
Basis of U.S. poverty line	Bell, 1987; Rowntree & Beveridge, discussed in Doron, 1990
Inadequacy of U.S. poverty line	Gustafsson & Lindblom, 1993; Veit-Wilson, 1992
Poverty in Great Britain	Benington, 1992
Homeless working poor	First & Toomey, 1989
Rationalizations of elderly poverty	Meier, Dittman, & Toyle, 1980
Employment trouble of aged	Regan, 1989
Feminization of poverty	Abramovitz, 1992
Stereotypes of the poor	Kluegel & Smith, 1986
Cure for poverty	Nichols-Casebolt & McClure, 1989
Culture of poverty	Lewis, 1966
Subsets of the poor	Hill, 1992
Scapegoating	Heap, 1966
Problems of the poor	Atherton, 1990
Shortcomings of welfare reform	Gans, 1995; Hagen, 1992

14. Persisting Unemployment

The problem of unemployment dates back to the beginnings of recorded history. Governments use many devices to obscure and minimize the extent of unemployment, including definitional and statistical methods, such as leaving out part-time workers who are desperately looking for full-time work, or not including discouraged workers who know they can no longer find jobs. The amount of unemployment deemed "acceptable" has risen for decades. Methods of maintaining employment figures include featherbedding, goldbricking, and overcounting. Working hours are decreasing, and productivity is rising. Social welfare policies based upon a full working population, or designed to prepare people for jobs, may have to be revised in light of past experience and future possibilities.

The problem of unemployment has been a concern since the earliest days of social work as a profession. With heavy societal emphasis on work as the only legitimate means of acquiring material and psychic rewards, people unable to find work are heavily disadvantaged. Today, the unemployed and those with problems stemming from unemployment are well represented in many social workers' caseloads, particularly in areas such as inner cities or in respect to certain client groups, such as youth or members of minorities. Both social welfare programs and social work activities center around the area of work.

Unemployment in History

The problem of maintaining maximum employment has occupied governments since antiquity. The pharoah who built the Great Pyramid at Giza took

239

100,000 farmers from their land and turned them into urban laborers for the twenty years of construction required. Due to the very shape of the structure, fewer and fewer laborers were required as the pyramid neared completion. The unemployed could not be returned to the farms that were no longer theirs. Some historians maintain that each of the later pyramids was begun when work on the previous one was about half completed. In short, the later pyramids were make-work projects to keep the laborers occupied.

Herod the Great used a similar strategy. When the Second Temple was finished, he began building a road around the Temple Mount in Jerusalem to give work to the 10,000 otherwise-unemployed temple builders. The Roman Emperor Vespasian forbade the use of rivers for moving construction materials, in order to give more jobs to people.

Obscuring Unemployment

Since ancient times, governments have engaged in a large variety of attempts to create jobs. When unsuccessful, they have tried to disguise the actual number of people ready, willing, and able to work who cannot find jobs—and particularly full-time year-round jobs. To do so, governments have often engaged in what might be called definitional deviousness and statistical skullduggery. In England, for example, people are not officially unemployed until they have been out of work for four weeks. Those who do not find work during an arbitrarily defined time period are declared unemployable and dropped from the unemployment statistics. Obviously, by lengthening the first period and shortening the second, unemployment could be statistically erased in Britain.

The United States uses similar obscuring devices. Unemployment is determined by a household survey of 60,000 families, in which the wage earners are asked, in effect, "Did you work last week?" If the answer is negative, the second question is, "Did you seek work last week?" If the answer is yes, then the person is unemployed. However, the definition of work, for purposes of this survey, is whatever takes more than one hour a week. Thus, paid baby-sitting for a couple of hours or running a paid errand that takes more than an hour constitutes working, and the respondent is not considered unemployed.

This leaves part-time workers out of the unemployment statistics. About 6.3 million part-time workers actually want full-time jobs but can't find them. Sixty percent of jobs created in 1993 were part-time jobs. Similarly, between 1 million and 7 million others are too discouraged to go out and look for work, and they, too, are omitted from the unemployment figures. When part-time workers who want to work full-time and discouraged workers were taken into account, the official unemployment figure of 6.8% in November 1993 rose to over 10%.[1]

The household survey to determine the unemployed rate does not ask why respondents did not seek work. A severe snowstorm, a transportation strike, illness, or other reasons beyond the individual's control can act to reduce the unemployment figure. Perhaps more important quantitatively, failure to look for work might arise from weeks, months, and sometimes years of fruitless search.

Official unemployment figures also omit transient workers, seasonal workers, domestic workers, agricultural laborers, school leavers, and illegal immigrants. Also excluded are the unemployed who are taking, or who are required to take, various kinds of training and retraining courses. They are listed as students receiving stipends rather than as unemployed workers receiving compensation. Others are "employed" with their salaries, or large parts of them, paid by the government, either directly or as a subsidy to the employer.

In Israel, a study found that the number of unemployed persons can vary from 19,000 to 115,000, depending on which official definition and method of counting is used. Sweden, which boasts an official 1.9% unemployment rate, may have 5.5% to 11% unemployed when such concealment is corrected. It may be necessary to increase official figures between 50% and 300% to cover the percentage of the labor force that is seeking but cannot find full-time work. For example, Schneiderman holds that real U.S. unemployment in 1993 was actually 14%, twice the 7% publicized.[2]

The Job Shortage

Despite temporary fluctuations, the unemployment rate throughout the Western world has been rising inexorably. Finding jobs for people—especially full-time, decent-paying jobs—is becoming increasingly difficult. After every recession or period of economic difficulty, the "floor" of unemployment rises. In 1930, Beveridge saw 2% unemployment among unskilled workers as the irreducible minimum. In 1946, Congress could not agree on a definition of full employment, but by 1973 the American Council of Economic

Advisors was speaking of 3.5% unemployment as the "natural" (read: un-avoidable) rate, and this quickly became 5%. In 1979, the Humphrey-Hawkins Act called 4% unemployment "full employment." In 1983, the same Council of Economic Advisors quoted above described 6% to 7% unemployment as the natural rate. In 1992, the definition of full employment used by government economists was 6% unemployment, although some argue that 3% of the labor force unemployed would constitute full employment in the United States. In Newfoundland, by contrast, 20% unemployment is considered full employment. At this writing, the unemployment rate in the United States hovers between 6% and 7%, and the Federal Reserve Board has made it clear that 8 million people officially unemployed would be considered full employment. In Europe, the rate varies from country to country, between 1% and 21%, with an average of about 11%.[3]

It has been charged that the United States, unlike Sweden, for example, has never been committed to a full employment economy. The U.S. government has never made a commitment to provide jobs for all who want them. In fact, there is a subtle feeling that unemployment is a hedge against inflation and that a supply of unemployed people makes for a harder-working, more amenable workforce.

REDUCED WORK HOURS

The rise in unemployment has occurred despite a continual reduction in hours of work. For example, in 1900 the average workweek in the United States was 53 hours; in 1979 it was 35.5 hours; in 1987 it was 34.8 hours, and in 1990 it was 34.5 hours. Over the past half-century, the average hours per year have been reduced by .5% to 1% a year. Average Americans have an estimated 4 hours a day more leisure time than their grandparents had, and if the rate of decrease continues as it has since 1880, the workweek will be cut in half by the time today's children retire. The 4-day week was introduced into some major industries as long ago as 1976.[4]

Although the curve is not a smooth one, with a slight growth in the workweek during the recent recession, the long-term trend of work hours continues to be downward, even taking into consideration second and unreported jobs. As the workweek has contracted and life expectancy has been extended, more than twenty-two years of leisure have been added to the average American's life. Between 1965 and 1985, free time increased from 35 to 40 hours a week. This trend is accelerating, as reductions in the length of the work year through longer vacations and added holidays are more prevalent than increases in overtime work.[5]

CONTINGENT WORKERS

One of the most potent factors in keeping the unemployment figure down is the increase in what are called "contingent workers." These part-time and short-term workers number about 30 million. Between 1980 and 1987 the number of part-time workers in the United States more than doubled. Of the 25 million part-time workers, approximately 40% are doing part-time work only because they can't find full-time jobs. About 20% of all new jobs are part-time. Of the jobs created between January and August 1993, nearly 60% were part-time.[6]

Productivity Growth

As hours of work shrink and unemployment grows, overall productivity has hardly been affected and has even increased. With productivity in 1980 considered as a statistical 100, productivity throughout the world rose to 130 by 1987. In the United States between 1977 and 1987, output per employee hour rose from 108 to 140. Between 1982 and 1987, output per employee year rose at an average annual rate of .8%. As companies continue the production rate while dismissing workers, per-worker productivity automatically increases. *The New York Times* reported a productivity increase of 1.9% from April through June 1991, and in 1993, productivity rose at a 2.7% average annual rate. For 1992, worker productivity—defined as output per number of hours worked—reached 2.8%, the best gain for American workers since 1972. In fact, there is hardly a product in the United States that is in short supply because too few workers are engaged in its manufacture. In Europe, a reported problem in industry is massive overcapacity.[7]

GOLDBRICKING AND FEATHERBEDDING

In addition to this clear reduction in working hours, there are also hidden reductions in working time. A growing amount of time is wasted on the job by those who are working (goldbricking). Very few employees report that they work as hard as they can. Cherrington studied building workers on the job and found that about 50% of their time was spent in activities other than work. Swisher's study found that 13 hours of a 40-hour workweek are wasted, with three of them devoted to simply daydreaming. Time wasted on the job is said to be increasing at about 1% per annum.[8]

Some jobs are maintained simply to provide work; the marketability of the product or service is of little concern. This is called featherbedding. Thus the U.S. government provided massive loans to Chrysler Corporation when it faced closure. This was in order to safeguard the jobs of workers, not to stave off a problematic shortage of Chrysler products. The Connecticut legislature voted down restrictions on cheap handguns and automatic weapons in order to preserve jobs in Hartford's Colt Manufacturing Company. Sources say President Bush was opposed to higher-mileage cars because they would result in lost jobs. When closure of a shipyard or a military installation is proposed, the question is never how this would affect national defense, but rather how many jobs it would cost—and in many cases the latter consideration prevails.

REBUILDING THE INFRASTRUCTURE

Because unemployment is such a major social problem, many solutions are proposed and tried. One of the most familiar is using the unemployed to rebuild the physical infrastructure, meaning roads, bridges, tunnels, sewers, and so on. The image of swarms of unemployed men (and perhaps women) spreading out over the countryside and working on the roads ignores the fact that most roadbuilding is done by enormous and sophisticated machines that clear the ground, mix the concrete, spread the asphalt, and so forth, with their operators sitting in air-conditioned cabs, often listening to the radio or tape cassettes.

It has been estimated that to insulate *all* the homes in Great Britain would occupy 30,000 workers; to rebuild the roads, tunnels, and so forth, including the North Sea tunnel, would occupy 62,000 more—a mere handful compared to the 3 million currently unemployed in Britain. In Israel, widening roads, building overpasses, extending the railroad to Eilat, building a tunnel from the Mediterranean to the Dead Sea, and all the similar works that proponents can imagine would occupy 20,000 people, leaving over 180,000 still unemployed. To build homes for *every family* in the Third World would employ 8 million people, whereas unemployment in India alone is in the tens of millions.[9]

Also these figures omit the cost of creating such jobs, which is often enormous. The American public works program in the early 1940s, one of the most extensive of historical efforts, cost about half of the defense expenditure for 1942. The Emergency Employment Act of 1971 managed to employ only about one in twenty-five of the unemployed at its peak, and in 1974 the Job Opportunities Program (JOBS) employed only 100,000 people at a cost of $13,881 per person per year. Job subsidy and job creation programs cost from $10,000 to $25,000 for each job, and less than half the jobs are new—15% to 65% of them simply displace other workers. Hence it is easy to overestimate the real employment potential of such projects and to underestimate their costs, while dwelling on the necessity and desirability of the end results.[10]

Increasing Services

It is more difficult to estimate how many of the currently unemployed could be trained and employed to bring the human services—teaching, nursing, and social work—to an optimum labor force. In 1988, for example, it was estimated that an additional 300,000 nurses, at most, would satisfy the need in that field. As for teachers, to reduce average classroom populations from today's average of twenty-four to a maximum of fifteen would require 1 million new teachers, and cost more than a $70 billion. As to social workers, membership in the National Association of Social Workers grew by about 6,000 per year from 1988 to 1991. Were this to double or triple in the next ten years, it would have almost no effect on total unemployment of about 10 million. In short, even if the economy could bear the cost of retraining, providing facilities, and paying enough nurses, teachers, and social workers to bring services to an optimal condition, it would not, by itself, result in full employment.[11]

An investment of $40 billion in the United States would have created 640,000 jobs in 1993 and 1.25 million jobs in 1994. This would have reduced the current official jobless rate by less than 20% and the real rate from 6% to 13%. The hard-core unemployed would probably not have benefited. In fact, unemployment might not have been reduced at all: If present trends continue, most new service jobs will be filled by previously nonworking women.[12]

A National Service Corps

A proposal to reduce unemployment that surfaces regularly is for some sort of national service corps that would use the unemployed for usually unspecified tasks, presumably in the public service or public works sector. The Civilian Conservation Corps (CCC) of the 1930s is often the model used. Past experience with such projects indicates a number of substantial problems, not the least of which is that they do not really reduce unemployment. Of those who served a six-month period in the CCC, 77% were still unemployed at the end, as were 58% of those who stayed in for a year. And the estimated value of the work done by each enrollee was $664, with per capita costs of $1,004.[13]

TRAINING AND RETRAINING

Training programs generally assume that jobs are available but that the unemployed people lack the skills to fill them. Such programs are beset with problems, the most important being that most programs are not based upon actual job openings, but rather on expectations (or hopes) that such jobs will be available. Even if jobs are available at the beginning of such courses, they may not be open at its completion. Not many employers are willing to hold jobs open until specific individuals finish training.

Many such courses have been called "preparing people for nonexistent jobs." Nor is everyone suitable for training courses. In 1982 only a quarter to a third of the AFDC caseload was considered employable. From 1977 to 1984 1.2 million U.S. workers received basic trade readjustment benefits, but only 70,000 of these began retraining, and only 28,000 stayed the course. Of those who finished, fewer than 4,500 found jobs that used their new skills. More recently, only one in five retrained workers landed jobs paying at least 80% of their former wage. The program has been labeled a "dud." A major study of the results of the Federal Job Training Partnership Act found that those who enrolled in the program earned 8% less than those who were given no training. In essence, the track record of training and retraining courses is dismal.[14] Neverthless, these efforts will probably be continued because there seems to be agreement that it is preferable to do something rather than nothing.[15]

SUMMARY

Unemployment has proved to be an intractable problem for generations, and it will probably grow worse, as hours of work continue to decrease and productivity continues to rise. Because much social welfare policy concerning employment and unemployment is based upon a series of myths—that work is abundant and necessary, that people have a deep, abiding need to work—it will take a long time for acceptance of grim reality to replace comforting mythology. If unemployment continues to be difficult to deal with, the future may demand a new and different view of work and unemployment, resulting in radically different methods of dealing with it.

EXERCISE

An unemployed person in the United States is one who did not work more than one hour in the previous week and is actively looking for work.

1. You are a full-time student in a school of social work, have an infant, and take care of a bedridden mother. Are you out of work? Are you unemployed? Are you underemployed?
2. Under the same circumstances, financial need causes you to advertise and seek work that you can do at home. Does this change your status?
3. Under the same circumstances, you are given envelopes to stuff at home on a per-piece basis, but you can devote only an hour a week to it. Does this change your status?
4. Under the same circumstances, you can devote six hours a week to stuffing envelopes. Does this change your status?
5. While devoting six hours a week to stuffing envelopes, you are still actively looking for work. Does this change your status?
6. Another ailing person moves into your house, and you take care of him or her as well as your mother, for which you receive a small payment from his or her parents. Does this change your status?
7. Suppose that after some months of this arrangement, you found you could no longer do more than take care of your infant and your parent. Would you be entitled to unemployment compensation? Why or why not?

Notes

1. Statistics are from the following sources: number of part-time workers, Uchitelle (1992) and Herbert (1993); number of discouraged workers, Schneiderman (1992); revised unemployment rate, Uchitelle (1993).

2. Statistics are from the following sources: on Israel, Sicron (1986); on Sweden, Macarov (1991b) and Jonzon (1991); the 50% to 300% estimates, Field (1977), Kogut & Aron (1980), Levinson (1980), Schwartz & Neikirk (1983), Yankelovich, Zettenberg, Strumpel, & Shanks (1983); Schneiderman (1992).

3. Statistics are from the following sources: 1930 rate, Beveridge (1930); the 3.5% rate of 1946, Reich (1983); the 5% rate, Sharp, Register, & Leftwich (1992); Humphrey-Hawkins Act, *World of Work Report* (1979; *4*, p. 29); 6%-7%, Reich (1983); the 1992 definition, Jones (1992); 3% argument, Sherraden (1991b); the Newfoundland figures, *The Future of Work* (1989); 8 million out of work, Kuttner (1994).

4. Statistics are from the following sources: reduction in work hours, *World of Work Report* (1980; *5*, p. 52), Kendrick (1979), and International Labour Office (1991); leisure in grandfather's time, Kaplan (1960); halving the workweek, Buckingham (1961).

5. Statistics are from the following sources: additional twenty-two years of leisure, Cunningham (1964); the increase from 1965 to 1985, Robinson (1991).

6. Statistics are from the following sources: 30 million contingent workers, Schneiderman (1992); the growth in part-time workers, Belous (1989); involuntary part-time work, *Monthly Labor Review* (1988; *111*, pp. 71-73); new part-time jobs, *The New York Times* (April 29, 1988; p. A38); the 1993 figure is from Herbert (1993).

7. Statistics are from the following sources: worldwide productivity, United Nations (1992b); U.S. output per employee hour, Plunkert (1990); 1991 productivity increase, *The New York Times* (September 6, 1991; IE5); 1993 productivity increase, Roach (1993); best gain, "US Productivity Keeps Climbing" (1993).

8. The studies are Cherrington (1980) and Swisher (1994); reports of increasing unproductive time are in Kendrick (1979) and Yankelovich & Immerwahr (1983).

9. Statistics are from the following sources: British estimates, House of Lords (1981); Israeli jobs, the *Jerusalem Post* (July 8, 1992; p. 8); the 8 million estimate, Sethuraman (1985); unemployment in India, *The New York Times* (April 29, 1988; p. A38).

10. The job creation figures are from Morris (1986).

11. Statistics are from the following sources: nurses, *The New York Times* (April 6, 1988; p. A23); teachers, *The New York Times* (April 29, 1988; p. A38); social workers, "Data Study" (1993).

12. The investment costs are from *The New York Times* (October 25, 1992; p. 41E); the jobless reduction and present trends are from Olsson (1987).

13. Macarov (1991b) asserts that service corps won't reduce unemployment; the figures are from Salmond (1967).

14. "Preparing people for non-existent jobs" is from Hall (1984) and Moroney (1991). Statistics are from the following sources: employability of caseload, Rein (1982); 1977-1984 record, *The New York Times* (August 10, 1986; p. A23); the most recent "dud" program, *Time Magazine* (October 29, 1993; p. 22); the study of FJTPA, DeParle (1993).

15. See Norris & Thompson (1995).

READ MORE ABOUT IT . . .

For more information on:	See these sources:
The pyramids	Mendelssohn, 1977
Vespasian	Garraty, 1978
Job creation methods	Taggart, 1977
British unemployment	Field, 1977; Sadan, 1993
Lack of definition of unemployment	Jones, 1992
Lack of U.S. commitment to full employment	Ginzberg, Williams, & Dutka, 1989
Four-day workweek	Kaplan, 1975; *Methods of Adjusting,* n.d.
Downward trend in workweek	*The New York Times* (October 25, 1992, p. IE2)
Second jobs	Feingold, 1991
Rising productivity	Herman, 1989; "The Economy," 1993
Overcapacity in Europe	Benington, 1992
Employees fail to work as hard as they can	Macarov, 1982; Walbank, 1980; Yankelovitz & Immerwahr, 1983
Connecticut gun law	"Gun Control vs. Jobs," 1992
Suggestion for service corps	Sherraden & Sherraden, 1991
Myths of employment	Jones, 1992
Some radical solutions	Macarov, 1988b

15. From Welfare State to Welfare Society and Welfare Reform

Some apparently intractable problems—such as poverty, unemployment, racism, and sexism—have led some planners to the conclusion that governmental provision of welfare services is inefficient, ineffective, or both. As a result, some people believe that responsibility for social welfare should be allotted more effectively between the government and private and voluntary sectors.

A current issue in welfare policy has to do with whether and how the welfare state should be changed. In the United States and elsewhere, there has been movement toward a more "mixed economy of welfare." In effect, this would turn over some government welfare responsibilities to not-for-profit voluntary agencies and private for-profit organizations. At the programmatic level, this means removing people from the public welfare rolls by making them dependent on the nongovernmental sector—primarily the marketplace, and on or voluntary organizations and families when the market fails them.

Defining the Welfare State

The term *welfare state* generally refers to countries that undertake to protect and/or to provide for their population in the manner once thought to be the province of the family, religious institutions, voluntary organizations, or the marketplace. The welfare state is usually considered coeval with insurance-type universal programs, although the welfare state may also contain means-tested programs, such as food stamps, AFDC, and general relief, as in the United States.

Creation of the welfare state was a governmental response to problems too widespread and too deep to be dealt with by nongovernmental bodies. Only the government, and usually the central government, was thought to have the resources and the structure to deal with such problems. The welfare state also expressed an ideology: that government, as the embodiment of the popular will, was responsible for providing welfare, just as it provided education, defense, roadways, and so forth. The objectives of the welfare state vary somewhat, but they may include the redistribution of income and services, innovations, reduction of social inequalities, and social integration. Some observers define welfare states as those that spend at least a specified portion of their gross national product on welfare.

HISTORY OF WELFARE STATES

Governmental responsibility for individual problems, although beset with ambivalence, has a long history. Although the term *welfare state* does not seem to have been used before 1941,[1] the concept of a state taking full responsibility for the needs of its citizens has its roots in antiquity.

For example, in the fourth century B.C., all full citizens of Athens received enough food and money to secure their livelihood. With the distribution of income from captured territories, Athens was an ancient approximation of the welfare state. In England, although the Elizabethan Poor Laws emphasized individual responsibility, they also established residency requirements and local responsibility, putting the burden indirectly on the community.

Although Bismarck instituted social insurance for political reasons, the result was a governmental system of payments in the event of contingencies—payments that were made by right and regulated by law, which could be anticipated by recipients. The United States took the road toward a welfare state with the passage of the Social Security Act in 1935, as a reaction to the continuing effects of the Great Depression.

In Britain, William Beveridge had issued a pamphlet in 1924 calling for "insurance for all and everything." Although it envisioned a complete welfare state, it wasn't until World War II, immediately after the terrible retreat from Dunkirk, that *The Times* (of London) issued a dramatic call for social justice, abolition of privilege, more equitable distribution of income and wealth, and other drastic changes in English life. As a result, Beveridge reviewed a series of surveys made between 1928 and 1937, coming to the conclusion that poverty and want in England were "needless." In 1942 he published *Social Insurance and Allied Services,* generally known as the Beveridge Report. More than any other single document, the Beveridge Report brought about a decision and a series of actions that turned Great Britain into a welfare state. This document provided seminal ideas that affected thinking about welfare in many other countries.

ALTERNATIVES TO
THE WELFARE STATE

Before the Beveridge Report, three possibilities were being considered in Great Britain. The socialist school believed that the capitalist system of private enterprise and a free market economy was inefficient and unjust and should be replaced by a rational order of things planned and directed by the state. Under socialism, normal needs would be met automatically, and some would cease to exist: There would be no more poverty or squalor. A second school held that the socioeconomic system could be remedied by state intervention to modify some of its operations. The third school contended that the existing system could correct whatever might be wrong in the normal course of events. Government intervention or control was unnecessary and even harmful.

The welfare state, as it emerged, drew on the positions of the first and second schools:

> The total ultimate responsibility of the State for the welfare of its people was recognized more explicitly than ever before. . . . The social services were not to be regarded as regrettable necessities to be retained only until the capitalist system had been reformed or socialized; they were a permanent and even a glorious part of the social system itself. They were something to be proud of, not to apologize for.[2]

The Modern Welfare State

Social welfare as a governmental responsibility became clearly accepted with Bismarck's insurance programs, Social Security in the United States, and the Beveridge Plan in Great Britain. Once established, such plans grew rapidly: from 57 countries with 142 programs in 1940, to 146 countries with

465 programs in 1991.[3] In addition, governments took responsibility for some noninsurance programs, such as school lunches, food stamps, rent vouchers, and direct relief.

During times of massive deprivation, such as the Great Depression, people not only accepted that the government must undertake social welfare activities but understood that only the government had the resources to do so. However, this assumption of responsibility is not enshrined in law. In the United States, for example, "The courts have not found in the Constitution a right to social welfare."[4] One cannot sue the government for welfare benefits, unless their denial is clearly discriminatory.

Titmuss referred to the "trichotomy" of social welfare systems, by which he meant their consideration of social, fiscal, and occupational needs.[5] Government, according to the British analyst, bears some responsibility for each of these. The welfare state represents the abandonment of a residual conception of social welfare, which sees the market and the family—and perhaps the church and voluntary groups—as the natural, desirable, first-line sources of help, with the government acting only to help the few who fall through that network. Instead, social welfare is built into the ongoing activities of government, as a structural component. The contrary view has been called "subsidiarity," which as previously mentioned, means that activities should be undertaken by the smallest or most local unit, such as the family, relatives, friends, voluntary organizations, commercial frameworks, and localities, followed, if necessary, by states. Welfare activities should be assumed by the state only when all else has failed.

For the past decade or so, the nature of the welfare state has been undergoing changes. Those that deal with programmatic changes are designed to change the welfare state into a welfare society. Those changes that generally aim to influence behavior of welfare recipients are referred to as welfare reform.

The Welfare Society

The welfare state's goal of protection for the citizenry (or the working population) from the cradle to the grave has never been universally accepted as a proper societal goal. President Herbert Hoover once described the welfare state as a "disguise for the totalitarian state" and declared that it put the United States on the "last mile to collectivism."[6] Others have pointed out that if the money individuals invest in contributory social welfare programs were used to buy private insurance, the costs would be less and the benefits greater. Many hold to the Jeffersonian theory of least government, arguing that government should not do what can be done by other societal institutions.

There does not appear to be any consensus about the dismantling of social welfare, although rising costs lead to calls for reducing government involvement. The proposal to do this is accompanied by the anticipation that the marketplace and voluntary organizations will increase their participation. This has been termed moving from a welfare state to a welfare society, or a mixed economy of welfare, or welfare pluralism.[7]

Governments use various methods to escape the burden of social welfare costs. The simplest is simply to reduce budgets for that purpose. Another method is to allow or require responsibility to fall on small government units, such as states, counties, and cities. Still another method is to turn over certain services to for-profit or voluntary agencies. A number of researchers have examined how to decide when the market, the voluntary sector, the government, partnerships between the government and other agencies, and even private citizens should take over such services.

PRIVATIZATION

There have always been private, for-profit social welfare activities, such as hospitals, homes for the elderly, and child care arrangements, and voluntary efforts also preceded government programs by centuries. The earliest Charity Organization Societies were purely voluntary, and until the 1930s, most social welfare activities in the United States were carried out by voluntary groups such as labor unions, fraternal orders, ethnic associations, religious groups, community centers, and settlement houses. There has also always been an intermingling of government, voluntary, and private service providers. However, since the implementation of the Social Security Act in the United States and the Beveridge Plan in Britain, government functioning in social welfare has far outstripped the voluntary and the private sectors, at least in terms of money spent. In the United States the cost of government programs increased from $23.5 billion in 1950 to $428.3 billion in 1979.[8] The sheer size of the welfare budget is what propels most efforts toward privatization of the social services. So-called entitlement programs have become the fastest-growing segment of the federal budget.

Today, in many countries, including the United States, government agencies, institutions, and services are being turned over to public, voluntary, and membership organizations and to the private for-profit sector. This process has variously been called a shift from the public to the private sectors, a new welfare "mix," loadshedding, dumping, and corporatization. It has also been called denationalization, decentralization, and transfer from public to private ownership. However, the most common term for this process of change is *privatization.*

Privatization includes turning services over to both voluntary nonprofit organizations and for-profit businesses. Voluntary nonprofit organization—called "the third sector," as distinct from government and business— are characterized by a formal structure, legal independence, nonprofit distribution, voluntary activities, and production of a public benefit. The concept of the third sector was first introduced in the 1970s, and public discussion and research concerning this sector has burgeoned enormously since then. Kramer estimates that over 200 researchers in forty countries are studying this phenomenon, and twenty research centers have been established internationally.

Privatization has even affected social insurance. In the United Kingdom, workers may now opt out of the government pension scheme in favor of portable personal pensions. In Belgium, the work-injury program and the occupational disease program have been transferred to the private sector. Peru has recently allowed employees to opt for private pension schemes in place of the government program.[9]

Privatization is not confined to social welfare. A private firm has been assigned to run schools in Arizona, Minnesota, and Florida, among other states, and some states are turning their prisons over to private operators. In Israel, a private company has begun developing leisure-time activities in governmental nature reserves. In Brazil, the Social Services of Industry (SESI) is a private group supported by entrepreneurs who intend to "provide progress and public tranquillity" by extending welfare services to workers.

The most compelling way to increase privatization is to cut funds for needed activities, making it both necessary and profitable for others to undertake them. Thus, between 1982 and 1986 there was a 35% cut in federal spending for social services, and by 1988 this had become 42%. The WIN program, which spent $365 million in 1980, had been cut to $93 million by 1988. Unfortunately for welfare clients, state and local governments replaced only about 25% of these lost federal dollars.[10]

NONPROFIT VOLUNTARY ORGANIZATIONS

The political right is said to view voluntary nonprofit organizations as a bulwark against further government intervention in the lives of citizens, and the political left sees them as a means of achieving a sense of community, humanism, and altruism. However, the presumed differentiation between government and voluntary organizations is blurred by the fact that voluntary agencies are increasingly dependent upon government support, either through direct subsidies or contracts for the delivery of services. Nonprofit organizations cost the government about $12 billion a year in tax exemptions alone. In New York City, 80% of the $1 billion spent for social services goes to private agencies under contract. Over half of all federally funded personal social services are now provided by nongovernmental organizations. One study indicates that purchase-of-services contracting ranked second among all revenue sources for the agencies studied, and even church-related agencies receive as much as 80% of their funding from government sources. In fact, many voluntary organizations would cease to exist without some sort of government support.[11]

The need to secure adequate financing makes both the nonprofit and for-profit sectors dependent on government subsidies, and it also may shape their activities. Morris has said that investor-owned services are more efficient when it comes to securing reimbursement, but not in service delivery. Gronjberg goes further and says that nonprofit organizations are so busy trying to find enough money to stay in existence that they must neglect the poor they are supposed to be serving. Nevertheless, the use of voluntary organizations is generally seen as resulting in lower costs, more flexibility, and fewer bureaucratic restrictions.[12]

FOR-PROFIT SOCIAL WELFARE ORGANIZATIONS

Although the major motivation for privatization is to save the government money, the rationalization often offered for this move is the efficiency and effectiveness that can be expected, especially from for-profit enterprises. Such organizations are also believed to be more innovative, more participatory, and more cost-effective. However, the evidence is far from conclusive. Because attempts at empirical evaluation of the results of privatization are relatively rare, the discussion is often "in metaphysical terms."[13] One study

shows that many contracts are issued to private firms not because of anticipated savings, but simply because the public agency does not have the staff
and expertise to perform some desired function.

The assumption that only a profit motive will lead to efficiency—and thus
cost-savings—is popular, but a study of work relief in the 1930s found that
worker cooperatives and worker-run idle factories were operated efficiently
by industrial standards. More recently, a study of homes for the aged done
in Great Britain found that small homes were more efficient when privately
run, whereas large institutions were less costly under government auspices.
The savings in the small homes resulted from the low wages paid, the lack
of employee unionization, and the fact that many were mom-and-pop operations where the proprietors often worked 70 hours a week each—and sometimes as many as 93 hours—without pay.

A study of for-profit and nonprofit hospitals concluded that for-profit
hospitals were costlier, and nonprofit institutions were no less efficient. In
fact, standards of quality do not seem markedly different whether the ownership is governmental, nonprofit, or for-profit. Most studies examine only
the costs to the organization, and not the cost to the clients or to the public
as a whole, to whom the costs may be shifted. Glennerster estimates that if
the whole social security system in Britain were to be transferred to for-profit
auspices, costs to the general public would rise from the one and a half
pounds sterling per week per person prevalent in 1990 to at least four pounds
sterling by 1999.[14]

After services are turned over to private operators, cost increases may
begin—involving one out of three private contracts in the sample studied.
Government agencies then find themselves powerless to control the prices
of private, for-profit firms. When they attempt to do so, they find it difficult
to obtain competitive bids. Therefore, "many governments are captives of
the private contractors providing services to their communities."[15]

On a more pragmatic level, it has been found that the more governmental
bodies continue to demand certain standards, apply regulatory constraints,
and evaluate results in privately run programs—which they do more in social
services than in other sectors—the less inclined for-profit organizations are
to engage in these enterprises.

The effectiveness/efficiency rationale for privatization clearly flows from
Adam Smith's theory that free competition and the economic man will
produce the best goods at the least cost. Smith never envisioned cartels,
monopolies, subsidies, protective tariffs, and worldwide interlocking fiscal

policies—all of which affect the free market today. His theory of "pure" competition is an ideology underlying many of the social and welfare changes that took place during the Reagan/Bush administration.

As Matthews says, advocates of privatization seem to see it as a form of theology, whereas others adopt the role of exorcists attacking a new form of demonology. But privatization is neither a panacea nor an abomination. There are no inherent reasons why a program run by a privately controlled entity will be any more or less expensive, any worse or better managed, than a publicly run program. Although privatization may be the preferred solution to some welfare problems, nongovernment agencies have their own problems and pathologies. It is therefore doubtful whether privatization will "magically overcome the mundane but common problems of poor management and greed."[16]

Welfare Reform

Welfare reform is often used as a euphemism for efforts to get persons seen as exploiting the welfare system off the welfare rolls and into employment. The major thrust is directed at categorical and grant programs, rather than at social insurance or universal programs. The result has been a proliferation of programs to punish people who do not work, who have children out of wedlock, who continue to have children although on welfare, whose children do not attend school regularly, and so forth. One facet has been the growth in programs to motivate and prepare welfare recipients for employment, despite past experience showing that these efforts produce only limited results.

Welfare reform, as distinct from privatization, has little effect on entitlement programs. It is targeted primarily at AFDC, general relief, and—to some extent—food stamps. Recognizing that complete government withdrawal from the social welfare area is neither possible nor desirable, one way to reduce government involvement is to enable people to help themselves. This has been called "the enabling state," rather than the welfare state. The role of government, in this view, is to enable people to deal with their own problems progressively, through education, training, motivating, and so forth. In most cases, the end goal is to get relief recipients to go to work or, put more euphemistically, "increasing the capacity of families to care for themselves through jobs."[17]

THE FEAR OF DEPENDENCY

As with entitlement programs, a major motivation of welfare reform has been the rising costs of welfare. However, there is also widespread concern that under the welfare state, individuals will lose their taste for responsibility, freedom, and decision making. Some worry that if people are not motivated by their fear of a possible future disaster to work, save, or plan ahead, the human race may become "amiable idiots," and the progress of civilization will cease.

There is little empirical support for the hypothesis that the welfare state has deleterious effects upon people's character. Instead, research indicates that changes in welfare levels do not, as charged, contribute to family disintegration. Studies examining the relationship between benefit levels and out-of-wedlock births have consistently shown no significant association. In fact, women on welfare want and have fewer children than those who are not on welfare.

Nor does the presumed work disincentive of welfare programs hold up in the face of research. In Britain, it was found that unemployment insurance did not influence the supply of labor or labor force participation between World Wars I and II. A more recent study examined the possible expansion in work patterns of the elderly if social welfare restrictions on their earnings were to be removed. It was found that this change would have no effect on 84% to 95% of the participants.[18] In a cross-national study, the question was whether the amount of welfare payments affects work patterns. The conclusion:

> No correlation appears between the level of replacement ratios in a country and the extent or depth of its belief, as expressed in popular, official and academic opinions, that replacement ratios are too high and act as a work disincentive.[19]

In other words, people will believe that welfare payments are too high and keep others from working—no matter how low payments actually are. If they are properly designed, controlled, and financed, the redistributive effects of welfare need have no depressing effect on work incentives. In fact, a proper welfare system increases wealth.

EXAMPLES FROM ABROAD

Critics of social welfare often denigrate the high level of welfare support in the Scandinavian countries by referring to the alcoholism and the suicide and divorce rates there, which they assume are correlated with generous financial support. Of course, correlation is not causation, but most important, studies indicate that the facts critics cite are spurious. It is almost impossible to compare alcoholism rates, due to the various definitions and methods of counting in different countries. Many Scandinavians attribute the alcoholism in their region to the long, severe winter. Suicide rates are also difficult to compare: In some places, suicides are listed as accidents or natural deaths if possible, sometimes to spare the family and sometimes for religious reasons in cultures where suicide is considered a sin. However, the United Nations publishes comparative national suicide rates, and Hungary—not noted for liberal social welfare policies—has higher suicide rates than do Sweden, Norway, Denmark, and Finland. Austria has a higher rate than do Sweden and Norway. As for divorce, the United States has one of the highest rates in the world. Denmark and Finland are surpassed by five other countries, and Sweden and Norway are well down on the list.[20]

WELFARE REFORM AND AFDC

Welfare reform expresses itself most clearly in policies regarding AFDC mothers. The avowed intent of the original ADC act was to allow and encourage mothers to stay home and take care of their children. The public image behind the law was of the genteel, middle-class, white widow unable to sustain herself and her children, forced to leave the children every day in order to go to work. Everyone saw her as deserving of help, and her children as precious assets entitled to the best education and other opportunities. However, when AFDC began to operate, the program took an unforeseen turn:

> The New Deal sponsors of AFDC had intended to help the widow with small children. The support she received would tide her over in the interim between the loss of her husband and the day when the children were old enough to take over her support. . . . By the fifties it had become embarrassingly, outrageously clear that most of these women were not widows. Many of them had not even been married. Worst of all, they didn't stop having babies after the first lapse [sic]. They kept having more. This had not been part of the plan.[21]

The AFDC program, in its various forms, has grown into the largest noninsurance welfare program in the United States. When it began as part of Social Security in 1936, 162,000 families received $49.7 million in benefits.

In 1975, more than 3.5 million families received assistance totaling more than $9 billion. By 1989, the average *monthly* number of recipient families was close to 4 million, representing over 11 million individuals; total payments were $17.5 billion dollars. The phenomenal growth in AFDC recipients and costs came to be seen by the general public and legislators alike not as an indication of the depth and breadth of poverty in the United States, but as evidence of the mendacity of the poor.[22]

Either as cause or as effect, the public image behind AFDC changed to that of an unmarried African American teenager who had children in order to receive more money. This view was bolstered by statistics showing that in 1960, 15% of non-white children were living in female-headed households, but by 1985 this figure had risen to 51%.[23] The movement for welfare reform, epitomized by the Family Support Act of 1988, was born in the 1980s out of a confluence of factors:

- the economic cost of supporting nonworking single parents who continued to have more children
- outrage at the presumed lack of morality exhibited by welfare recipients, their lack of appreciation for what was being done for them, and their purported acceptance of dependency rather than undertaking to improve themselves by working
- racism expressed in the imputation that most such recipients are non-white
- the reagan/Bush ideology of "least government"

The major foci of welfare reform were AFDC and general assistance, with the latter playing a minor role. It is interesting that these are means-tested programs; universal programs that cost the same and support some of the same recipients were hardly criticized. The Social Security Administration, through its Old-Age, Survivors', and Disability Insurance (OASDI) program and through the Supplemental Security Income (SSI) program, pays out nearly as much money as the AFDC program in a typical month, but these do not provoke public outrage.

AFDC AND MOTIVATION TO WORK

Before the Family Support Act of 1988 was adopted, AFDC used a number of devices to force mothers to go to work—on pain of withholding payments. The program was responsible in great part for the proliferation of child care programs, which were generally established, not as educational or family-welfare programs, but as baby-sitting operations that removed the excuse of child care duties from mothers viewed as basically lazy. With the adoption of the Work Incentive Program (WIN) in 1967, which required applicants to accept any job available or undergo training, a double standard for families was established. White middle-class women were insisting on equal pay and equal opportunities; women in welfare families were expected to take any job, at any pay.

AFDC has used a number of other devices that are basically antifamily. Because married couples living together were not eligible for AFDC at one point, regardless of income, desertion was rewarded. If the mother knew the whereabouts of her husband, she was required to notify law enforcement officers (known in welfare jargon as NOLEO—notice to law enforcement officers). To be eligible for help, she was legally required to name the father. Midnight raids on welfare households to detect signs of a man in the house—a hat, a cigar—were common.

The WIN regulations of AFDC became operative in 1967, but by 1980 WIN was doing very little actual training. The 1973 Comprehensive Employment and Training Act (CETA) was intended to provide disadvantaged adults with temporary public sector jobs. So many recipients returned to welfare or unemployment benefits that Congress replaced it in 1982 with the Job Training and Partnership Act, which emphasized private training schemes rather than public sector employment. However, a New York study concluded that few welfare recipients obtain jobs after taking government-financed training at private schools. Only 4% found jobs and left the welfare rolls.[24]

The Omnibus Budget and Reconciliation Act of 1981 and the Tax Equity Fiscal Responsibility Act of 1982 were mandatory workfare and training programs, in the sense that refusal to take part in them could lead to a reduction or loss of benefits. Examination of a hundred welfare studies since 1975 by the General Accounting Office found no firm evidence that welfare greatly discouraged people from working, broke up families, or encouraged unmarried women to become pregnant just to receive benefits. However, public opinion continued to hold that welfare, and particularly AFDC, caused immorality, broken families, and avoidable dependency.

DEPENDENCE AND PAUPERISM

The words *dependent, dependence,* and *dependency* have taken on a pejorative aspect, although babies are dependent on their parents, citizens are dependent in many ways on their governments, businesses are dependent on laws and regulations, and in society as a system, people are dependent on one another. Nevertheless, in social welfare jargon, dependency has become a synonym for pauperism. Dependency is seen as purposeful malingering—not merely reliance on benefits, but refusal to join the mainstream work and family system. It is seen as an aberration to be cured, shelved, or "treated" as a disease. Some fear that public assistance creates dependency and that this dependency gives rise to a deviant and persistent subculture—a subset of the poor whose poverty is somehow attributable to their behavior. Rees notes that if the effort had been termed *welfare support,* or *welfare strengthening,* rather than *welfare reform,* the actions that followed would have been quite different.[25]

THE FAMILY SUPPORT ACT OF 1988

The 1988 Family Support Act provides a good example of welfare reform. It arose from a combination of motivations:

- the burgeoning of costs
- the presumed acceptance, if not support, of immoral behavior, represented by unwed, often teen-age, mothers
- the lack of social responsibility attributed to absent fathers and nonworking mothers
- the fostering of poverty by simply supporting the poor
- the feared political repercussions of being seen as soft on welfare cheats

The act emphasizes the short-term, temporary nature of public assistance and reemphasizes that all parents, regardless of income, have an obligation to support their children financially. Even mothers with preschool children are expected to work, if child care is available. The act also made it possible for states to experiment with various means of coping with the problem. Among other things, the act provides for universal withholding from a parent's wages of court-ordered child support payments, even if this impairs the relationship between the parents. Mothers with children 3 years or older are required to participate in job training programs, but states have the option of lowering the child's age to 1 year if appropriate child care facilities are available.

Some states immediately took advantage of the act to change their regulations. New Jersey now denies additional benefits to mothers on welfare who have more children. The program also requires that welfare parents whose youngest child is at least 2 years old —almost all of them single mothers—participate in educational, employment, or job training programs. Recipients of AFDC whose youngest child is under age 2 are required to take part in vocational assessment and counseling in preparation for the job market. Virginia is experimenting with a program that would pay a bonus to AFDC parents whose children have good school attendance records and would cut payments by one-third to parents convicted of educational neglect. Maryland cuts payments for poor school attendance or for not getting preventive health care. Wisconsin cuts payments by as much as 43% for truancy or dropouts.

Some states now offer "marriage bonuses" and deny additional benefits for children born to women on welfare. "Wedfare" or "bridefare" proposals require women on welfare to marry and have fewer children in order to qualify for aid. "Edfare" and "learnfare" programs cut benefits to families who fail to keep kids in school. "Healthfare" penalizes families who do not see a doctor. "Housefare" cuts payments to parents who fail to pay rent on time. Seeking fraud, some states now also fingerprint welfare mothers.

One of the most intensively pursued goals of the Family Support Act is to require and/or increase personal responsibility. One aspect of this is taking legal measures to require fathers—married or not—to contribute to the support of their children. Another part is to transform welfare recipients—popularly viewed as unwed, African American, teenage mothers—into respectable, responsible, working women by furnishing child care facilities for their children, while motivating, training, and helping them to find and take jobs.

Workfare provisions of welfare reform are intended to reduce (a) welfare costs, (b) welfare dependency and its negative effect on recipients, and (c) the unfair burden imposed on taxpayers, who are carrying their own weight and should not have to sustain those who choose to live without working.

WORKFARE

Most states have undertaken some kind of job training for relief recipients, in many cases contracting this out to for-profit agencies. The general acronym for these programs is WEPs, or Welfare Employment Programs. The individual programs bear a variety of names, many of them also acronyms, such as JJI, EPP, CWEP, TRADE, WDP, TOPS, OJT, ESP, JOBS, GAIN, and MATCH. A few have full names, such as MAXIMUS and America Works.

Evaluations of such programs include the lyrical descriptions of sponsors countered by great cynicism toward others.

The WEPs have trouble finding eligible participants. Despite popular mythology, only a minority of welfare recipients are employable. Whereas one third of AFDC mothers seem employable, the rest are working, in training, incapacitated, or needed at home. Employable mothers constitute a tiny 6.7% of all 17 million welfare recipients; the rest are children, elderly, or people with disabilities. Almost 55% of the caseload in 1984 had health-related problems or child care responsibilities that prevented or limited their ability to work. In 1992, the JOBS program served only 11% of welfare recipients, and they were often clients already motivated to improve their circumstances—people who would probably have left welfare on their own. About half of those in the program chose some form of education—only 3% were in community work experience or workfare. Only a minority of AFDC adults participate in GAIN.[26]

A study of GAIN and JOBS programs found that the employment rate was 17% higher among participants than among controls, and that there was a 5% drop in welfare rolls. However, a General Accounting Office study in 1987 found only a 5% to 7% difference in employment between experimental and control groups. Nor did finding a job necessarily mean going off welfare. Most jobs found by participants were part-time and low paid, and thus in half of the programs reporting, more than 48% of the participants remained on AFDC. In a careful study of thirteen demonstration WEP programs, it was found that no one's earnings were increased by as much as $1,000 a year. However, costs of the programs ranged from $158 per participant to $3,060, averaging over $600 per participant. Ellwood found that a participant's income is usually increased $200 to $750 annually, and a *New York Times* study found that program participants earned an average of $1,902 a year more than members of a control group.[27]

Employment training programs show short-term results for some—usually white males. For most welfare recipients, success is usually a short-term job with a high probability of returning to the welfare rolls. Of the approximate 21% who left welfare because of earnings between 1968 and 1981, only 30% had annual earnings of more than $8,000, not enough to push a family of four above the poverty line of that period. In addition, 40% of all women who leave with an earnings increase eventually return to welfare. As many people are leaving work for welfare as the reverse. Abramovitz points out that although such programs may improve the self-esteem and even employability of some workers, they also may displace others by giving a job to a welfare mother instead of another worker, or by taking a job away from someone, who must the apply for AFDC. There have been few studies of such trade-offs.[28]

Proponents of welfare reform have greeted workfare with enthusiasm, but all of the programs combined have not put a noticeable dent in the total welfare caseload. The most successful programs reduced welfare rolls by 10%. Congress, as it enacted workfare requirements, expected a modest impact: removal of 1.3% of families from the welfare rolls after five years. There is no reliable, generalizable, replicable evidence that workfare gets people off welfare. In 1831 Earl Grey called upon parliament to promote "habits of industry" among the working class, and Lord Attwood pointed out that under the circumstances, with millions of people unsuccessfully seeking work, such an attitude was a "cold insult" to them. One could say the same about workfare today. Atherton, for one, holds that there is no reason to suppose that the provisions of Family Support Act will be more effective than similar programs have been during the past 400 years.

In the short run, this type of welfare reform costs more than welfare itself. Helping people become self-supporting is extremely expensive. Training usually costs more than the wage that many of the trainees receive in the way of increased personal income. Thus, it may be that the aim of saving money and the aim reforming welfare are mutually exclusive.

SUMMARY

For a number of reasons, including the rising cost of social welfare expenditures and the persistence of problems such as poverty and unemployment, there has been a move to turn government-sponsored services over to for-profit and nonprofit groups. This has been phrased as moving from a welfare state to a welfare society. In contrast, welfare reform puts emphasis on reshaping programs to get people off the dole and into the workforce. Unfortunately, studies indicate that laudable as this goal may be, reforms have done little to reduce cost, increase independence, or reduce the burden on the taxpayer.

EXERCISES

A.   A proposal has been made to turn the university or school in which you study over to an international conglomerate, which will operate it for the highest profit possible. What would you foresee as a result in terms of:

1. the composition of the student body?
2. course offerings?
3. faculty?
4. competence of graduates?
5. effect on the student community as a whole?

B.   A proposal has been made to sell shares in the university or school in which you study on the stock exchange, with the provision that the institution will be run, for profit, by a joint committee of stockholders and students. What would you foresee as a result, in terms of:

1. the composition of the student body?
2. course offerings?
3. faculty?
4. competence of graduates?
5. effect on the student community as a whole?

C.   A proposal has been made to give all students equal shares in the university or school in which you study—sharing in both financial gains or losses and in the direction of the institution.
   Would you be in favor of such a move? Why, or why not?

D.   A proposal has been made to give all students both financial and policy making powers in the university or school in which you study. The higher your grades, the more shares and voting power will be con- ferred on you.
   Would you be in favor of such a move? Why, or why not?

E.   It has been said that the cause of problems is solutions. Welfare reform is intended as a solution to the problems of the social welfare system. How would you evaluate the following attempts to deal with these problems?

1. If all welfare clients were required to hold jobs, even if some of these jobs were meaningless make-work, what would be the effect on:
   a.   individuals?
   b.   infants and children?
   c.   the economy?
   d.   society?

2. If all welfare programs paid one half of their current rates, what would be the effect on:
   a.   individuals?
   b.   employment?
   c.   poverty?
   d.   dependent people and those with disabilities?
   e.   the economy?
   f.   society at large?

3. If all welfare programs paid twice their current rates, what would be the effect on:
   a.   individuals?
   b.   employment?
   c.   poverty?
   d.   dependent people and those with disabilities?
   e.   the economy?
   f.   society at large?

Notes

1. The 1941 date is from Temple (1967).
2. The quotation is from Marshall (1965).
3. Statistics on the growth of programs are from U.S. Department of Health and Human Services (1992).

4. The quotation is from Kurland (1974).

5. Titmuss (1967).

6. President Hoover is quoted by Titmuss (1967) and by Schlesinger (1967).

7. The phrases *welfare society* and so on are from Barretta-Herman (1992).

8. Costs of programs are from McMillan & Bixby (1980).

9. The statistics are from Kramer (1993), as are the characteristics of the "third sector."

10. Statistics are from the following sources: 35% cut, Wolch (1990); 42% cut, Johnson (1989); WIN program cuts, Gueron & Long (1990); replacement rate, Wolch (1990).

11. Statistics are from the following sources: cost of tax exemptions, Ferris & Graddy (1989); New York City expenses, Netting, McMurty, Kettner, & Jones-McClintic (1990); one half to nongovernment organizations, Kramer (1993); 80% of funds from government, Netting et al. (1990). Moskowitz (1989) predicted the end of organizations without government support.

12. Morris (1987); Gronjberg (1990).

13. The phrase is from Van Horn (1991), who also provides the reason for many contracts.

14. Glennerster (1992).

15. The quotation is from Van Horn (1991).

16. Matthews (1989); the quotation is from Van Horn (1991), as is the conclusion that privatization is neither panacea nor abomination.

17. *Enabling state* is from Gilbert & Gilbert, 1989; the quotation is from Nichols-Casebolt & McClure (1989).

18. The statistics are from Packard (1990).

19. The quotation is Reubens (1989).

20. Suicide and divorce rates are from United Nations (1992c).

21. The quotation is from Murray (1984).

22. The growth in AFDC funds is from Current Operating Statistics (1977). The other figures are from *Social Security Bulletin* (1991; *54*[6], 10).

23. The 1960 figure on children in female-headed households is from Berrick (1991); the 1985 figure is from Taylor, Chatters, Tucker, & Lewis (1991).

24. The 4% figure is from Berger (1989).

25. Rees (1992).

26. The 6.7% figure is from Dear (1989), and the 55% figure is from Nichols-Casebolt & McClure (1989).

27. Statistics are from the following sources: the 17% employment rate, Riccio & Friedlander (1992); the General Accounting Office study, Abramovitz (1992); the thirteen demonstration programs, Greenberg & Wiseman (1992); Ellwood (1989); the *The New York Times* (October 25, 1992; p. 41E).

28. The 21% figure is from Nichols-Casebolt & McClure (1989); Moroney (1991) mentions the movement from work to welfare; Abramovitz (1992).

READ MORE ABOUT IT . . .

For more information on:	*See these sources:*
Definitions of the welfare state	Mishra, 1990; Pampel & Williamson, 1989; Pierson, 1991
Objectives of the welfare state	Jackson, 1989; Papadakis & Taylor-Gooby, 1987
Welfare in Athens	Hasebroek, 1933; Gouldner, 1969
Welfare in Britain	Titmuss, 1959
Beveridge's activities	Woodroofe, 1962
Alternatives to the welfare state	Marshall, 1965
Structural and residual concepts of social welfare	Wilensky & Lebeaux, 1958
Argument for private insurance	Murray, 1984
Sharing welfare responsibilities	Gormley, 1991; Loewenberg, 1992
"Shift" from public to private sector	Jackson, 1989
Welfare "mix"	"Experts Consultation," 1986
Privatization	Starr, 1985
in the United Kingdom	U.S. Department of Health and Human Services, 1989
in Belgium	U.S. Department of Health and Human Services, 1989
in Peru	U.S. Department of Health and Human Services, 1992
in schools	*Baltimore Sun* (July 23, 1992; p. 3B)
in prisons	Matthews, 1989
in Israel	"Leisure Company Opens," 1991
in Brazil	*SESI: Procedures and Objectives,* n.d.

For more information on:	*See these sources:*
Dumping	Karger & Stoesz, 1989
Corporatization	Karger & Stoesz, 1989
Loadshedding	Bendick, 1985
Efficiency of for-profit agencies	Savas, 1987
Innovativeness of for-profit agencies	Brenton, 1985
Inconclusiveness of studies	Karger & Stoesz, 1989; Kramer, 1981; Morris, 1987; Thayer, 1987
Worker-run industries	Rose, 1989
British homes for the aged	Judge & Knapp, 1985
Hospital cost-efficiency studies	Carroll, Conant, & Easton, 1987; Karger & Stoesz, 1989
No differences despite ownership	Hollingsworth & Hollingsworth, 1986; Kramer, 1993
Cost increases under private owners	Van Horn, 1991
Effect of government demands on for-profits	Matthews, 1989; Pack, 1991
Welfare reform not affecting entitlement programs	Macarov, 1993
"The enabling state"	Gilbert & Gilbert, 1989; Menzies, 1992
Lack of evidence that welfare state ruins character	Goodin, 1988
Relationship between benefits and births	Aponte, Neckerman, & Wilson, 1985
Effects of British unemployment	Reubens, 1989
Welfare increasing wealth	Mitchell, 1992

For more information on:	*See these sources:*
Cost of Social Security vs. AFDC	"Security for America's Children," 1992
White middle-class vs. welfare women	Hareven, 1974
History of AFDC	Handler & Hollingsworth, 1971
WIN and other training programs	Hill, 1992
The Omnibus Budget and Reconciliation Act	Hill, 1992
The GAO study of welfare's effects	Zimmerman, 1988
Dependency as pauperism	Katz, 1986
Dependency as malingering	Hill, 1992
Dependency as an aberration	Morris, 1986
Dependency as a subculture	Hill, 1992
Preschool children and Family Support Act	Hagen, 1992
New Jersey AFDC rules	*The New York Times* (July 26, 1992, p. 18)
AFDC in Virginia, Maryland, and Wisconsin	*Washington Post* (July 21, 1992, p. D4)
Fingerprinting welfare mothers	Abramovitz, 1992
Acronyms for training programs	Greenberg & Wiseman, 1992
JOBS and GAIN programs	Offner, 1992
Congressional intent for workfare	Hill, 1992
Effects of workfare	DeParle, 1994; Hill, 1992; Offner, 1992

For more information on:	*See these sources:*
Expense of making people self-supporting	Hill, 1992
Earl Grey/Attwood Debate	Hugo, 1965
Saving and reform mutually exclusive	Dear, 1989

16. Description, Prediction, and Prescription

This chapter suggests four very probable changes in society that will necessitate changes in the welfare system and offers a riskier prediction concerning culmination of current trends.

In the preceding fifteen chapters, the motivations and influences that shape current social welfare have been described. The context within which that shape is molded—such as the composition of the population, the structure of the economy, and the legislative process—have been taken as givens. However, in looking toward the future, it may be easier to predict changes in these contexts than to predict changes in human motivations or attitudes. Motivations and attitudes are notoriously difficult to predict, in part because they are themselves reactions to changes in social contexts. Hence, the predictions that follow deal with structures, situations, and processes that will require changes in social welfare policy.

Predicting the future is a risky business. One of the dilemmas of the human condition is that all experience and knowledge is about the past, whereas decisions must be made about the future. However, unanticipated events usually occur in addition to, rather than in place of, anticipated changes. Economic projections, at least, are usually accurate for up to ten years, although some much longer range forecasts have also proved themselves. For example, of the 137 devices imagined by George Orwell in his book *1984*, written over forty years ago, over a hundred are now in use.[1]

Some changes can be likened to tidal waves—suddenly, within a relatively short time, immense changes take place. The emergence of AIDS and homelessness as social problems fits this pattern. Other changes are more like an incoming tide; they slowly but inexorably proceed until they become visible. Growth in the number of the elderly and variations in family structures are cases in point. Finally, some changes are like underground water—they have to be searched out. An example is the effect of technology on social welfare.

Four Probable Predictions

Some changes are rooted in current situations. The predictions that follow are drawn from the data and analysis of the preceding chapters. Predictions will be made about (a) growth in the aged population, (b) changes in the working population, (c) technological innovations, and (d) the growing permanency of unemployment.

GROWTH IN THE AGED POPULATION

The aged stratum of the population will certainly grow quickly in the years to come. People already alive will move into their later years in ever-increasing numbers as life expectancy continues to lengthen (as noted in Chapter 10). Those now being born will live much longer than those born a generation or more ago. The rise in life expectancy arises from improvements in housing, nutrition, medicine, sanitation, and a number of other factors that will not reverse themselves. Thus if life expectancy stops increasing, it will certainly not become shorter.

An anticipated growth in the number and proportion of the elderly will be accompanied by more poverty among those dependent primarily on pensions. No existing insurance programs—government, private, or commercial—are actuarially based on paying premiums for ten, twenty, thirty, and more years. Moreover, 40% of the elderly have no prospect of a pension other than Social Security. One in five households have no net assets, and one in seven has no health insurance.[2]

Increasing taxation of the young to support the elderly will reach a point at which it is neither sufficient nor capable of further increase. Attempts to raise taxes further will result in political repercussions. Attempts to raise retirement ages to allow the elderly to keep working will clash with efforts to reduce unemployment by providing jobs for younger people.

In addition, the increase in the number of the aged will mean more ill or incapacitated people, many of whom will need years and even decades of care, as conditions that once resulted in relatively early death become treatable. The existence of more incapacitated elders will interfere with the desire of traditional caregivers—daughters—to enter the labor force. Among the healthy aged, the need for satisfying leisure activities will be felt. The increasing number of widows compared to the smaller increase in widowers will create social problems for both sexes. Repeated marriages and divorces will result in a web of various relationships with children, grandchildren, relatives by marriage, and the like.

The altruistic and humanitarian efforts demanded by the needs of the elderly will collide with economic and political realities. Relatives' responsibility will be increasingly cited and regularly resisted. Eventually, structural changes in social welfare will be needed to support the aged, and particularly to minister to those who are incapacitated.

CHANGES IN THE WORKING POPULATION

A recent phenomenon has been the move from an industrial to a service economy. At one time over 90% of the population engaged in agriculture, and today less than 3% in the United States do so. In the same way, industry provided the bulk of U.S. jobs, but today they provide less than 20%. By the end of this century, service employment is likely to constitute from 95% to 97% of all employment.[3]

By their nature, service jobs are more easily divided into several part-time jobs, which can often be filled by what are called "contingent" workers— hired when needed and fired with ease. This both facilitates and exploits the hiring of previously nonworking women in firms that have declared their intention to be "lean and mean." Many women are not available for full-time or permanent jobs due to family conditions; others want full-time work but settle for part-time jobs as the only positions available to them. Indeed, about 40% of part-time workers would rather work full-time.[4] Many part-time and contingent workers will be employed in care of the elderly—health aides, home care aides, companions, and so forth. "Workfare" provisions, which require mothers even of infants to work, will require increasing child care facilities, again offering some low-paying jobs to basically unskilled child care help.

The needs for elder care and child care will in large part be handled by part-time, temporary women workers, many of them entering the labor force for the first time. Unless their low pay is merely supplementing the full-time income of another family worker, they will join the "working poor" category. Because part-time and temporary workers are hardly covered under OASDI and unemployment compensation programs, are rarely unionized, and have few benefits such as vacations and holidays, increasing their numbers should also increase demands for changes in current social welfare policies. Because most of such workers will be new entrants into the labor force, the impact of their new jobs in reducing unemployment will be minimal.

TECHNOLOGICAL INNOVATIONS

One of the striking phenomena of modern times is the growth, and the pace of growth, of technology. Technology is sought and used for four major reasons: to simplify work, to increase production, to reduce costs, and to overcome problems too difficult for human hands. One effect of widespread use of technology is to change the nature and the content of work. It would be a mistake to think of robots replacing humans in their present jobs. One early proponent of automation, writing in 1971, confessed that he could not visualize a robot, instead of a milkman, placing a milk bottle on his porch in the morning.[5] Most readers of this book have probably never seen a milkman delivering milk, or milk in a glass bottle, or even a porch. Technology changes entire systems, not just individual jobs.

Technology often begins with those jobs that are difficult, dangerous, dirty, or demeaning—in short, the jobs that humans tend to avoid. In this sense, work becomes easier and cleaner. In addition, work safety records indicate that jobs today are much safer than they were in the past. Built-in "fail safe" devices, better engineering and construction, activities that are mechanically or electronically confined to safe limits, and other such devices all have contributed to the reduction in occupational accidents.

The introduction of automation in its various forms may reduce workers' tasks to pushing buttons and watching dials—a deskilling of work—with subsequent changes in their attitudes, gratifications, and self-images. Some fear that work will also become dehumanized, as workers and clients relate to machines rather than to people. One aspect of this prediction has to do with the relationships of workers in the workplace. Instead of relating to other people—talking to one another, sharing in the completion of tasks, and playing out social roles—workers will be relating to machines. This will mean a loss of social contacts and sociability and a frustration of gregarious needs. So strong is the need for relationships that workers in technologically centered jobs have been known to name their machines and to talk to and about the machine as though it were a person. On the other side, use of new technology increases free time on the job, with subsequent opportunities for socializing with other workers.

As a result of technology, the labor force may become polarized between a minority with challenging, interesting, ego-satisfying work, in power-wielding and influential positions, and a majority with banal, monotonous jobs. Continuing growth of technology will lead to many other changes, both within and outside the area of work. From a social welfare point of view, the major impact will be in the field of employment.

PERMANENT UNEMPLOYMENT

The problem of unemployment will probably become more urgent with the passage of time. Although some disagree, a large and growing number of people believe that technological changes will reduce the need for human labor in the future. For example, microelectronic devices are much simpler to manufacture than the products they replace, require much less labor to operate, and have longer life expectancies. As a consequence of technology, productivity of the individual worker rises constantly: In 1850 people used 13% of their total energy at work; today they use less than 1%. In 1950, every employed civilian worker in the United States produced $5,000 of the Gross National Product. In 1975, this had risen to $16,000. It is predicted that by the year 2000, this will be $85,000. If current increases continue, by the year 2100 every worker will produce $5 million worth of the GNP.[6]

Continuing unemployment has given rise to a generally accepted categorization that includes *frictional, structural,* and *cyclical* unemployment, each of which is time-limited, requiring only short-term or temporary help. However, as unemployment grows, especially among inner-city African American youths, an additional category has emerged as a growing challenge to social welfare policy makers: permanent unemployment. The importance of permanent unemployment is emphasized by the finding that a 1% increase in unemployment is correlated with 30,000 deaths, 20,000 of them from heart attacks.[7]

Current social welfare policy ignores the possibility of permanently unemployed people, holding to the myth that jobs are available but that people are either untrained or unmotivated. Social workers seek solutions to unemployment within this framework, with increasing frustration as the result. Current arrangements will not suffice in the face of the growing numbers of the permanently unemployed.

Prescriptions

As the population—and hence the workforce—grows, and as technology continues to enlarge the productivity capacity of every worker, society will have to alter the present attitudes and expectations about work: that everyone who can work must work and that jobs can be provided for each of them—even if they are part-time, low-paying jobs. Another method of distributing the resources of society will have to be found, and with it will come a dethroning of work as the highest value of society, the measure of human beings, and the only acceptable role for individuals.

A number of possibilities have been suggested, including redefining paid work to include home making, child rearing, volunteering, and community activity. Another suggestion goes further, proposing to pay people for engaging in what are now considered recreational activities, such as playing musical instruments, engaging in sports, writing memoirs, and so forth. Still more radical suggestions include the ownership of technology by groups of (former) workers; forming cooperatives of workers in which all income from every source would be divided equally; and forming collectives, like the Israeli kibbutz, in which everyone is provided the necessities and luxuries of life without regard for their activities.

Methods of arriving at new distribution systems in the almost-workless world to come include adoption of family allowances where they do not currently exist; expanding such allowances to provide basic living costs; and changing them to individual allowances, thus distributing the resources created by technology to everyone and assuring everyone a basic income.

Although plans are diverse, there is growing unanimity that some day in the not-too-distant future work will have to replaced as the basis of society, simply because there won't be enough of it to go around.

Changes of this sort will create very different motivations and influences on the social welfare system, resulting in a completely different structure. Conversely, a new societal order will emerge only insofar as mutual aid, humanitarianism, religion, and so forth, will permit, encourage, discourage, or shape it.

Conclusion

Social welfare arises from various motivations, such as mutual aid, religion, politics, economics, and ideology; it is acted upon by a number of influences, among them the ideas of Luther, Darwin, and Adam Smith. Social welfare takes place within the context of existing societal structures, situations, processes, and events. At present, four major problems confront the social welfare establishment: poverty, unemployment, attempts to change the welfare state into a welfare society, and program amendments subsumed under the heading of welfare reform.

Future changes in the overarching framework that will affect social welfare include the growth of the aged sector of the population, the entry of increasing numbers of women into the labor force, the growth of part-time and temporary work, continued growth of technology, and the emergence of permanent unemployment.

As these become manifest, they will require major societal changes, which will be affected by and have impacts upon social welfare. Perhaps Pogo has phrased it best: "We are confronted by insurmountable opportunities."

EXERCISES

A. Envision a society in which goods and services are provided by technology and in which religiosity is the highest value.

1. Who would be the elite of such a society?
2. Who would be the middle class?
3. Who would be the neglected, isolated, rejected?

B. Envision such a technologized society in which education is the highest value.

1. Who would be the elite of such a society?
2. Who would be the middle class?
3. Who would be the neglected, isolated, rejected?

C. Envision such societies, a society, in which music is th e highest value.

1. Who would be the elite in such a society?
2. Who would be the middle class?
3. Who would be the neglected, isolated, rejected?

D. Envision such a society, in which sports is the highest value.

1. Who would be the elite in such a society?
2. Who would be the middle class?
3. Who would be the neglected, isolated, rejected?

E. Envision such a society, in which personal strength is the highest value.

1. Who would be the elite in such a society?
2. Who would be the middle class?
3. Who would be the neglected, isolated, rejected?

Notes

1. Jaffe & Froomkin (1968) studied ten-year predictions, and Rada (1980) studied Orwell's predictions.
2. Figures are from "Away From Politics" (1993).
3. Service job estimates are from Stellman (1982).
4. Figures are from *Monthly Labor Review* (1988; *111*, 71-73).
5. Gabor (1971) is the early prophet.
6. The 1% figure is from Ministry of Health (1988); the 2100 prediction is from Calloway (1976).
7. The heart attack and death figures are from Pelletier (1983).

READ MORE ABOUT IT....

For more information on:	See these sources
Prediction	Lamm, 1982
Unanticipated events	Ferkiss, 1969
Anticipated changes in social welfare practice	Macarov, 1991a
Daughters as traditional caregivers	Brody, 1981
Employers as "lean and mean"	Hall, 1984; Kumpke, 1986
Impact of service jobs on unemployment	McKinlay, 1978
Beginnings and growth of technology	Macarov, 1982
Permanent unemployment	Rankin, 1983
Microelectronics	Norman, 1981
Social workers and unemployment	Macarov, 1988b
Methods of distributing resources	Macarov, 1985

References

Abramovitz, M. (1988). *Regulating the lives of women: Social welfare policy from colonial times to the present*. Boston: South End Press.

Abramovitz, M. (1989). Everyone is on welfare: "The role of redistribution in social policy" revisited. In I. C. Colby (Ed.), *Social welfare policy: Perspectives, patterns, insights* (pp. 34-46). Chicago: Dorsey.

Abramovitz, M. (1992). *Spreading the word about low-income women's activism: Challenging the myths of welfare reform*. New York: Hunter College.

Abramovitz, M. (1993). Question: Is the social welfare system inherently sexist and racist? Answer: Yes. In H. J. Karger & J. Midgley (Eds.), *Controversial issues in social policy*. New York: Allyn & Bacon.

Adler, P. (1970). The 1943 Zoot-Suit riots: Brief episode in a long conflict. In M. P. Servin (Ed.), *The Mexican Americans: An awakening minority* (pp. 124-142). Beverly Hills, CA: Glencoe.

Allardt, E. (1973). A welfare model for selecting indicators of national development. *Policy Sciences, 4*(1), 63-74.

Altmeyer, A. J. (1966). *The formative years of social security*. Madison: University of Wisconsin Press.

Ambassade de France. (n.d.). *Social security and national health insurance in France*. New York: Author.

American Association of Retired Persons. (1985). *A profile of older Americans 1985*. Washington, DC: Author.

Anthony, P. (1978). *The ideology of work*. London: Social Science Paperback.

Aponte, R., Neckerman, K. M., & Wilson, W. J. (1985). *Race, family structure, and social policy* (Working paper 7: Race and policy). Washington, DC: National Conference on Social Welfare.

Aptekar, H. H. (1967). The values, functions, and methods of social work. In *An intercultural exploration: Universals and differences in social work values, functions, and practice* (pp. 3-59). New York: Council on Social Work Education.

Aquilino, W. S. (1990). *Unlaunched adult children and parental well-being*. Madison: University of Wisconsin, Center for Demography and Ecology.

Aquirre, B. E., & Marshall, M. G. (1988). Training family daycare providers using self-study written and video materials. *Child and Youth Care Quarterly, 47,* 115-130.

Arab Information Center. (1965). *The Arab world.* New York: Author.

Ardrey, R. (1966). *The territorial imperative.* New York: Delta.

Ardrey, R. (1976). *The hunting hypothesis.* New York: Atheneum.

Atherton, C. R. (1990). A pragmatic defense of the welfare state against the ideological challenge from the right. *Social Work, 35*(1), 41-45.

Atherton, C. R. (1992). A pragmatic approach to the problem of poverty. *Social Work, 37*(3), 197-201.

Attlee, D. R. (1920). *The social worker.* London: Bell.

Away from politics. (1993, June 19). *International Herald Tribune,* p. 3.

Axinn, J., & Levin, H. (1975). *Social welfare: A history of the American response to need.* New York: Dodd, Mead.

Babuscio, J. (1988). *We speak for ourselves: The experiences of gay men and lesbians.* London: SPCK.

Bachrach, P., & Baratz, M. S. (1970). *Power and poverty: Theory and practice.* New York: Oxford University Press.

Back, K. W. (1989). *Family planning and population control: The challenges of a successful movement.* Boston: Twayne.

Ball, R. M. (1978). *Social security today and tomorrow.* New York: Columbia University Press.

Bane, M. J. (1980). Toward a description and evaluation of United States family policy. In J. Aldous & W. Dumon (Eds.), *The politics and programs of family policy.* Notre Dame, IN: University of Notre Dame Press.

Bankoff, E. A. (1983). Aged parents and their widowed daughters: A support relationship. *Journal of Gerontology, 38,* 226-230.

Barker, R. L. (1991). *The social work dictionary.* Silver Spring, MD: National Association of Social Workers.

Barnett, S. A. (1921). *Canon Barnett: His life, work, and friends.* London: Murray.

Barretta-Herman, A. (1992). *Biculturalism and monetarism: Restructuring New Zealand's social services.* Paper presented at the 26th International Congress of Schools of Social Work, Washington, DC.

Barringer, F. (1993, May 9). So who are we? Ethnic pride confounds the census. *The New York Times,* p. 2IE.

Barton, L. (1991). A cross-cultural comparison of child care as an employer-provided benefit. *International Journal of Sociology and Social Policy, 11*(5), 34-45.

Bell, D. (1960). *The end of ideology.* New York: Free Press.

Bell, W. (1987). *Contemporary social welfare.* New York: Macmillan.

Belous, R. S. (1989). How human resource systems adjust to the shift toward contingency workers. *Monthly Labor Review, 112,* 7-12.

Bendick, M. (1985). *Privatizing the delivery of social welfare service* (Working paper 6: Privatization). Washington, DC: National Council on Social Welfare.

Benington, J. (1992). Local strategies to combat poverty and unemployment in the UK. *INUSW Newsletter, 21,* 2-6.

Benson, R. S., & Wolman, H. (Eds.). (1971). *A blueprint for changing national priorities.* New York: Praeger.

Berger, G. (1976). Strengths and limitations in present attempts at preparing workers for Jewish communal service. In G. Berger (Ed.), *Innovation by tradition: Articles on Jewish communal life.* New York: Federation of Jewish Philanthropies.

Berger, J. (1989, June 18). Study of welfare clients says trade schools fail. *The New York Times,* p. A1.

Berkowitz, E. D. (1989). Wilbur Cohen and American social reform. *Social Work, 34,* 293-299.

Berrick, J. D. (1991). Welfare and child care: The intricacies of competing social values. *Social Work, 36*(4), 345-351.

Bertman, S. L. (1991). *Facing death: Images, insights, and interventions.* New York: Hemisphere.

Beveridge, W. H. (1930). *Unemployment.* New York: Longmans, Green.

Beveridge, W. H. (1942). *Social insurance and allied services.* New York: Macmillan.

Bird, C. (1966). *The invisible scar.* New York: Pocket Books.

Birenbaum, A., & Sagarin, E. (1972). *Social problems: Private troubles and public issues.* New York: Scribners.

Bixby, A. K. (1992). Public social welfare expenditures, fiscal year 1989. *Social Security Bulletin, 55*(2), 61-62.

Black, B. J. (1965). Vocational rehabilitation. In *Encyclopedia of social work.* New York: National Association of Social Workers.

Blau, J. (1992). A paralysis of social policy? *Social Work, 37*(6), 558-562.

Bluhm, W. T. (1974). *Ideologies and attitudes: Modern political culture.* Englewood Cliffs, NJ: Prentice Hall.

Boodman, S. G. (1992, July 28). The enduring legacy of deprivation. *Washington Post* (Health section), p. 16.

Brenton, M. (1985). Privatisation and voluntary sector social services. In C. Jones & M. Brenton (Eds.), *Yearbook of social policy research.* London: Routledge & Kegan Paul.

Brieland, D. (1975). *Contemporary social work.* New York: McGraw-Hill.

Briggs, A. (1965). The welfare state in historical perspective. In M. N. Zald (Ed.), *Social welfare institutions* (pp. 37-90). New York: John Wiley.

British Information Services. (1975). *Social services in Britain.* New York: Author.

Brocas, A-M., Cailloux, A-M., & Oget, V. (1990). *Women and social security: Progress towards equality of treatment.* Geneva: International Labour Office.

Brody, E. M. (1981). Women in the middle and family help to older people. *The Gerontologist, 21,* 471-480.

Brody, J. A., Cornoni-Huntley, J., & Patrick, C. H. (1981). Research epidemiology as a growth industry at the National Institute on Aging. *Public Health Reports, 96,* 269-273.

Brosse, T. (1950). Altruism and creativity as biological factors in human evolution. In P. A. Sorokin (Ed.), *Exploration in altruistic love and behavior.* Boston: Beacon.

Brown, J. C. (1940). *Public relief 1929-1939.* New York: Holt.

Browning, R. X. (1986). *Politics and social welfare policy in the United States.* Knoxville: University of Tennessee Press.

Buckingham, W. (1961). *Automation.* New York: Mentor.

Burghardt, S., & Fabricant, M. (1987). Radical social work. In A. Minahan (Ed.), *Encyclopedia of social work.* Silver Spring, MD: National Association of Social Workers.

Burkhauser, R. V. (1978). *Are women treated fairly in today's social security system?* Madison: University of Wisconsin, Institute for Research on Poverty.

Callahan, D. (1991). Abortion in a pluralistic society. In B. S. Kogan (Ed.), *A time to be born and a time to die.* New York: Aldine de Gruyter.

Callicutt, J. W. (1987). Mental health services. In A. Minahan (Ed.), *Encyclopedia of social work.* Washington, DC: National Association of Social Workers.

Calloway, M. D. (1976). Men, machines, and social security. *Black Aging, 1,* 20-22.

Campbell, J. (Ed.). (1971). *The portable Jung.* New York: Viking.

Cannon, H. G. (1959). *Lamarck and modern genetics.* Westport, CT: Greenwood Press.

Carabine, J. (1992). "Constructing women": Women's sexuality and social policy. *Critical Social Policy, 12*(1), 23-37.

Carlton-LaNey, I. (1992). Elderly Black farm women: A population at risk. *Social Work, 37*(6), 517-523.

Carrera, J. (1987). Aid to families with dependent children. In A. Minahan (Ed.), *Encyclopedia of social work.* Silver Spring, MD: National Association of Social Workers.

Carroll, B. J., Conant, R. M., & Easton, T. A. (Eds.). (1987). *Private means, public ends: Private business in social service delivery.* New York: Praeger.

Cates, J. R. (1983). *Insuring inequality.* Ann Arbor: University of Michigan Press.

Census bureau ups 65+ population estimates. (1993). *AARP Bulletin, 34*(2), 3.

Cetron, M., & Davies, O. (1991). Trends shaping the world. *The Futurist, 25*(5), 11-21.

Cetron, M., & O'Toole, T. (1982). *Encounters with the future: A forecast of life into the 21st century.* New York: McGraw-Hill.

Charles, S., & Webb, A. (1986). *The economic approach to social policy.* Brighton: Wheatsheaf.

Charnow, J. (1943). *Work relief experience in the United States.* Washington, DC: Social Science Research Council.

Chatterjee, Farkas investigate fiscoholism. (1992). In *MSASS Action.* Cleveland: Case Western Reserve University.

Chen, Y-P. (1985). Economic status of the aging. In R. H. Binstock & E. Shanas (Eds.), *The handbook of aging and the social sciences.* New York: Van Nostrand Reinhold.

Cherrington, D. J. (1980). *The work ethic: Working values and values that work.* New York: Amacom.

Chesler, E. (1992). *Woman of valor: Margaret Sanger and the birth control movement in America.* New York: Simon & Schuster.

Chilman, C. S., Nunnally, E. W., & Cox, F. M. (Eds.). (1988). *Variant family forms.* Newbury Park, CA: Sage.

Clark, L. L. (1984). *Social Darwinism in France.* University: University of Alabama Press.

Clarke, J., Cochrane, A., & Smart, C. (1987). *Ideologies of welfare: From dreams to disillusion.* London: Hutchinson.

Cloward, R. A., & Piven, F. F. (1975). The acquiescence of social work. *Social Science and Modern Society, 14,* 55-63.

Code of Federal Regulations, Public Welfare, Parts 200 to 499. (1974). Washington, DC: Office of the Federal Register, General Services Administration.

Colcord, J. (1936). *Cash relief.* New York: Russell Sage.

Colborn, D. (1992a, July 28). Medicaid—a safety net with some holes. *Washington Post* (Health section), p. 19.

Colborn, D. (1992b, July 28). A vicious cycle of risk. *Washington Post* (Health section), p. 10.

Colborn, D. (1992c, July 28). Who is poor? *Washington Post* (Health section), p. 12.

Coleman, J. S. (1959). *Community conflict.* New York: Free Press.

Coll, B. D. (1969). *Perspectives in public welfare.* Washington, DC: U.S. Department of Health, Education, and Welfare.

Commission on Private Philanthropy and Public Needs. (1975). *Giving in America: Toward a stronger voluntary sector.* Washington, DC: Author.

Compendium of social statistics and indicators—1988. (1991). New York: United Nations.

Conference Board. (1985). *The working woman: A progress report.* New York: Author.

Congressional Budget Office. (1987). *Workfare—introduction.* Washington, DC: Government Printing Office.

Connell, S. (1987). Homelessness. In A. Minahan (Ed.), *Encyclopedia of social work.* Silver Spring, MD: National Association of Social Workers.

Constantelos, D. (1968). *Byzantine philanthropy and social welfare.* New Brunswick, NJ: Rutgers University Press.

Constantino, C. (1981). Intervention with battered women: The lawyer-social worker team. *Social Work, 26*(6), 456-460.

Conze, E. (1959). *Buddhism: Its essence and development.* New York: Harper & Row.

Cooke, K. (1988). The costs of unemployment. In R. Walker & G. Parker (Eds.), *Money matters: Income, wealth and financial welfare* (pp. 81-98). London: Sage.

Coughlin, B. J. (1965). *Church and state in social welfare.* New York: Columbia University Press.

Council on Social Work Education. (1992). *Statistics on social work education in the United States, 1991.* Alexandria, VA: Author.

Cunningham, R. L. (1964). *The philosophy of work.* New York: National Association of Manufacturers.

Current operating statistics. (1977, April). *Social Security Bulletin, 40,* 83-84.

Cutler, D., Bigelow, D., & McFarland, B. (1992). The cost of fragmented health financing: Is it worth it? *Community Mental Health Journal, 28*(2), 121-133.

Cutright, P. (1965). Political structure, economic development, and national social security programs. *American Journal of Sociology, 70,* 537.

Darwin, C. The orgin of the species. (1959). London: Murry.

Darwin, F. (1888). *The life and letters of Charles Darwin.* New York: Appleton.

Data study shows a "greening" of NASW. (1993). *NASW News, 38*(2), 12.

Davis, K. (1984). Wives and work: The sex role revolution and its consequences. *Population and Development Review, 10,* 397-417.

Davis, M. F., & Abramovitz, M. (1992, May 21). The myth that welfare policies don't work. *Christian Science Monitor,* p. 19.

Dear, R. B. (1989). What's right with welfare? The other face of AFDC. *Journal of Sociology and Social Welfare, 16*(2), 5-44.

Demographic yearbook, 1951. (1953). New York: United Nations.

Demographic yearbook, 1987. (1989). New York: United Nations.

Demographic yearbook, 1989. (1991). New York: United Nations.

Demographic yearbook, 1990. (1991). New York: United Nations.

Demographic yearbook, 1991. (1992). New York: United Nations.

DeParle, J. (1992, July 8). When giving up welfare for a job doesn't pay. *The New York Times,* pp. 1, 15.

DeParle, J. (1993, November 7). Debris of past failures impedes poverty policy. *The New York Times,* p. 2IE.

DeParle, J. (1994, March 6). Gauging workfare's employability. *The New York Times,* p. 2IE.

Department of Health and Social Security. (1986). *Client access to records: Current and future practice.* London: Author.

Department of Public Welfare. (1962). *Social welfare in Thailand.* Bangkok: Ministry of the Interior.

deSchweinitz, K. (1943). *England's road to social security.* Philadelphia: University of Pennsylvania Press.

DiNitto, D. M., & Dye, T. R. (1987). *Social welfare: Politics and public policy.* Englewood Cliffs, NJ: Prentice Hall.

Dixon, J. (1984). *Prospectus.* Canberra: International Fellowship for Economic and Social Development.

Dixon, J. (Ed.). (1987a). *Social welfare in Africa.* London: Routledge.

Dixon, J. (Ed.). (1987b). *Social welfare in the Middle East.* London: Routledge.

Dixon, J. (1992). China. In J. Dixon & D. Macarov (Eds.), *Social welfare in socialist countries.* London: Routledge.

Dixon, J., & Kim, H. S. (Eds.). (1985). *Social welfare in Asia.* London: Routledge.

Dixon, J., & Macarov, D. (Eds.) (1992a). *Social welfare in socialist countries.* London: Routledge.

Dixon, J., & Macarov, D. (1992b). Preface In J. Dixon & D. Macarov (Eds.), *Social welfare in socialist countries.* London: Routledge.

Dixon, J., & Scheurell, R. (Eds.). (1990). *Social welfare in developed market countries.* London: Routledge.

Dixon, J., & Scheurell, R. (Eds.). (1991). *Social welfare in Latin America.* London: Routledge.

Dixon, S. L. (1987). *Working with people in crisis.* Toronto: Merrill.

Doolittle, F. C. (1987). Social welfare financing. In A. Minahan (Ed.), *Encyclopedia of social work.* Silver Spring, MD: National Association of Social Workers.

Doron, A. (1990). Definition and measurement of poverty. *Social Security: Journal of Welfare and Social Security Studies, 2,* 27-49.

Douglas, E. T. (1970). *Margaret Sanger: Pioneer of the future.* New York: Holt, Rinehart & Winston.

Doyal, L., & Gough, I. (1991). *A theory of human need.* London: Macmillan.

Drachman, D., & Halberstadt, A. (1992). A stage migration framework applied to recent Soviet émigrés. *Journal of Multicultural Social Work, 2*(1), 63-78.

Drucker, H. M. (1974). *The political uses of ideology.* New York: Barnes & Noble.

Drucker, P. F. (1973). Why service institutions do not perform. In P. F. Drucker (Ed.), *Management: Tasks, responsibilities, practices.* New York: Harper & Row.

Dugdale, R. L. (1970). *The Jukes: A study in crime, pauperism, disease, and heredity.* New York: Arno.

Eagle, E. (1960). Charges for care and maintenance in state institutions for the mentally retarded. *American Journal of Mental Deficiency, 65,* 199.

Eckardt, R. W., Jr. (1974). *Evangelical Christianity and professional social work: A study of the beliefs and practices of the social work majors of Philadelphia College of the Bible and Temple University.* Unpublished doctoral dissertation, University of Pennsylvania.

Economic and Social Council. (1992). *Social development questions: Social development.* New York: United Nations.

The economy—but many are left behind. (1993, January 31). *The New York Times,* p. IE5.

Eddy, J. P., Lawson, D. M., Jr., & Stilson, D. C. (1983). *Crisis intervention: A manual for education and action.* New York: University Press.

Eekelaar, J. (1978). *Family law and social policy.* London: Weidenfeld & Nicolson.

Eisenberg, R., Gwatkin, S., & Tracy, E. (1991). Exploring the Jewish roots of voluntarism: A seminar for Jewish big brothers and big sisters. *Journal of Jewish Communal Service, 68*(1), 24-30.

Ellwood, D. T. (1989). *Poor support: Poverty in the American family.* New York: Basic Books.

Encyclopedia Judaica, Vol. 5. (1971). Jerusalem: Keter.

Encyclopedia of Social Work. (1987). Silver Spring, MD: National Association of Social Workers.

Enkes, S. (1967, May/June). The economic case for birth control in underdeveloped nations. *Challenge Magazine.*

Erikson, E. H. (1958). *Young man Luther: A study in psychoanalysis and history.* New York: Norton.

Estes, R. J. (Ed.). (1992). *Internationalizing social work education: A guide to resources for a new century.* Philadelphia: University of Pennsylvania.

Etzioni, A. (1964). *Modern organizations.* Englewood Cliffs, NJ: Prentice Hall.

Evaluation of family planning in health services. (1975). Geneva: World Health Organization.

Experts consultation on planning the welfare mix. (1986). Vienna: European Centre for Social Welfare Training and Research.

Faris, E. (1930). *Intelligent philanthropy.* Chicago: University of Chicago Press.

Feder, L. H. (1936). *Unemployment relief in periods of depression.* New York: Russell Sage.

Feine, Z. (1974). *Interagency collaboration in drug rehabilitation.* Richmond: Virginia Department of Mental Health and Mental Retardation.

Feingold, S. N. (1991). The Futurist quiz. *The Futurist, 25*(5), 54.

Ferkiss, V. C. (1969). *Technological man: The myth and the reality.* New York: Mentor.

Ferris, J. M., & Graddy, E. (1989). Fading distinctions among the nonprofit, government, and for-profit sectors. In V. A. Hodgkinson & R. W. Lyman (Eds.), *The future of the nonprofit sector* (pp. 123-139). San Francisco: Jossey-Bass.

Field, F. (1977). Making sense of the unemployment figures. In F. Field (Ed.), *The conscript army.* London: Routledge & Kegan Paul.

Field, M. G. (1953). Structured strain in the role of the Soviet physician. *American Journal of Sociology, 63,* 493.

Finch, J. (1989). Social policy, social engineering and the family in the 1990s. In M. Bulmer, J. Lewis, & R. Piachaud (Eds.), *The goals of social policy.* London: Unwin Hyman.

Fink, A. E. (1974). *The field of social work.* New York: Holt, Rinehart & Winston.

First, R. J., & Toomey, B. G. (1989). Homeless men and the work ethic. *Social Service Review, 63*(1), 113-126.

Fisher, G. M. (1992). Poverty guidelines for 1992. *Social Security Bulletin, 55*(1), 43-46.

Fitzpatrick, J. P. (1971). *Puerto Rican Americans: The meaning of migration to the mainland.* Englewood Cliffs, NJ: Prentice Hall.

Fogarty, J. P. (1962). *Hearings.* Subcommittee of the committee on appropriations, House of Representatives, 87th Congress, 2nd session. Washington, DC: Department of Health, Education, and Welfare.

Folsom, M. B. (1965). Measures to reduce poverty. In M. S. Gordon (Ed.), *Poverty in America.* San Francisco: Chandler.

Fowles, D. (1983). The changing older population. *Aging, 339,* 6-11.

Francome, C. (1986). *Abortion practice in Britain and the United States.* London: Allen & Unwin.

Frank, J. (1992, September 7). Reports: Poverty spreads in US. *Jerusalem Post,* p. 8.

Frederico, R. C. (1973). *The social welfare institution: An introduction.* Lexington, MA: D. C. Heath.

Freud, S. (1958). *Civilization and its discontents.* New York: Paperback.

Friedman, M. (1962). *Capitalism and freedom.* Chicago: University of Chicago Press.

Friedman, P. R. (1974). The mentally handicapped citizen and institutional labor. *Harvard Law Review, 87,* 567-587.

Furstenberg, F. F., Jr., & Spanier, G. B. (1984). *Recycling the family: Remarriage after divorce.* Beverly Hills, CA: Sage.

The future of work: Consultation report. (1989). Ottawa: Canadian Council on Social Development.

Futurist, The. (1989). *23*(6).

Gabor, D. (1971). *Inventing the future.* New York: Knopf.

Galper, J. H. (1975). *The politics of social services.* Englewood Cliffs, NJ: Prentice Hall.

Galper, J. H. (1980). *Social work practice: A radical perspective.* Englewood Cliffs, NJ: Prentice Hall.

Gans, H. J. (1995). *The war against the poor: The underclass and antipoverty policy.* New York. Basic Books.

Garraty, J. A. (1978). *Unemployment in history: Economic thought and public policy.* New York: Harper & Row.

Garrison, K. C., & Jones, R. F. (1969). *The psychology of human development.* Scranton, PA: International Textbook.

Gauthier, M. (1992). Follow the dirt road. *Bulletin of the International Communal Studies Association, 11,* 25.

Gelb, J., & Palley, M. L. (1982). *Women and public policies.* Princeton, NJ: Princeton University Press.

General Services Administration. (1974). *Code of federal regulations: Public welfare, parts 200 to 499.* Washington, DC: Office of the Federal Register.

Gilbert, D. (1973). The changing work ethic and rehabilitation. *Journal of Rehabilitation, 39,* 14-17.

Gilbert, N., & Gilbert, B. (1989). *The enabling state.* New York: Oxford University Press.

Gilbert, N., & Specht, H. (1974). *Dimensions of social welfare policy.* Englewood Cliffs, NJ: Prentice Hall.

Ginzberg, E., Williams, T., & Dutka, A. (1989). *Does job training work? The client speaks out.* Boulder, CO: Westview.

Ginzberg, L. D. (1990). *Women and the work of benevolence: Morality, politics, and class in the nineteenth-century United States.* New Haven, CT: Yale University Press.

Glassman, U., & Kates, L. (1990). *Group work: A humanistic approach.* Newbury Park, CA: Sage.

Glennerster, H. (1992). *Paying for welfare in the 1990s.* New York: Harvester Wheatsheaf.

Glennerster, H., & Midgley, J. (Eds.). (1991). *The radical right and the welfare state.* Savage, MD: Barnes & Noble.

Glick, P. C. (1984). Marriage, divorce, and living arrangements. *Journal of Family Issues, 5,* 7-26.

Goddard, H. H. (1973). *The Kallikak family: A study in the heredity of feeble-mindedness.* New York: Arno. (Original work published 1912)

Goldman, E. F. (n.d.). *Rendezvous with destiny: A history of modern American reform.* New York: Vintage.

Goldsen, R. K. (1950). *Puerto Rican journey.* New York: Harper & Row.

Goldston, R. (1968). *The Great Depression: The United States in the thirties.* Greenwich, CT: Fawcett.

Goodin, R. E. (1985). The priority of needs. *Philosophy and Phenomenological Research, 45,* 615-625.

Goodin, R. E. (1988). *Reasons for welfare: The political theory of the welfare state.* Princeton, NJ: Princeton University Press.

Goodwin, L. (1972). *Do the poor want to work? A social-psychological study of work orientations.* Washington, DC: The Brookings Institution.

Gormley, W. T., Jr. (1991). The privatization controversy. In W. T. Gormley, Jr. (Ed.), *Privatization and its alternatives* (pp. 3-16). Madison: University of Wisconsin Press.

Gottlieb, N. (1987). Sex discrimination and inequality. In A. Minahan (Ed.), *Encyclopedia of social work.* Silver Spring, MD: National Association of Social Workers.

Gouldner, A. W. (1969). *The Hellenic world: A sociological analysis.* New York: Harper & Row.

Graham, J. J. (1970). *The enemies of the poor.* New York: Random House.

Greenberg, D., & Wiseman, M. (1992). What did the OBRA demonstrations do? In C. F. Manski & I. Garfinkel (Eds.), *Evaluating welfare and training programs* (pp. 25-75). Cambridge, MA: Harvard University Press.

Greenstreet, R. L. (1988). *Cost-effective alternatives in alcoholism treatment.* Springfield, IL: Charles C Thomas.

Greif, G. L. (1990). *The daddy track and the single father: Coping with kids, housework, a job, an ex-wife, a social life, and the courts.* Lexington, MA: Lexington Books.

Greve, R. M., & Gladstone, A. (1983). Framework paper. In D. Gaudart, R. M. Greve, & A. Gladstone (Eds.), *Changing perceptions of work in industrialized countries: Their effect on and implications for industrial relations.* Geneva: International Institute of Labour Studies.

Griffiths, D. (1974). *The waiting poor: An argument for abolition of the waiting period on unemployment and sickness benefits.* Fitzroy, Victoria, Australia: Brotherhood of Saint Laurence.

Griswold v. Connecticut. 381 U.S. 479 (1965).

Gronjberg, K. A. (1990). Poverty and nonprofit organizational behavior. *Social Service Review, 64,* 208-243.

Gross, A. M. (1978). *The use of cost effectiveness analysis in calculating the cost of providing alternative living environments for the elderly and mentally retarded.* Unpublished doctoral dissertation, Brandeis University, Waltham, MA.

Gueron, J. M., & Long, D. A. (1990). Welfare employment policies in the 1980s. In L. A. Ferman, M. Hoyman, J. Cutcher-Gershenfield, & E. J. Savoie (Eds.), *New developments in worker training: A legacy for the 1990s* (pp. 191-223). Madison, WI: Industrial Relations Research Association.

Guest, G. (1989). The boarding of the dependent poor in colonial America. *Social Service Review, 63*(1), 92-112.

Gun control vs. jobs. (1992, July 7). *The New York Times,* p. B5.

Gurin, C., & Gurin, P. (1976). Personal efficacy and the ideology of individual responsibility. In B. Strumpel (Ed.), *Economic means for human needs: Social indicators of well-being and discontent.* Ann Arbor: University of Michigan Press.

Gustafsson, B., & Lindblom, M. (1993). Poverty lines and poverty in seven European countries, Australia, Canada, and the USA. *Journal of European Social Policy, 3*(1), 21-38.

Gutman, H. G. (1976). *Work, culture, and society in industrializing America.* New York: Knopf.

Guttmacher, A. F. (1968). Family planning: Humanism and science. In F. Haselkorn (Ed.), *Family planning and the role of social work.* Garden City, NY: Adelphi University School of Social Work.

Habib, J. (1985). The economy and the aged. In R. H. Binstock & E. Shanas (Eds.), *The handbook of aging and social sciences.* New York: Van Nostrand Reinhold.

Habib, J., & Lerman, R. (1976). *Alternative benefit formulas in support programs for the aged.* Jerusalem: Brookdale Institute.

Hagen, J. L. (1992). Women, work, and welfare: Is there a role for social work? *Social Work, 37*(1), 9-14.

Hall, K. (1984). How shall we ever get them back to work? *International Journal of Manpower, 5,* 24-32.

Hampden-Turner, C. (1975). *From poverty to dignity.* Garden City, NY: Anchor.

Handler, J. F., & Hollingsworth, E. J. (1971). *The "deserving poor": A study in welfare administration.* New York: Academic Press.

Hansen, M. L. (1964). *The immigrant in American history.* New York: Harper & Row.

Hardcastle, D. A. (1978). Aging now and in the future. *Journal of Social Welfare, 5,* 41-49.

Hardy, T. (1869). *Far from the madding crowd.* New York: H. A. Winston.

Hareven, T. K. (1974). Societal problems. In C. A. Chambers (Ed.), *A century of concern: 1873-1973.* Columbus, OH: National Conference on Social Welfare.

Harper, R. F. (1955). The code of Hammurabi, King of Babylon. In J. Bartlett (Ed.), *Familiar quotations.* Boston: Little, Brown.

Harrington, M. (1963). *The other America.* New York: Macmillan.

Hartman, A. (1990). Aging as a feminist issue. *Social Work, 35*(5), 387-388.

Hasebroek, J. (1933). *Trade and politics in ancient Greece.* London: Bell.

Hatch, S. (Ed.). (1980). *Mutual aid and social and health care.* London: Bedford Square.

Hatch, S., & Hinton, T. (1986). *Self-help in practice: A study of Contact a Family, community work, and family support.* Sheffield, UK: Joint Unit for Social Services Research.

Heap, K. (1966). The scapegoat role in youth groups. *Case Conference, 12,* 215.

Heaton, T. B. (1984). Religious homogamy and marital satisfaction reconsidered. *Journal of Marriage and the Family, 46,* 729-733.

Heilbroner, R. L. (1953). *The worldly philosophers.* New York: Simon & Schuster.

Herbert, B. (1993, August 8). The 6.8% illusion. *The New York Times,* p. IE7.

Herman, A. S. (1989). Productivity continued to rise in many industries in 1987. *Monthly Labor Review, 112,* 13-20.

Herzberg, F. (1966). *Work and the nature of man.* Cleveland: World.

Herzberg, F., Mausner, B., & Snyderman, B. B. (1959). *The motivation to work.* New York: John Wiley.

Herzberg, W. (1955). *Protestant, Catholic, and Jew: An essay in American religious sociology.* Garden City, NY: Doubleday.

Hill, D. (1992). The American philosophy of welfare: Citizenship and the "politics of conduct." *Social Policy and Administration, 26*(2), 117-128.

Hoffer, E. (1969). *Working and thinking on the waterfront.* New York: Harper & Row.

Hoffman, I. L. (1958). *The concept of need in social work.* St. Paul, MN: Wilder Foundation.

Hofstadter, R. (1944). *Social Darwinism in American thought.* Boston: Beacon Press.

Hokenstad, M. D. (1992). Cross-national trends and issues in social service provision and social work practice for the elderly. *Journal of Gerontological Social Work, 12*(1/2), 1-15.

Holgersson, L., & Lundstrom, S. (1975). *The evolution of Swedish social security.* Stockholm: The Swedish Institute.

Hollingsworth, J. R., & Hollingsworth, E. J. (1986). *A comparison of non-profit, for-profit, and public hospitals in the United States: 1935 to the present* (Working paper #113, Program on Nonprofit Organizations). New Haven, CT: Yale University, Institution for Social and Policy Studies.

Holmes, T. R., & Hokenstad, M. C. (1991). Mental health services: An international perspective. *Journal of Sociology and Social Welfare, 18*(2), 5-24.

Holtzman, A. (1963). *The Townsend movement.* New York: Bookman.

Homans, G. C. (1951). *The human group.* London: Routledge & Kegan Paul.

Horowitz, D., & Kolodny, D. (1969). The foundations: Charity begins at home. *Ramparts, 7,* 39-48.

House of Lords. (1981). *Report of the House of Lords Select Committee on Unemployment.* London: Her Majesty's Stationery Office.

Howard, D. S. (1943). *The WPA and federal relief policy.* New York: Russell Sage.

Huff, D. D. (1992). Upside-down welfare. *Public Welfare, 50*(1), 36-40.

Hugo, V. (1965). *The hunchback of Notre Dame.* London: Dent.

Hunger amid the plenty. (1993, March 7). *The New York Times,* p. IE5.

Hunnicutt, B. K. (1990, January 4). Are we all workaholics? *Wall Street Journal.*

Hurwitz, D. S. (1987). Retirement and pension plans. In A. Minahan (Ed.), *Encyclopedia of social work* (pp. 507-512). Silver Spring, MD: National Association of Social Workers.

International Labour Office. (1970). *Introduction to social security: A workers' education manual.* Geneva: Author.

International Labour Office. (1991). *Yearbook of labour statistics.* Geneva: Author.

Jackson, J. E. (1989). Choosing institutions. *Institute for Social Research Newsletter, 16,* 7-9.

Jacobsen, T. (1965). Babylonia and Assyria. In W. E. Preece (Ed.), *Encyclopedia Britannica* (Vol. 2, pp. 951-979). London: Benton.

Jacobson, T. (1992). *The oppression of benevolence.* Unpublished doctoral dissertation, Lund University, Lund, Sweden.

Jaffe, A. J., & Froomkin, J. (1968). *Technology and jobs: Automation in perspective.* New York: Praeger.

James, E. (1975). Income and employment effects of women's liberation. In C. B. Lloyd (Ed.), *Sex, discrimination, and the division of labor.* New York: Columbia University Press.

Jansson, B. S. (1984). *Theory and practice of social welfare policy: Analysis, processes, and current issues.* Belmont, CA: Wadsworth.

Jehle, F. F. (1991). *The complete & easy guide to social security and medicare, with sections on disability and SSI programs.* Madison, CT: Fraser.

Johnson, A. B. (1990). *Bedlam: The truth about deinstitutionalization.* New York: Basic Books.

Johnson, L. C., & Schwartz, C. L. (1991). *Social welfare: A response to human need.* Boston: Allyn & Bacon.

Johnson, N. (1989). The privatization of welfare. *Social Policy and Administration, 23,* 17-30.

Joint Economic Committee. (1980). *The cost of racial discrimination.* Washington, DC: Government Printing Office.

Jolly, D., & Gerbaud, I. (1992). *The hospital of tomorrow.* Geneva: World Health Organization.

Jones, E. F., Farina, A., Hastorf, A. H., Markus, H., Miller, D. T., & Scott, R. A. (1984). *Social stigma: The psychology of marked relationships.* New York: Freeman.

Jones, L. (1992). The full employment myth: Alternative solutions to unemployment. *Social Work, 37,* 359-364.

Jonzon, B. (1991). Labour market policy and manpower provision in the Swedish model. In C. de Neubourg (Ed.), *The art of full employment* (pp. 439-451). North-Holland, The Netherlands: Elsevier Science Publishers.

Joravsky, D. (1970). *The Lysenko affair.* Cambridge, MA: Harvard University Press.

Jorns, A. (1969). *The Quakers as pioneers in social work.* Montclair, NJ: Patterson Smith.

Joseph, J. A. (Ed.). (1989). *The charitable impulse: Wealth and social conscience in communities and culture outside the United States.* New York: The Foundation Center.

Judge, K., & Knapp, M. (1985). Efficiency in the production of welfare: The public and private sectors compared. In R. Klein & M. O'Higgins (Eds.), *The future of welfare.* Oxford, UK: Basil Blackwell.

Kagan, S. L., Powell, D. R., Weissbourd, S., & Zigler, E. F. (1987). *American's family support programs: Perspectives and prospects.* New Haven, CT: Yale University Press.

Kahn, A. J. (1973). *Social policy and social services.* New York: Random House.

Kahn, S. (1991). *Organizing: A guide for grass-roots leaders.* Silver Spring, MD: National Association of Social Workers.

Kamerman, J. B. (1988). *Death in the midst of life: Social and cultural influences on death, grief, and mourning.* Englewood Cliffs, NJ: Prentice Hall.

Kamerman, S. K., & Kahn, A. J. (1978). *Family policy: Government and families in fourteen countries.* New York: Columbia University Press.

Kamm, P. S. (1991). *Remarriage in the middle years and beyond.* San Leandro, CA: Bristol.

Kane, R. A., & Kane, R. L. (1991, August 28). Time to rethink the nursing home. *The New York Times,* p. 61E.

Kaplan, J. (1975). *Leisure: Theory and policy.* New York: John Wiley.

Kaplan, M. (1960). *Leisure in America: A social inquiry.* New York: John Wiley.

Karger, H. J., & Stoesz, D. (1989). *The future of American social welfare.* New York: Longmans.

Kasarda, J. D. (1989, January). Urban industrial transition and the underclass. *The Annals (AAPSS), 501,* 26-47.

Kateb, G. (1963). *Utopia and its enemies.* New York: Schocken.

Kates, R. W., & Millman, S. (1990). On ending hunger: The lessons of history. In L. F. Newman, W. Crossgrove, R. W. Kates, R. Matthews, & S. Millman. (Eds.), *Hunger in history: Food shortage, poverty, and deprivation* (pp. 389-407). Cambridge, MA: Basil Blackwell.

Katz, A. H., & Bender, E. I. (1990). *Helping one another: Self-help groups in a changing world.* Oakland, CA: Third Party Publishing.

Katz, M. B. (1986). *In the shadow of the poorhouse: The social history of welfare in America.* New York: Basic Books.

Kelly, P. (1992). The application of family systems theory to mental health services for southeast Asian refugees. *Journal of Multicultural Social Work, 2*(1), 1-13.

Kendrick, J. W. (1979). Productivity trends and the recent slowdown. In W. E. Fellner (Ed.), *Contemporary economic problems.* Washington, DC: American Enterprise Institute.

Kennedy, D. M. (1970). *Birth control in America: The career of Margaret Sanger.* New Haven, CT: Yale University Press.

Kerbo, H. R., & Shaffer, R. A. (1992). Lower class insurgency and the political process: The response of the U.S. unemployed, 1890-1940. *Social Problems, 39*(2), 139-154.

Kershaw, J. A. (1965). The attack on poverty. In M. S. Gordon (Ed.), *Poverty in America.* San Francisco: Chandler.

Kilpatrick, A. C., & Holland, T. P. (1990). Spiritual dimensions of practice. *The Clinical Supervisor, 8*(2), 125-140.

King, S. S. (1979, May 1). Doctors say federal food plans have slashed gross malnutrition. *The New York Times,* p. B9.

Kivisto, P., & Blanck, D. (Eds.). (1990). *American immigrants and their generations: Studies and commentaries on the Hansen thesis after fifty years.* Chicago: University of Illinois Press.

Kluegel, J. R., & Smith, E. R. (1986). *Beliefs about inequality: Americans' views of what is and what ought to be.* New York: Aldine de Gruyter.

Kogut, A., & Aron, S. (1980). Toward full employment policy: An overview. *Journal of Sociology and Social Welfare, 7,* 85-99.

Kohler, K. (1903). Charity. In I. B. Singer (Ed.), *The Jewish encyclopedia* (Vol. 3). New York: Funk & Wagnalls.

Kohs, S. C. (1966). *The roots of social work.* New York: Association Press.

Kotz, N. (1971). *Let them eat promises.* Garden City, NY: Doubleday.

Kraft, L., & Bernheimer, C. J. (1954). *Aspects of the Jewish Community Center.* New York: National Association of Jewish Center Workers.

Kramer, R. (1981). *Voluntary agencies in the welfare state.* Berkeley: University of California Press.

Kramer, R. (1993). *Reflections on the voluntary nonprofit sector in Israel: An international perspective.* Paper delivered as the Arnulf M. Pins Memorial Lecture, Paul Baerwald School of Social Work, The Hebrew University, Jerusalem.

Kropotkin, P. (1925). *Mutual aid: A factor in evolution.* New York: Knopf.

Kumpke, T. (1986). *Works organization in the post-industrial company.* Paper delivered at the conference on New Technologies and the Future of Work, European Centre for Work and Society, Maastricht.

Kurland, P. B. (1974). The judicial road to social welfare. *Social Service Review, 48,* 481-493.

Kurtz, L. F. (1990). The self-help movement: Review of the past decade of research. *Social Work with Groups, 13*(3), 101-115.

Kus, R. J. (Ed.). (1990). *Keys to caring: Assisting your gay and lesbian clients.* Boston: Alyson.

Kuttner, R. (1994, June 19). The welfare perplex. *The New York Times,* p. IE7.

Lader, L. (1955). *The Margaret Sanger story and the fight for birth control.* Garden City, NY: Doubleday.

Lamm, R. D. (1982). Why the U.S. closed its border. *The Futurist, 16,* 4-8.

LaPiere, R. T. (1934). Attitudes versus actions. *Social Forces, 13,* 230-237.

Law and population. (n.d.). New York: United Fund for Population Activities.

Leahy, W. H. (1976). An economic perspective of public employment programs. *Review of Social Economics, 34,* 198.

Leary, D. T. (1970). Race and regeneration. In M. P. Servin (Ed.), *The Mexican-Americans: An awakening minority* (pp. 13-27). Beverly Hills, CA: Glencoe.

Lee, J. A. B., & Swenson, C. R. (1986). The concept of mutual aid. In A. Gitterman & L. Shulman (Eds.), *Mutual aid groups and the life cycle.* Itasca, IL: Peacock.

Lee, P., & Raban, C. (1983). Welfare and ideology. In M. Loney, D. Boswell, & J. Clarke (Eds.), *Social policy and social welfare.* London: Open University Press.

Leiby, J. (1987). History of social welfare. In A. Minahan (Ed.), *Encyclopedia of social work* (pp. 755-777). Silver Spring, MD: National Association of Social Workers.

Leichter, H., & Mitchell, W. (1967). *Kinship and casework.* New York: Russell Sage.

Leisure company opens. (1991, June 25). *Jerusalem Post,* p. 6.

Lens, S. (1969). *Poverty: America's enduring paradox.* New York: Crowell.

Lerner, M. (1971). Respectable bigotry. In M. Friedman (Ed.), *Overcoming middle-class rage.* Philadelphia: Westminster Press.

Leuchtenberg, W. E. (1963). *Franklin D. Roosevelt and the New Deal.* New York: Harper & Row.

Levinson, A. (1980). *The full employment alternative.* New York: Coward, McCann & Geoghehan.

Levitan, S. A. (1985). *Programs in aid of the poor.* Baltimore, MD: The Johns Hopkins University Press.

Levitas, R. (1990). *The concept of utopia.* New York: Philip Allan.

Lewis, O. (1966). The culture of poverty. *Scientific American, 215*(19).

Lieberman, S., & Black, D. (1987). Loss, mourning and grief. In A. Bentovim, G. G. Barnes, & A. Cooklin (Eds.), *Family therapy: Complementary frameworks of theory and practice* (pp. 251-266). London: Academic Press.

Lingg, B. A. (1990). Women beneficiaries aged 62 or older, 1960-1988. *Social Security Bulletin, 53,* 2-12.

Lipsey, M. W. (1984). Is delinquent prevention a cost-effective strategy? *Journal of Research in Crime and Delinquency, 21*(4), 279-302.

Loewenberg, F. M. (1992). Ideology or pragmatism? Further reflections on voluntary and public sector relations in the nineteenth century. *Nonprofit and Voluntary Section Quarterly, 21,* 119-133.

Loewenberg, F. M., & Dolgoff, R. (Eds.). (1972). Preface. In *The practice of social intervention: Goals, roles, and strategies.* Itasca, IL: Peacock.

Longman, P. J. (1990). Financing the future: Is social security the problem or the solution? In H. J. Aaron (Ed.), *Social security and the budget.* New York: University Press.

Lorenz, K. (1971). *On aggression.* New York: Bantam.

Lubove, R. (1973). *The professional altruist: The emergence of social work as a career—1880-1930.* New York: Atheneum.

Ludington, N. (1993, May 12). World population growing at record rate. *Jerusalem Post,* p. 5.

Macarov, D. (1968). *Report of an evaluative study of the statewide information and consultation service.* New York: State Communities Aid Association.

Macarov, D. (1970a). The concept of empathy and the educational process. *Applied Social Studies, 2,* 107.

Macarov, D. (1970b). *Incentives to work.* San Francisco: Jossey-Bass.

Macarov, D. (1975). The Israeli community center during the Yom Kippur war. *Journal of Jewish Communal Service, 51,* 340.

Macarov, D. (1977a). *Ambiguities and misconceptions in public attitudes toward the poor: An Israeli example.* Unpublished manuscript, Paul Baerwald School of Social Work, The Hebrew University, Jerusalem.

Macarov, D. (1977b). Political ideologies and social welfare. *International Social Work, 20,* 44-50.

Macarov, D. (1977c). Social welfare as a by-product: The effect of neo-mercantilism. *Journal of Sociology and Social Welfare, 4,* 1135-1144.

Macarov, D. (1978a). *The design of social welfare.* New York: Holt, Rinehart & Winston.

Macarov, D. (1978b). Empathy: The charismatic chimera. *Journal of Education for Social Work, 14,* 86-92.

Macarov, D. (1980). *Work and welfare: The unholy alliance.* Beverly Hills, CA: Sage.

Macarov, D. (1982). *Worker productivity: Myths and reality.* Beverly Hills, CA: Sage.

Macarov, D. (1985). Planning for a probability: The almost workless world. *International Labour Review, 123,* 629-642.

Macarov, D. (1987a). *Caution, confidentiality and concealment: Thoughts on clients' access to personal records.* Paper delivered at International Expert Meeting on Client Access to Personal Social Services Records, European Centre for Social Welfare Training and Research, Anugraha, Egham/Surrey, United Kingdom.

Macarov, D. (1987b). Israel. In J. Dixon (Ed.), *Social welfare in the Middle East* (pp. 32-70). London: Routledge.

Macarov, D. (1987c). *Social workers' attitudes toward work with the aged.* Paper delivered at the European Regional Group Meeting, International Association of Schools of Social Work, Sitges, Spain.

Macarov, D. (1988a). *Quitting time: The end of work.* Patrington, Hull, UK: MCB University Press.

Macarov, D. (1988b). Reevaluation of unemployment. *Social Work, 33,* 23-28.

Macarov, D. (1988c). The work personality: A neglected element in research. *International Journal of Manpower, 3,* 2-8.

Macarov, D. (1989). *The service society: Knowledge, ignorance, hopes and fears.* Paper delivered at the Fourth World Congress, International Society for Social Economics, Toronto.

Macarov, D. (1991a). *Certain change: Social work practice in the future.* Silver Spring, MD: National Association of Social Workers.

Macarov, D. (1991b). Full employment is neither feasible nor desirable. *International Journal of Sociology and Social Policy, 11*(1/2/3), 171-191.

Macarov, D. (1993). Self-reliance versus entitlement programs: Or, where should we put the deck-chairs on the *Titanic? International Social Work, 36,* 133-141.

Macarov, D., Akbar, A., Kulkarni, D. V., & Wertheimer, M. (1967). Consultants and consultees: The view from within. *Social Service Review, 41*(3), 283-297.

Macarov, D., & Fradkin, G. (1973). *The short course in development training.* Ramat-Gan, Israel: Massada.

Macarov, D., & Meller, J. (1985). Studying satisfactions in human service organizations: An exploration. *International Journal of Sociology and Social Policy, 5,* 1-15.

Macarov, D., & Meller, J. (1986a). Research in progress: Studying social workers' satisfactions. *Social Work Education, 5,* 26.

Macarov, D., & Meller, J. (1986b). Social workers' satisfactions: Methodological notes and substantive findings. *Journal of Sociology and Social Welfare, 13,* 740-760.

Macarov, D., & Rothman, B. (1977). Confidentiality: A constraint on research? *Social Work Research and Abstracts, 13,* 16.

Macarov, D., & Yanay, U. (1974). *A study of centers for discharged reservists.* Jerusalem: Ministry of Labour.

Macaulay, J., & Berkowitz, L. (Eds.). (1970). *Altruism and helping behavior: Social psychological studies of some antecedents and consequences.* New York: Academic Press.

MacDonald, D. (1963, January 16). Our invisible poor. *New Yorker.*

Machlowitz, M. M. (1981). *Workaholics: Living with them, working with them.* New York: Mentor.

MacIver, R. M. (1948). Introduction. In F. Gross (Ed.), *European ideologies.* New York: Philosophical Library.

MacKay, R. C., Hughes, J. R., & Carver, E. J. (Eds.). (1990). *Empathy in the helping relationship.* New York: Springer.

Manchester, W. (1973). *The glory and the dream: A narrative history of America, 1932-1972.* Boston: Little, Brown.

Mandelbaum, A. (1977). Mental health and retardation. In J. B. Turner (Ed.), *Encyclopedia of social work.* Washington, DC: National Association of Social Workers.

Manser, G. (1987). Volunteers. In A. Minahan (Ed.), *Encyclopedia of social work* (pp. 842-851). Silver Spring, MD: National Association of Social Workers.

March, M. S., & Newman, E. (1971). Financing social welfare: Governmental allocation procedures. In *Encyclopedia of social work.* New York: National Association of Social Workers.

Marcus, S. (1965). Hunger and ideology. In M. N. Zald (Ed.), *Social welfare institutions.* New York: John Wiley.

Marland, S. P., Jr., (1974). *Career education: A proposal for reform.* New York: McGraw-Hill.

Marmor, T. D., Mashaw, J. L., & Harvey, P. L. (1990). *America's misunderstood welfare state: Persistent myths, enduring realities.* New York: Basic Books.

Marshall, T. H. (1965). *Social policy.* London: Hutchinson.

Martin, J. M. (1966). *Lower-class delinquency and work programs.* New York: New York University Press.

Maslow, A. H. (1954). *Motivation and personality.* New York: Harper.

Maton, K. I., & Pargament, K. I. (1991). Towards the promised land: Prospects for religion, prevention, and promotion. *Prevention in Human Services, 10*(1), 1-8.

Matthews, A. (Ed.). (1989). *Privatizing criminal justice.* London: Sage.

Maududi, A. A. (1974). *Birth control: Its social, political, economic, moral and religious aspects.* Lahore, Pakistan: Islamic Publications.

Mayadas, N. S., & Elliott, D. (1992). Integration and xenophobia: An inherent conflict in international migration. *Journal of Multicultural Social Work, 2*(1), 47-62.

Mayo, E. (1933). *The human problems of an industrial civilization.* New York: Macmillan.

McAll, C. (1990). *Class, ethnicity, and social inequality.* Montreal: McGill-Queens University Press.

McFarland, K. (1957). Why men and women get fired. *Personnel Journal, 25,* 307.

McKillip, J. (1987). *Need analysis; Tools for the human services and education.* Newbury Park, CA: Sage.

McKinlay, J. B. (1978). The limits of human service. *Social Policy, 8,* 29-34.

McMillan, A., & Bixby, A. K. (1980). Social welfare expenditures, fiscal year 1978. *Social Security Bulletin, 43,* 3-17.

McWilliams, C. (1970). The borderlands are invaded. In M. P. Servin (Ed.), *The Mexican-Americans: An awakening minority* (pp. 30-54). Beverly Hills, CA: Glencoe.

Measuring poverty. (1985). Washington, DC: Congressional Budget Office.

Meier, E. L., Dittman, C. C., & Toyle, B. B. (1980). *Retirement income goals.* Washington, DC: President's Commission on Pension Policy.

Meiss, K. A. (1991). *Work, welfare, and social work practice.* Stockholm: School of Social Work, Stockholm University.

Mendelssohn, K. (1977). *The riddle of the pyramids.* London: Sphere.

Menzies, K. (1992). *The enabling state: Welfare and the creation of the possibility of participation.* Ontario, Canada: University of Guelph.

Methods of adjusting to automation and technological change. (n.d.). Washington, DC: U.S. Department of Labor.

Michielse, H. C. M., & vanKrieken, R. (1990). Policing the poor: J. L. Vives and the sixteenth century origins of modern social administration. *Social Service Review, 64*(1), 1-21.

Middleman, R. R., & Goldberg, G. (1974). *Social service delivery: A structural approach to social work practice.* New York: Columbia University Press.

Miles, I. (1985). *Social indicators for human development.* London: Pinter.

Miller, B. C., Card, J. J., Paikoff, R. L., & Peterson, J. L. (Eds.). (1992). *Preventing adolescent pregnancies.* Newbury Park, CA: Sage.

Miller, H. (1961). Government's role in social welfare. In B. J. Coughlin (Ed.), *Church and state in social welfare.* New York: Columbia University Press.

Minahan, A. (Ed.). (1987). *Encyclopedia of social work.* Silver Spring, MD: National Association of Social Workers.

Ministry of Health. (1988). *How to avoid heart disease.* Jerusalem: Author.

Mishra, R. (1990). *The welfare state in capitalist society: Policies of retrenchment and maintenance in Europe, North America, and Australia.* New York: Harvester Wheatleaf.

Mitchell, D. (1992). Welfare states and welfare outcomes in the 1980s. *International Social Security Review, 45*(1/2), 73-90.

Mollison, A. (1991, September 18). Report paints depressing picture of widespread poverty in America. *Atlanta Journal and Constitution,* p. B1.

Morgan, L. A. (1984). Changes in family interaction following widowhood. *Journal of Marriage and the Family, 46,* 323-334.

Morner, M. (1970). First meeting of the races in America. In M. P. Servin (Ed.), *The Mexican-Americans: An awakening minority* (pp. 2-27). Beverly Hills, CA: Glencoe.

Moroney, R. M. (1991). *Social policy and social work: Critical essays on the welfare state.* New York: Aldine de Gruyter.

Morris, R. (1986). *Rethinking social welfare: Why care for the stranger?* New York: Longman.

Morris, R. (1987). Re-thinking welfare in the United States: The welfare state in transition. In R. R. Friedmann, N. Gilbert, & M. Sherer (Eds.), *Modern welfare states: A comparative view of trends and prospects.* New York: New York University Press.

Moskowitz, J. (1989). Increasing government support for nonprofits: Is it worth the cost? In V. A. Hodgkinson & R. W. Lyman (Eds.), *The future of the nonprofit sector: Challenges, changes, and policy considerations.* San Francisco: Jossey-Bass.

Moss, P., & Fonda, N. (1980). *Work and the family.* London: Temple Smith.

Moynihan, D. P. (1967, February 5). The case for a family allowance. *The New York Times Magazine,* pp. 13, 68-73.

Moynihan, D. P. (1973). *The politics of a guaranteed income: The Nixon administration and the family assistance plan.* New York: Vintage.

Munday, B. (1987). *Client access to personal social services records* (Eurosocial reports No. 30). Vienna: European Centre for Social Welfare Training and Research.

Murphy, P. (1993, June 21). When saving the family only makes matters worse. *International Herald Tribune,* p. 6.

Murray, C. (1984). *Losing ground: American social policy—1950-1980.* New York: Basic Books.

Murray, C. (1988). *In pursuit of happiness and good government.* New York: Simon & Schuster.

Myles, J. (1989). *Old age in the welfare state: The political economy of public pensions.* Lawrence: University Press of Kansas.

Nanavatty, S. M. C. (1992). Reflections on ICSW [Special issue]. *ICSW Information, 12,* 14.

Near, H. (1992). *The kibbutz movement: A history, origins and growth, 1909-1939.* Oxford, UK: Oxford University Press.

Netting, F. E., McMurty, S. L., Kettner, P. M., & Jones-McClintic, S. (1990). Privatization and its impact on nonprofit service providers. *Nonprofit and Voluntary Sector Quarterly, 19*(1), 33-46.

New York State Department of Social Services. (1976). *How I found a way to eat better for less money.* Albany: Author.

Nichols-Casebolt, A. M., & McClure, J. (1989). Social work support for welfare reform: The latest surrender in the war on poverty. *Social Work, 34*(1), 77-80.

Niebuhr, R. (1932). *The contribution of religion to social work.* New York: Columbia University Press.

Nisbet, R. (1973). *The social philosophers: Community and conflict in Western thought.* New York: Crowell.

Norman, A. (1982). *Mental illness in old age: Meeting the challenge.* London: Centre for Policy on Aging.

Norman, C. (1981). The new industrial revolution: How microelectronics may change the workplace. In J. O'Toole, J. L. Schreiber, & L. C. Woods (Eds.), *Working: Changes and choices.* New York: Human Sciences Press.

Norris, D. F., & Thompson, L. (1995). *The politics of welfare reform.* Thousand Oaks: Sage.

Norton, A. J., & Glick, P. G. (1986). One-parent families: A social and economic profile. *Family Relations, 35*(1), 177-181.

Norton, M. (1989). *Raising money from trusts.* London: Directory of Social Change.

O'Donnell, E. J., & Reid, O. M. (1971). The multiservice neighborhood center: Preliminary findings from a national survey. *Welfare in Review, 9,* 1.

Oettinger, K. B., & Stansbury, J. D. (1972). *Population and family planning: Analytical abstracts for social work educators and related disciplines.* New York: International Association of Schools of Social Work.

Offner, P. (1992). JOBS: How are we doing? Where are we going? *Public Welfare, 50*(3), 8-12.

Oliner, S. P., & Oliner, P. M. (1988). *The altruistic personality: Rescuers of Jews in Nazi Europe.* New York: Free Press.

Olsson, S. (1987). Towards a transformation of the Swedish welfare state. In R. R. Friedmann, N. Gilbert, & M. Sherer (Eds.), *Modern welfare states: A comparative view of trends and prospects.* New York: New York University Press.

Orfield, G. (1985). *Race and the federal agenda: The loss of the integrationist dream, 1965-1974* (Working paper No. 7: Race and policy, pp. 1-43). Washington, DC: National Conference on Social Welfare.

Orshansky, M. (1965a). Counting the poor: Another look at the poverty profile. In L. A. Ferman, J. L. Kornbluh, & A. Haber (Eds.), *Poverty in America.* Ann Arbor: University of Michigan Press.

Orshansky, M. (1965b). Who's who among the poor. *Social Security Bulletin, 28*(3).

Ostrander, S. A. (1989). The problem of poverty and why philanthropy neglects it. In V. A. Hodgkinson & R. W. Lyman (Eds.), *The future of the nonprofit sector: Challenges, changes, and policy considerations.* San Francisco: Jossey-Bass.

Ozawa, M. E. (1989). Conclusions. In M. E. Ozawa (Ed.), *Women's life cycle and economic insecurity: Problems and proposals.* New York: Praeger.

Pack, J. R. (1991). The opportunities and constraints of privatization. In W. T. Gormley, Jr. (Ed.), *Privatization and its alternatives* (pp. 281-306). Madison: University of Wisconsin Press.

Packard, M. D. (1990). The earnings test and the short run work response to its elimination. *Social Security Bulletin, 53,* 2-16.

Page, R. M. (1984). *Stigma.* London: Routledge.

Palfrey, C., Phillips, C., & Thomas, P. (1991). *Efficiency, economy, and the quality of care.* Norwich, CT: Social Work Monographs.

Palmer, G. H. (1970). *Altruism: Its nature and varieties.* Westport, CT: Greenwood Press.

Palmer, S., & Humphrey, J. A. (1990). *Deviant behavior: Patterns, sources, and control.* New York: Plenum.

Pampel, F. C., & Williamson, J. B. (1989). *Age, class, poltics and the welfare state.* Cambridge, UK: Cambridge University Press.

Papadakis, E., & Taylor-Gooby, P. (1987). *The private provision of public welfare.* New York: St. Martin's.

Parmar, S. L. (1970). What good is economic betterment? *CERES, 3,* 21.

Patterson, J. T. (1986). *America's struggle against poverty—1900-1985.* Cambridge, MA: Harvard University Press.

Paul, N. L., & Miller, S. J. (1986). Death and dying and the multigenerational impact. In M. A. Karpel (Ed.), *Family resources: The hidden partner in family therapy.* New York: Guilford.

Payne, S. (1991). *Women, health, and poverty: An introduction.* New York: Harvester Wheatsheaf.

Pear, R. (1993, October 10). Poverty 1993: Bigger, deeper, younger, getting worse. *The New York Times,* p. IE4.

Pearson, K. (1912). *Darwinism, medical progress and eugenics.* London: University College.

Pechman, J. A., & Timpane, P. M. (Eds.). (1975). *Work incentives and income guarantees: The New Jersey negative income tax experiment.* Washington, DC: The Brookings Institution.

Peck, E., & Senderowitz, J. (1974). *Pronatalism: The myth of Mom and apple pie.* New York: Crowell.

Pelletier, K. R. (1983, September 8). The hidden hazards of the modern office. *The New York Times.*

Perlmutter, F. M. (Ed.). (1988). Alternative social agencies: Administrative strategies [Special issue]. *Administration in Social Work, 12*(2).

Persons, S. (1959). Darwinism and American culture. In S. Persons, *The impact of Darwininan thought on American life and culture.* Austin: University of Texas Press.

Persson, I. (Ed.). (1990). *Generating equality in the welfare state: The Swedish experience.* Oslo, Norway: Universitetsforlaget.

Peterson, D. A. (1990). Personnel to serve the aging in the field of social work: Implications for educating professionals. *Social Work, 35*(5), 412-415.

Petrovich, J. (1989). The future of Hispanics and philanthropy. In V. A. Hodgkinson & R. W. Lyman, (Eds.), *The future of the nonprofit sector: Challenges, changes, and policy considerations* (pp. 237-247). San Francisco: Jossey-Bass.

Pierson, C. (1991). *Beyond the welfare state?* Cambridge, UK: Polity Press.

Pimlott, J. A. R. (1935). *Toynbee Hall.* London: Dent.

Piven, F. F. (1971). Federal interventions in the cities: The new urban programs as a political strategy. In E. O. Smigel (Ed.), *Handbook on the study of social problems*. Chicago: Rand McNally.

Plunkert, L. M. (1990). The 1980s: A decade of job growth and industry shifts. *Monthly Labor Review, 113*, 3-16.

Powell, T. J. (1987). *Self-help organizations and professional practice*. Silver Spring, MD: National Association of Social Workers.

Prabhupada, A. C. B. (1972). *The perfection of Yoga*. Los Angeles: International Center for Krishna Consciousness.

Price, C. (1969). The study of assimilation. In J. A. Jackson (Ed.), *Migration*. Cambridge, UK: Cambridge University Press.

Quinney, R. (1975). The future of crime. In A. Inciardi & H. A. Siegel (Eds.), *Emerging social issues: A sociological perspective*. New York: Praeger.

Rada, J. (1980). *The impact of micro-electronics*. Geneva: International Labour Office.

Rafter, N. H. (1992). Claims-making and socio-cultural context in the first U.S. eugenics campaign. *Social Problems, 39*(1), 17-34.

Raichele, D. R. (1980). The future of the family. In F. Feather (Ed.), *Through the '80s: Thinking globally, acting locally*. Bethesda, MD: World Future Society.

Raiklin, E. (1990). The colours and dresses of racism in America [Special issue]. *International Journal of Social Economics, 17*(7/8).

Rankin, M. (1983). *Strategies for mutual support among unemployed people*. Paper delivered at Third World Congress, International Society for Social Economics, Fresno, CA.

Ranks of poor, uninsured are continuing to grow. (1992). *AARP Bulletin, 33*(9), 13.

Raskin, A. H. (1976, October 8). Shorter workweek: A new breakthrough. *The New York Times*, p. 14.

Reasoner, S. H., & Mercer, S. O. (1991). Catastrophic health care bill: A postmortem. *Gerontological Social Work, 18*(1/2), 39-53.

Rees, S. (1992, July 18-22). *Responding to economic rationalism by developing social justice: The priority issue in enhancing empowerment*. Paper delivered at the 12th International Symposium of the International Federation of Social Workers, Washington, DC.

Regan, P. (1989). Unemployment in Lancaster and Morecambe. *International Journal of Manpower, 10*, 20-23.

Reich, R. B. (1983). An industrial policy for the right. *The Public Interest, 7*, 3-17.

Rein, M. (1982). Work in welfare: Past failures and future strategies. *Social Service Review, 56*, 211-229.

Reingold, J., Wolk, R. L., & Schwartz, S. (1972). Attitudes of adult children whose aging parents are members of a sheltered workshop. *Aging and Human Development, 3*, 331-337.

Reischauer, R. D. (1989). The welfare reform legislation: Directions for the future. In P. H. Cottingham & D. T. Ellwood (Eds.), *Welfare policy for the 1990s*. Cambridge, MA: Harvard University Press.

Reports on elder abuse, effectiveness of reporting laws, and other factors. (1991). Washington, DC: General Accounting Office.

Rescher, N. (1972). *Welfare: The social issues in philosophical perspective*. Pittsburgh: University of Pittsburgh.

Reuben, S. C. (1987). *But how will you raise the children?* New York: Pocket Books.

Reubens, B. G. (1989). Unemployment insurance in the United States and Europe, 1973-1983. *Monthly Labor Review, 112*, 22-31.

Riccio, J., & Friedlander, D. (1992). GAIN and the prospect of JOB's success. *Public Welfare, 50*(3), 22-32.

Rich, D. Z. (1989). *The economics of welfare: A contemporary analysis.* New York: Praeger.

Richan, W. C. (1987). *Beyond altruism: Social welfare policy in American society.* New York: Haworth.

Richardson, J. (1976). *Food stamp program reform: 94th Congress.* Washington, DC: Library of Congress.

Ringer, B. B. (1983). *We the people and others: Duality and America's treatment of its racial minorities.* London: Tavistock.

Ringer, B. B., & Lawless, E. R. (1989). *Race, ethnicity, and society.* London: Routledge.

Roach, S. S. (1993, March 14). The new majority: White-collar jobless. *The New York Times,* p. IE7.

Roberts, P., & Schulzinger, R. (1988). *Family support policy: A state advocacy guide for combatting poverty.* Washington, DC: Center for Law and Social Policy.

Robinson, J. P. (1991). How Americans use time. *The Futurist, 25*(5), 23-25.

Rodman, H. (1950). On understanding lower class behavior. *Social and Economic Studies, 8,* 441.

Roe v. Wade. 410 U.S. 113 (1973).

Roethlisberger, F. A., & Dickson, W. J. (1939). *Management and the worker.* Cambridge, MA: Harvard University Press.

Rogers, G. (1980). *Pension coverage and vesting among private wage and salary workers in 1979.* Washington, DC: Office of Research and Statistics, Social Security Administration.

Rose, N. E. (1989). Work relief in the 1930s and the origins of the Social Security Act. *Social Service Review, 63*(1), 83-91.

Rosenheim, M. K. (1969). *Shapiro v. Thompson:* "The beggars are coming to town." *Supreme Court Review,* vol. 303.

Ross-Sheriff, F. (1990). Displaced populations. In L. Ginsberg, S. Khinduka, J. A. Hall, F. Ross-Sheriff, & A. Hartman (Eds.), *Encyclopedia of social work* (18th ed., 1990 Supplement, pp. 78-93). Silver Spring, MD: National Association of Social Workers.

Rothman, D. J. (1971). *The discovery of the asylum: Social order and disorder in the new republic.* Boston: Little, Brown.

Rothman, S. M. (1977, January-February). Sterilizing the poor. *Social Science and Modern Society, 514,* 36-40.

Roueche, B. (1965). *Eleven blue men.* New York: Berkley.

Rubin, G. E. (1992). The multicultural curriculum: Why Jews are concerned. *Journal of Jewish Communal Service, 68*(3), 210-218.

Rubinow, I. M. (1966). What do we owe to Peter Stuyvesant? In R. Morris & M. Freund (Eds.), *Trends and issues in Jewish social welfare in the United States, 1899-1952.* Philadelphia: Jewish Publication Society of America.

Rue, V. M. (1973). A U.S. Department of Marriage and the Family. *Journal of Marriage and the Family, 35,* 89-99.

Ryan, W. (1974). Blaming the victim: Ideology serves the establishment. In P. Roby (Ed.), *The poverty establishment.* Englewood Cliffs, NJ: Prentice Hall.

Sadan, S. (1993, March 18). Shetreet blasts Namir's "immediate jobs" program. *Jerusalem Post,* p. 2.

Saha, A. (1990). Traditional Indian concept of time and its economic consequences. *International Journal of Sociology and Social Policy, 10*(7), 58-79.

Saha, A. (1992). Basic human nature in Indian tradition and its economic consequences. *International Journal of Sociology and Social Policy, 12*(1/2), 1-50.

Saint George (Szent Gyorgy), A. (1970). *The crazy ape.* New York: Philosophical Library.

Salaman, L. (1987). *Of market failure, voluntary failure, and third party government.* Washington, DC: The Urban Institute.

Salmond, J. A. (1967). *The CCC, 1933-1942: A New Deal case study.* Durham, NC: Duke University Press.

Saltzman, A., & Proch, K. (1990). *Law in social work practice.* Chicago: Nelson-Hall.

Sands, R. G., & Nuccio, K. (1992). Postmodern feminist theory and social work. *Social Work, 37*(6), 489-494.

Sanger, M. (1938). *Margaret Sanger: An autobiography.* New York: Norton.

Savas, E. S. (1987). *Privatization: The key to better government.* Chatham, NJ: Chatham House Press.

Savin-Williams, R. C. (1990). *Gay and lesbian youth: Expressions of identity.* New York: Hemisphere.

Scheler, M. F. (1954). *The nature of sympathy.* London: Routledge & Kegan Paul.

Schermerhorn, R. A. (1970). *Comparative ethnic relations.* New York: Random House.

Schindler, R. (1980). Mutual aid as mutual exclusion in the development of welfare services— the case of Israel. *International Social Work, 23*(3), 48-52.

Schindler-Rainman, E. (1992, Spring). Values in a changing world: Challenges and choices. *The Journal of Volunteer Administration,* pp. 6-9.

Schlesinger, A., Jr. (1967). The welfare state. In C. I. Schottland (Ed.), *The welfare state.* New York: Harper & Row.

Schneiderman, L. (1992). *The American welfare state: A family perspective.* Paper delivered at the International Conference on Social Welfare, Seoul, Korea.

Schorr, A. L. (1960). *Filial responsibility in the modern American family.* Washington, DC: Government Printing Office.

Schorr, A. L. (1965a). Income maintenance and the birth rate. *Social Security Bulletin, 28,* 2.

Schorr, A. L. (1965b). *Social security and social services in France.* Washington, DC: Government Printing Office.

Schottland, C. I. (1963). *The social security program in the United States.* New York: Appleton-Century-Crofts.

Schottland, C. I. (1974). The changing roles of government and family. In P. E. Weinberger (Ed.), *Perspectives on social welfare: An introductory anthology.* New York: Macmillan.

Schulz, J. H. (1992). "Poverty level"—Worn-out words to hide the truth. *AARP Bulletin, 33*(3), 18.

Schwartz, E. E. (1963). A way to end the means test. *Social Work, 4*(3).

Schwartz, G. G., & Neikirk, W. (1983). *The work revolution.* New York: Rawson.

Scott, R. F. (1970). The Zoot-Suit riots. In M. P. Servin (Ed.), *The Mexican-Americans: An awakening minority* (pp. 116-124). Beverly Hills, CA: Glencoe.

Secretaries of State for Health, Social Security, Wales and Scotland. (1989). *Caring for people: Community care in the next decade and beyond.* London: Her Majesty's Stationery Office.

Security for America's children: A report from the annual conference of the National Academy of Social Insurance. (1992). *Social Security Bulletin, 55*(1), 57-62.

Select Committee on Nutrition and Human Need, U.S. Senate. (1975). *Who gets food stamps?* Washington, DC: Goverment Printing Office.

Service Directory of National Voluntary Health and Social Welfare Organizations. (1974). New York: National Assembly of National Voluntary Health and Social Welfare Organizations.

SESI: Procedures and Objectives. (n.d.). Rio de Janeiro: Cediv Coordenacao de Eventos e Divulgacao.

Sethuraman, S. V. (1985). Basic needs and the informal sector: The case of low-income housing in developing countries. *Habitat International, 9,* 299-316.

Shapiro v. Thompson. 394 U.S. 618 (1969).

Shapiro, T. M. (1985). *Population control politics: Women, sterilization, and reproductive choice.* Philadelphia: Temple University Press.

Sharp, A. M., Register, C. A., & Leftwich, R. H. (1992). *Economics of social issues.* Homewood, IL: Irwin.

Sheldon, S. (1978). *Bloodline.* London: Fontana.

Shemmings, D. (1991). *Client access to records: Participation in social work.* Aldershot, UK: Avebury.

Sheridan, M. J., Bullis, R. K., Adcock, C. R., Berlin, S. D., & Miller, P. C. (1992). Practitioners' personal and professional attitudes and behaviors toward religion and spirituality: Issues for education and practice. *Journal of Education for Social Work, 28*(2), 190-203.

Sherraden, M. (1988). Rethinking social welfare: Toward assets. *Social Policy, 18*(3).

Sherraden, M. (1991a). *Assets and the poor: A new American welfare policy.* New York: Sharpe.

Sherraden, M. (1991b). Full employment and social welfare policy. *International Journal of Sociology and Social Policy, 11*(1/2/3), 192-211.

Sherraden, M., & Sherraden, M. S. (1991). One type of youth employment service: Non-military service in Canada and Mexico. In D. Macarov (Ed.), *Persisting unemployment: Can it be overcome?* Patrington, Hull, UK: MCB University Press.

Sicron, M. (1986). *How many unemployed are there in Israel?* Paper delivered at the annual meeting of Israel Industrial Relations Association, Bar-Ilan University, Ramat Gan, Israel.

Silverstone, B., & Burack-Weiss, A. (1983). *Social work practice with the frail elderly and their families.* Springfield, IL: Charles C Thomas.

Simon, B. L. (1992). U.S. immigration policies, 1798-1992: Invaluable texts for exploring continuity and change in racism and xenophobia. *Journal of Multicultural Social Work, 2*(2), 53-63.

Smith, A. (1937). *The wealth of nations.* New York: Modern Library.

Smith, A. D. (1955). *The right to life.* Chapel Hill: University of North Carolina Press.

Smith, H. W. (1989). Corporate contributions to the year 2000: Growth or decline? In V. A. Hodgkinson & R. W. Lyman (Eds.), *The future of the nonprofit sector.* San Francisco: Jossey-Bass.

Social Security at a glance. (1992). *Social Security Bulletin, 55*(2), 129.

Social Security Bulletin. (1991). *54*(6), 10.

Specht, H. B. (1992). A less complex statement of social work's mission. *Social Security Review, 66*(1), 152-159.

Spencer, H. (1852). A theory of population, deduced from the general law of animal fertility. *Westminster Review, 57,* 468-501.

Spickard, P. R. (1989). *Mixed blood: Intermarriage and ethnic identity in twentieth-century America.* Madison: University of Wisconsin Press.

Spindler, A. (1979). *Public welfare.* New York: Human Sciences Press.

Squires, P. (1990). *Anti-social policy: Welfare, ideology, and the disciplinary state.* New York: Harvester Wheatsheaf.

Stack, C. B. (1974). *All our kin: Strategies for survival in a black community.* New York: Harper & Row.

Stallings, R. A. (1973). The community context of crisis management. *American Behavioral Scientist, 16,* 312.

Starr, P. (1985). *The meaning of privatization* (Working paper No. 6: Privatization). Washington, DC: National Council on Social Welfare.

Stein, J. (Ed.). (1966). *The Random House dictionary of the English language.* New York: Random House.

Steiner, G. Y. (1966). *Social insecurity: The politics of welfare.* Chicago: Rand McNally.

Stellman, J. (1982). *Human and public health aspects of telecommunication.* Paper delivered at Fourth General Assembly, World Future Society, Washington, DC.

Stoesz, D., & Karger, H. J. (1990). *The corporatization of the welfare state.* Unpublished manuscript.

Stoesz, D., & Karger, H. (1992). The decline of the American welfare state. *Social Policy and Administration, 26*(1), 3-17.

Stoner, M. R. (1989). *Inventing a non-homeless future: A public policy agenda for preventing homelessness.* New York: Peter Lang.

Story, D. C. (1992). Volunteerism: The "self-regarding" and "other-regarding" aspects of the human spirit. *Nonprofit and Voluntary Sector Quarterly, 21*(1), 3-18.

Stotland, E., Mathews, K. E., Jr., Sherman, S. E., Hansson, R. O., & Richardson, B. Z. (1978). *Empathy, fantasy, and helping.* Beverly Hills, CA: Sage.

Strauss, A. (1956). *George Herbert Mead on social psychology.* Chicago: University of Chicago Press.

Strauss, A. (1962). Transformations of identity. In A. M. Rose (Ed.), *Human behavior and social processes.* Boston: Houghton Mifflin.

Striner, H. E. (1975). Recurrent educational and manpower training in Great Britain. *Monthly Labor Review, 98,* 30-34.

Strumpel, B. (1976). Introduction and model. In B. Strumpel (Ed.), *Economic means for human needs: Social indicators of well-being and discontent* (pp. 1-12). Ann Arbor: University of Michigan.

Suffolk County Department of Social Services. (1974). *Guidelines on reporting child abuse and maltreatment.* Hauppage, NY: Author.

Sullivan, M. (1987). *Sociology and social welfare.* Boston: Allen & Unwin.

Summaries of elder abuse. (1990). Washington, DC: National Aging Resource Center.

Sumner, W. G. (1963). *Social Darwinism.* Englewood Cliffs, NJ: Prentice Hall.

Swisher, K. (1994, April 21). Dreaming on the job. *Jerusalem Post,* p. 7.

Taggart, R. (Ed.). (1977). *Job creation: What works?* Salt Lake City, UT: Olympus.

Tannen, D. (1991). *You just don't understand.* London: Virago.

Tatara, T. (1990). Federal social welfare: Recent trends. In S. Ginsberg, S. Khinduka, J. A. Hall, F. Ross-Sheriff, & A. Hartman (Eds.), *Encyclopedia of social work* (18th ed., 1990 supplement). Silver Spring, MD: National Association of Social Workers.

Tawney, R. H. (1948). *The acquisitive society.* New York: Harcourt, Brace & World.

Tawney, R. H. (1958). Economic virtues and prescriptions for poverty. In H. D. Stein & R. A. Cloward (Eds.), *Social perspectives on behavior.* New York: Free Press.

Taylor, F. W. (1911). *The principles of scientific management.* New York: Harper.

Taylor, R. J., Chatters, L. M., Tucker, M. B., & Lewis, E. (1991). Developments in research on black families: A decade review. In A. Booth (Ed.), *Contemporary families: Looking forward, looking back* (pp. 275-296). Minneapolis, MN: National Council on Family Relations.

Teegardin, C. (1992, September 4). U.S. poor increase by 2 million. *Atlanta Journal and Constitution,* p. A1.

Temple, W. (1967). The state. In C. I. Schottland (Ed.), *The welfare state.* New York: Harper & Row.

Terrell, K. (1992). Female-male earnings differentials and occupational structure. *International Labour Review, 131,* 387-404.

Thayer, F. C. (1987). Privatization: Carnage, chaos, and corruption. In B. J. Carroll, R. M. Conant, & T. A. Easton (Eds.), *Private means, public ends: Private business in social security delivery.* New York: Praeger.

Theisen, W. M. (n.d.). *The right to work: Wage labor in a market economy.* Des Moines: School of Social Work, Univerity of Iowa.

Thoenes, P. (1966). *The elite in the welfare state.* New York: Free Press.

Thompson, K. (1986). *Beliefs and ideology.* London: Tavistock.

Tietze, C., & Murstein, M. J. (1975). Induced abortion: 1975 factbook. *Reports on Population/Family Planning, 14,* 1-76.

Titmuss, R. M. (1959). *Essays on "the welfare state."* New Haven, CT: Yale University Press.

Titmuss, R. M. (1967). The welfare state: Images and reality. In C. I. Schottland (Ed.), *The welfare state.* New York: Harper & Row.

Titmuss, R. M. (1971). *The gift relationship.* London: Allen & Unwin.

Titmuss, R. M. (1974). *Social policy: An introduction.* New York: Pantheon.

Tutvedt, O., & Young, L. (Eds.). (1991). *Social work and the Norwegian welfare state.* Oslo: Norwegian State College of Local Government Administration and Social Work.

Uchitelle, L. (1992, September 6). America isn't creating enough jobs and no one seems to know why. *The New York Times,* p. 1-2.

Uchitelle, L. (1993, November 7). How the job count is off. *The New York Times,* p. 2IE.

United Nations. (1965). *Social reconstruction in the newly independent countries of North Africa.* New York: Author.

United Nations. (1976). *World population growth and response: 1965-1975—A decade of global action.* New York: Author.

United Nations. (1992a). *Abortion policies: A global review.* New York: Author.

United Nations. (1992b). *Population and vital statistics report: Data available as of 1 April 1992.* New York: United Nations Department of Economic and Social Development.

United Nations. (1992c). *Statistical yearbook, 37th issue.* New York: Author.

United Nations. (1992d). *Trends in Social Security, 2,* 11-12.

United Nations. (1992e). *World population monitoring, 1991.* New York: Author.

United Nations Technical Assistance Program. (1963). *Local government in selected countries.* New York: Author.

U.S. Department of Commerce. (1987). *Statistical abstract of the United States 1988.* Washington, DC: Bureau of the Census.

U.S. Department of Health and Human Services. (n.d.). *Answers about aging: New pieces to an old puzzle.* Washington, DC: Author.

U.S. Department of Health and Human Services. (1987a). *Research advances in aging, 1984-1986.* Washington, DC: Author.

U.S. Department of Health and Human Services. (1987b). *Social security programs throughout the world—1987.* Washington, DC: Author.

U.S. Department of Health and Human Services. (1989). *Social security programs throughout the world, 1988.* Washington, DC: Author.

U.S. Department of Health and Human Services. (1991). *Social security bulletin annual statistical supplement 1991.* Washington, DC: Author.

U.S. Department of Health and Human Services. (1992). *Social security programs throughout the world—1991.* Washington, DC: Author.

U.S. Department of Health, Education, and Welfare. (1977). *Social security programs throughout the world—1977.* Washington, DC: Author.

US productivity keeps climbing. (1993, March 11). *Jerusalem Post,* p. 6.

Van Horn, C. E. (1991). Myths and realities of privatization. In W. T. Gormley, Jr. (Ed.), *Privatization and its alternatives* (pp. 261-280). Madison: University of Wisconsin.

Van Praag, B. M. S., & Van Beek, K. W. H. (1991). Unemployment and the social security trap. In C. de Neubourg (Ed.), *The art of full employment* (pp. 283-303). New York: Elsevier North-Holland Science Publishers.

Veit-Wilson, J. H. (1992). Muddle or mendacity? The Beveridge committee and the poverty line. *Journal of Social Policy, 21,* 269-301.

Verba, S. (1961). *Small groups and political behavior.* Princeton, NJ: Princeton University Press.

Vianello, M., Siemienska, R., Damian, N., Lupri, E., Coppi, R., D'Arcangelo, E., & Bolasco, S. (1990). *Gender inequality: A comparative study of discrimination and participation.* London: Sage.

Vigilante, J. L. (1976). Back to the old neighborhood. *Social Service Review, 50*(2), 194-208.

Visher, E. B., & Visher, J. S. (1988). *Old loyalties, new ties: Therapeutic strategies with stepfamilies.* New York: Brunner/Mazel.

Wagner, D. (1989). Radical movements in the social services: A theoretical framework. *Social Service Review, 63*(2), 264-284.

Wagner, D. (1990). *The quest for a radical profession.* New York: University Press of America.

Walbank, M. (1980). Effort in motivated work behaviour. In K. D. Duncan, M. M. Gruneberg, & D. Wallis (Eds.), *Changes in working life.* Chichester, UK: Wiley.

Watson, D. (1980). *Caring for strangers.* London: Routledge & Kegan Paul.

Weber, M. (1952). *The Protestant ethic and the spirit of capitalism.* New York: Scribners.

Weber, N. (Ed.). (1988). *Giving USA: The annual report on philanthropy for the year 1987.* New York: American Association for Fund-Raising Counsel Trust for Philanthropy.

Weinberg, D. H. (1985). Measuring poverty. *Family Economics Review, 2,* 9.

Wellness Newsletter. (1994). *5*(1).

Whyte, W. F. (1955). *Money and motivation.* New York: Harper.

Wilding, P. (Ed.). (1986). *In defense of the welfare state.* Manchester, UK: Manchester University Press.

Wilensky, H. L. (1975). *The welfare state and equality: Structural and idological roots of public expenditures.* Berkeley: University of California Press.

Wilensky, H. L., & Lebeaux, C. N. (1958). *Industrial society and social welfare.* New York: Free Press.

Wineberg, R. J. (1991). A community study of the ways religious congregations support individuals and the local human services network. *Journal of Applied Social Sciences, 15*(1), 51-72.

Wineberg, R. J. (1992). Local human services provision by religous congregations: A community analysis. *Nonprofit and Voluntary Sector Quarterly, 21*(2), 107-118.

Wingen, M. (1992). Theoretical and practical issues in family policy. In G. Kiely (Ed.), *In and out of marriage: Irish and European experiences.* Dublin: Family Studies Centre.

Winston, E. (1969). A national policy on the family. *Public Welfare, 27,* 54.

Wirtz, W., & Goldstein, H. (1975). Measurement and analysis of work training. *Monthly Labor Review, 98*(9), 19-34.

Witte, E. W. (1962). *The development of the Social Security Act.* Madison: University of Wisconsin Press.

Wolch, J. R. (1990). *The shadow state: Government and voluntary sector in transition.* New York: The Foundation Center.

Woodroofe, K. (1962). *From charity to social work in England and the United States.* Toronto: University of Toronto Press.

World of Work Report. (1979). *4*(29). (1980). *5*(52).

Wuthnow, R., & Hodgkinson, V. A. (Eds.). (1990). *Faith and philanthropy in America: Exploring the role of religion in America's voluntary sector.* San Francisco: Jossey-Bass.

Yakabe, K. (1974). *Labor relations in Japan: Fundamental characteristics.* Tokyo: International Society for Educational Information.

Yankelovich, D., & Immerwahr, J. (1983). *Putting the work ethic to work.* New York: Public Agenda Foundation.

Yankelovich, D., Zettenberg, H., Strumpel, B., & Shanks, M. (1983). *Work and human values: An international report on jobs in the 1980s and 1990s.* New York: Aspen Institute.

Yans-McLaughlin, V. (1990). Introduction. In V. Yans-McLaughlin (Ed.), *Immigration reconsidered: History, sociology, and politics.* New York: Oxford Press.

Zald, M. N. (Ed.). (1965). *Social welfare institutions.* New York: John Wiley.

Zastrow, C. (1992). *Social problems: Issues and solutions.* Chicago: Nelson-Hall.

Zimmerman, S. L. (1988). *Understanding family policy: Theoretical approaches.* Newbury Park, CA: Sage.

Index

About the Author

David Macarov is Emeritus Professor at the Paul Baerwald School of Social Work, Hebrew University, Jerusalem. He has been Visiting Professor at Adelphi University, University of Melbourne, and University of Pennsylvania, among others. He is the founder of the Society for the Reduction of Human Labor and the Israel Chapter of the World Future Society and a Life Fellow of the International Society for Social and Economic Development. His two previous books published by Sage are *Work and Welfare: The Unholy Alliance* (1980) and *Worker Productivity: Myths and Reality* (1982). Other books include *Quitting Time: The End of Work* and *Certain Change: Social Work Practice in the Future*.